John Cairney

CONTENTED wi' little and cantie wi' mair, John Cairney looks back at the paradise he lost and blames Willie McGonagall rather than Rabbie Burns.

Cairney returned to Scotland in 1971 "like a Border reiver, having made his pile from 'This Man Craig'" and that man Burns. About half the promise of the good life, living in his beautiful National Trust house at Pittenweem, working for the Royal Lyceum Company, doing an occasional bit of touring, walking with his children, looking at the sea. Then came McGonagall.

McGonagall was meant to kill off Burns, but he just about killed off Cairney. An old Dundee man sold him McGonagall would bring him nothing but bad luck, and, sure enough, Cairney found himself swept up on a new popular tide and working harder than ever. Early last year he collapsed with stomach trouble and spent many weeks recuperating. He resolved, of course, to take things easier. But even today he can hardly remember when he last spent three consecutive days at home.

Burns wrote once of his fears that "the popular tide shall recede with silent celerity and leave me a barren waste of sand." Perhaps it is something akin to Burns's apprehension that draws Cairney relentlessly into places and projects which many of his fellow-actors would avoid, whether for reasons of stamina, ability or taste.

Perhaps it is something else: "The only time I'm totally relaxed is when I'm standing in front of an audience or kneeling down in church on Sunday." There are moments, too, in his zippy, stereo-wired Mini-Cooper, when Cairney feels himself "safely encapsulated with Mahler on the motorway" and allows himself to take his foot off the accelerator.

But at other times it is all unbelievable go—a sequence of writing, acting, reading, talking, doing, being that takes your breath away just to hear about it.

'The only time I'm totally relaxed is when I'm standing in front of an audience or kneeling down in church on Sunday'

John Cairney and Alannah O'Sullivan.

Why John Cairney has publicly executed Burns

The loneliness of the long-distance actor
by Cordell Marks

FOR 18 YEARS John Cairney has been Robert Burns. And you can watch him put to several hour of identity sweeping...

A wee pause wi' Robert Burns
By WILLIAM RUEHLMANN
Ledger-Star Staff Writer

NORFOLK — Scots poet Robert Burns was on his hands and knees in furious search of his socks. "They're around here somewhere," he said in a rich, boggy burr.

Well, not Burns, precisely, but his very image. Actor John Cairney, whose...

people television advice entertainment
Wednesday, April 8, 1981

The Daily Break
THE LEDGER-STAR LEISURE TIME SECTION

Robert Burns To the Life
5 APR 1977

John Cairney is almost Robert Burns to the life, his poetry a...

The people's voice had a Scottish accent
28 JUN 1990

CAIRNEY SAYS FAREWELL TO THE BURNS IMAGE

ACTOR John Cairney, who sprang to renown for his portrayal of Robert Burns in "There Was A Man," is taking on the Laird of Pittenweem personal role...

Final Fling

The Man Who Played Robert Burns

THE MAN
WHO PLAYED
ROBERT BURNS
—— AN ——
AUTOBIOGRAPHICAL
JOURNEY

JOHN
CAIRNEY

MAINSTREAM
PUBLISHING

All rights reserved.
First published in Great Britain in 1987 by
MAINSTREAM PUBLISHING COMPANY (EDINBURGH) LIMITED
7 Albany Street
Edinburgh EH1 3UG

ISBN 1-85158-070-0

British Library Cataloguing in Publication Data

Cairney, John
   The man who played Burns: an autobiographical journey.
   1. Acting
   I. Title
   792'.028'0924   PN2065

   ISBN 1-85158-070-0

Typeset in Imprint by Bookworm Typesetting Ltd, Edinburgh
Printed in Great Britain by Adlard & Son Ltd, The Garden City Press, Letchworth, Herts

for Jim and Fran

To the late William Cowan of Kelty

John Connolly

1996

Acknowledgements

I would like to thank the following for their correspondence, co-operation, assistance, and encouragement, without which it would have been impossible to assemble and collate the memories of a very significant time in my life: Andy Stewart, Jimmy Logan, Tom Wright, Gerard Slevin, John Calder, Jim Haynes, Richard Demarco, Haldane Duncan, Mike Westcott, John Worth, Neil Ross, Colin Wright, James Donald, Clare Brotherwood, Graham Buchanan, Bob Keedick, David Roy, Tom Raffel, Maureen Braid, James Mackay, Bill Anderson, Stuart Mackenzie, Alanna Knight, Nan Vinnel, Mike Paterson, Paul and Stephanie Morris, Jack and Jane Turnbow and Bob and Ellen Lapthorne. Not to mention all the other friends and relations, colleagues, the ladies and gentlemen of the press, fellow Burnsians and the countless ordinary men and women who have been part of my Burns story along the way.

For the photographs, I am indebted to Gerald McGrath of Glasgow, Douglas Corrance and the Scottish Tourist Board and particularly to David Pashley of Napier College, Edinburgh for his splendid front cover photograph and for the use of his overcoat!

I am grateful to the learned Professor and Doctor, David Daiches, for his scholarship and friendship, to James Hutcheson for his cover design, and to my editor, Judy Moir, for her invaluable suggestions. I want to thank my publishers, Bill Campbell and Peter Mackenzie, for their courage and trust. And a similar debt is due to my daughter, Jennifer, for reading the original mansucript at a single sitting!

Finally, I want to thank my wife, Alannah – for everything.

JOHN CAIRNEY
GLASGOW
3 JULY, 1987

I have taken a whim to give you a history of myself. My name has made a little noise in my own country and there have been many interested themselves on my behalf. I think it time, however, I spoke for myself. I will give you an honest narrative, though this might give me some pain in the telling, for I commence on this history under some twitching qualms of conscience, arising from a suspicion I am doing what I ought not to be doing. A predicament I have been in more than once before.

ROBERT BURNS
(1759-1796)

The First Burns, 1965.

PROLOGUE

O wad some pow'r the giftie gie us
To see ourselves as others see us...

The Crichton, as it's called locally, is a Scottish medical establishment specialising in psychiatric care. In 1968 I was playing Robert Burns in *There Was A Man* in my own production at the Theatre Royal in Dumfries and was asked by the matron to visit the Crichton Hospital as a guest during its birthday celebrations. That old barnstormer, Elliot Williams, who so often acted as my "minder" in the Dumfries area, was instructed to bring me. We were met at the main door by the matron – who turned out to be a man! He thanked me politely for coming and said that the patients were all ready to meet me and were "very excited" about my visit. You must bear in mind that I was then at the height of my celebrity phase in Scotland, having had a high profile in television that year, not only as Burns on Scottish Television, but simultaneously as *This Man Craig* on BBC. The combination of both at the time had given me something of a national fame, and personal appearances such as this were usually rather hectic and hysterical affairs.

On this occasion, however, there were no girls, no crowds, no fuss; only the matron, old Elliot and myself. "This way then," she – I mean, he – said briskly. We were taken first into the men's ward where, to my amazement, the patients were sitting by their beds, almost at attention, neat and tidy in their day clothes. There was not a sound. Just a roomful of seated, silent men. It was so quiet our footsteps echoed like a cavalry charge as we made our way up one side and stopped at the first bed. The matron leaned down to the old man beside it.

"George, I would like you to meet John Cairney. You know, the man who plays Robert Burns." George looked quite unimpressed, and stared at me impassively. I put on my professional smile, and held out my hand. George made no move to take it, so it just hung about uselessly in space before I pulled it back again. By which time the matron moved us quickly on to the next bed-space.

11

"William, I want you to meet John Cairney. He's an actor you know, and he plays Robert Burns on the telly."

"Oh, aye," said William, staring at his boots. At this I put my hands behind my back. But we were already moving on. I followed like the Duke of Edinburgh.

We were now at bed three.

"Albert, this is John Cairney," the matron was saying gallantly. "You've seen him as Rabbie Burns."

"Hiv ah?" said Albert, and turned to look out of the window.

"Yes, you have," replied the matron. "Many times, Albert." But Albert only grunted and the matron was already moving on. "It's a nice day," I heard Elliot say to somebody. By this time we had reached the end of one side. The matron was quite unperturbed and only said, "You mustn't mind them, Mr Cairney. They're just shy."

"Of course," I said. The matron rubbed his hands – "Shall we carry on, then?"

"Oh," I said, "Sure, why not?" But I exchanged a wry look with Elliot, who put his fingers to his lips, and said quickly to the matron, "I don't think Mr Cairney has very much time this mornin'."

"That's right," I said lamely. "Not much time." I looked wistfully at the back door right at hand.

"And we have the women to do yet," added Elliot. The matron understood.

"I see," he said. "Look, if we go out the back way here we can cut across the lawn, and get into the women's ward from the side. It'll save going round all the corridors." God, I thought to myself, have I got to go through all this again with the women?

"This way, then," said the matron, and we all followed after him.

It was a beautiful July day and the windows of the men's ward were wide open. No one was paying any attention to us as we passed. There was a hum of conversation coming from inside but we couldn't help overhear Albert confiding very loudly to William, *They've took away that man that thought he was Robert Burns!*

W E live in a story, and that's the truth of it. This is my story of a particular time of my life and it's as true as I can remember it. I suppose it all really began in 1959. I was 29 and one of my Christmas presents that year was a book – *Robert Burns, the Man and his Work* by Hans Hecht, first published at Heidelberg in 1919, and reissued to mark Burns' Centenary Year. It was given to me by my father-in-law, Willie Cowan. No doubt Mrs Cowan bought it, but I think it was Willie's idea. Willie Cowan was a real Burns man. All that year he had been celebrating 200 years of his favourite poet and Scotland's acknowledged National Bard. For most of that time his chocolate-box likeness (Burns', not Willie's) had been hung in Scottish homes and a volume of the poetical works lay with the Bible in a place of honour and, like the Bible, was revered but unread. Like many Scots, I had grown up with Burns too but it had never occurred to me to actually read him.

That particular Christmas I had to go into Maidenhead Hospital for a minor operation. I came out to occupy – somewhat gingerly – the cockpit of a mock-up plane at Pinewood in a TV film series called *Interpol*, starring Charles Korvin, in which I played an Indian airline pilot. So effective was my Indian make-up that I played no less than three Indians in the two weeks. They just changed the wardrobe for each script. It was while playing these various Singhs that the Christopher Mann Agency rang to say that Jimmy Logan wanted me to play Robert Burns in a sketch he was preparing for a television show he was doing for BBC to go out in January 1960.

And so, between an episode of *Laramie* and the 9 o'clock news, I went out live as Robert Burns for the very first time with Jimmy Logan and, as part of a sketch, recited "A Man's a Man" after the Carlu Carter trio and before a singing duo, Nina and Frederick.

I had little to do other than occupy a large, life-size picture frame and look like Robert Burns. As I sat there waiting for the red light and for Jimmy to cue me, he noticed on the rear side of the frame, the legend

"For Rabbi Burns – BBC/TV". "Perhaps we should've put out the show from Golders Green?" he whispered, then we were "on".

Nobody seemed to notice my Burns debut, and I forgot about it. After all it was just another job. But viewers had noticed, and they wrote letters to the BBC and to me. So I took notice, and something registered at the back of my mind about Robert Burns. I even read Willie Cowan's book. I began to get ideas about maybe doing something about Burns one day.

I started to make some notes. Could there be a play in this – better still, a film? But there was little time to ponder on it then. I had to go off to Aden on a film location. I came back to do another TV series, this time with Frank Finlay, then a BBC play at Riverside Studios where I got to play the leader of a rock-'n'-roll group and sing Ewan McColl's *The First Time Ever I Saw Your Face* for the first time ever. I next went up to the Glasgow Citizens to play *Hamlet*. It was that kind of year. All of 1961 was spent on the Continent, first of all playing Gulliver for Columbia Pictures and then *Jason and the Argonauts* for the same company who loaned me to Twentieth Century Fox for Elizabeth Taylor's *Cleopatra* until suddenly it was January 1962.

I never seemed to be out of work around that time, but all the time, wherever I went, whatever the job, I now had a Burns book by me, and a notebook which by then was getting rather full. I began to read Burns' *Collected Letters*. I had the idea that if I could organise the best of the poetry, the best of the songs, and link them with snatches of the letters, I might have a script. But I wasn't a writer. Who did I know who was? I remembered Eddie Boyd, whose work had so impressed me in Glasgow, but where was he now? I wrote to the BBC and enquired. Jimmy Crampsey replied that they had no idea where Eddie was. He could either be with Granada in Manchester, or with Hugh Leonard in Dublin, or even in London or Paris. I learned years later he was actually in Maryhill all the time, less than a mile from the BBC! Should I try Robert Kemp? After all, he'd already written a play on Burns? Or Robert McLelland perhaps? Time passed . . ..

I don't know what waiting-room I was in, or what magazine it was. I think it was the *Scottish Field*. I know it was coloured and glossy, and it was all about Robert Burns. I couldn't believe my luck. I read on, and I liked what I was reading. Who was this writer? I looked for the name – Tom Wright. Never heard of him. Still, that doesn't mean anything. Wait a minute, didn't I meet him during the *Hamlet*? I read on. By the end I was convinced this was the writer who could write a Burns play for me. Perhaps even a one-man show. That's it – a one-man show. A one-man show on Robert Burns. What a fabulous idea. Why had I never thought

14

of it before? I decided to do something about it before the idea grew cold on me. I must confess now that I stole the magazine, and that night wrote to him care of it:

"Dear Tom Wright . . .".

I had a reply by return.

"Dear John,
I remember you very well and am flattered that you remember me. I think the kind of programme you suggest could be very interesting . . . I think I more or less have the idea. Using the letters, poems and what have you . . .".

Later:

"The Burns proceeds. I'm just getting the first two acts typed and the third is under way . . .. Still unemployed and struggling – but making out. Cuthie phoned . . .".

Then later:

"I am pushing the Burns thing as hard as I can . . . It is my intention to get it finished as soon as possible and then have a nervous breakdown for a fortnight or so . . .".

Later still:

"Herewith your copy of the play, mate. It incorporates most, I think all, of the changes we agreed on . . .".

Later again:

"I hope you have seen the script – and like it . . . What a good Burns you will make . . . Yours, Tom."

I ran into Gerry Slevin at the Edinburgh Festival. He was directing Marlene Deitrich in her late-night show. I asked him if he'd like to direct me as Burns if Tom and I could work something out.

"A Catholic Burns?" he said. (He had helped me to found the Catholic Arts Guild in our student days.) "Sounds interesting."

"Catholic meaning Universal of course!" I hurriedly pointed out.

"Of course," grinned Gerry. "Right, you're on. Drop me a line about it – just to make it official." So I did.

"Dear Gerry – Further to our recent discussion . . .".

In this fragment of correspondence is all the reality of what making a play is about – the solitary writer, the vulnerable actor, the creative director all see the thing as their own. This is the real-life drama of individual passions caught up in a particular project, the comedy of egos jostling for positions, always the race against time, and always having to compromise. A one-man play is no different. In fact, with the focus so concentrated on one person all the ordinary problems of seeing a production from the script to the stage are all the more intensified.

Tom, as the writer, is voluble, intense, given to muttering and to calling everybody "mate". He is a professional bachelor, small, bearded, intensely shy, although you'd never think it. A little resentful and frustrated but only being what he always wanted to be – a writer. Doesn't trust me entirely but is willing to give me the benefit of the doubt, for the moment. After all, the whole project was my idea. And –

> "Facts are chiels that winna ding
> And donna be disputed . . ."

Gerard Slevin was the director. He and I, as I said, had first met years ago but he wasn't going to let a little thing like friendship stand in the way of getting his own way in every detail of the production. Like the name of the piece for instance. I think Tom might have been working under a title like "There Was A Lad" taken from one of his songs, or even "A Man's A Man". It was Gerry who suggested the combination – hence, *There Was A Man.*

"*Ecce homo,*" he said.

"Amen," said I.

"Fair enough," mumbled Tom.

Thus we had our title and we all shook hands on it. Like all good titles it was as if it had always been. Now we could really get on with it. We were an odd trio, but it was a trinity whose very differences gave it its strength, and we had Robert Burns on our side. He had plenty to say for himself, and by far the greatest part of the script is his, as Tom will readily admit, but in the beginning it was a matter of which words, and where and how. Gradually, however, a production shape emerged. Frank Spedding, now Dr Spedding, late of the Royal Scottish Academy of Music, was the composer. Frank thought the whole thing "first-rate" and was optimistic from the very beginning. So, while Tom burrowed among his mountain of words, and I fussed over his shoulder, Frank arranged lovely sounds of the period for violin, harpsichord and guitar, a different sound for every act. Gerry worked on a very simple and portable stage design, and I talked to anyone who'd listen about the project.

16

First of all, to "Cuthie", that is big Iain Cuthbertson, director at the Citizens, who was not so sure that Burns outside the Burns season was valid theatrical fare. He saw that I might be a draw, but would the subject appeal to a general audience? Michael Goldberg, a lovely man, was Chairman of the Citizens' Board at the time. After the *Hamlet*, he thought I could recite the telephone book and get a house in Glasgow – but a telephone book in an old Scots dialect? He wasn't so sure. Neither was Perth nor Dundee. I even wrote to the General Cigar Company in New York who made "Robbie Burns" cigars – but not a puff!

What was slightly more problematical, however, was the fact that during all this I was working full time on other things. This was fine, in that it allowed me to commission Tom and start him off with some cash and also pay him the several stage payments. He was to get a hundred down, a hundred when it went into rehearsal and get a hundred on the first night plus his normal percentage on performances. It was a good deal for me, and Tom was glad of the break.

It was my original intention to retain the performing rights of the piece, but since we worked so closely on the project together, it was thought better to make a company to produce it ourselves, but somehow this never happened. I got my original money back, eventually, and all rights naturally reverted to Tom. Which was a pity. It led to so much misunderstanding and bitterness later.

I spent two months in Cardiff on a BBC serial, another two in Glasgow playing *The Master of Ballantrae*, lost the part of Dr Finlay to Bill Simpson and *Tunes of Glory* to John Fraser, but came up to the Edinburgh Festival to play James Boswell.

At Gerry's invitation, I stayed on to play Rashleigh in *Rob Roy* and meet the Queen at the Lyceum, but all the time, by telephone and letter, and trays of beers at the Ivanhoe, the Red Lion, the Grafton and sundry other hostelries in Glasgow, Tom, Gerry and I discussed, disagreed, swore, quarrelled, kissed and made up, laughed and cried over an opus called *There Was A Man*. We still hadn't found a theatre, nor could we fix an opening date. I came back to London. It looked as if it were all going to drift away from us. It was now January 1963.

Maurice Lindsay at Border TV booked me to read some Burns with Mary Marquis and to sing a song with Moira Anderson. He also gave me his Burns Encyclopaedia, which gave us more grist to the mill. I hoped that we might have agreed a rehearsal script for *There Was A Man* by this time, but it still needed cuts, needed tightening. And rewrites. Especially rewrites. By now Tom was really going off me. He didn't realise that the actor sees the script only as a blueprint, nothing more. It is a working guide to physical externals and emotional intentions to be realised by him in performance with the help of the director for the benefit of the audience. It is not a Bible, or a sacred text, or holy writ. Certainly every actor will try to personify the playwright's intention, but he cannot populate his mind. And, until he performs it, an actor will worry his rehearsal text like a dog with a rubber ball. It made for some rowdy sessions. And for some extra letter-writing:

> "With the best will in the world I cannot go on repeating myself . . . when we have gone over it so many times, I find it incomprehensible that you feel capable of rewriting it . . . This, John, is my play. I own it – every part of it. You cannot have final word on the script . . . (so) don't keep changing it – please . . . believe me I have no antagonism about this, but unless we agree that the writing is my job and the acting is yours . . . I feel I have wasted my time."

Well, that was me told! But we still didn't have a venue. Even Gerry was getting impatient. For me it wasn't the end of the world. I had a lovely wife and three lovely daughters. As well as this treasure, I now had a personal manager, Barry Krost. He arranged my London West End debut as Captain Absolute in Sheridan's *The Rivals*. My father died on the first night. I went on in a daze and got my best ever notices. Not that I cared much as I got the plane to Glasgow the next morning. It was the first time I had flown. After the funeral, I learned that Hammer Films wanted me to sign for something called *Devil-Ship Pirates*. Barry was urging me to forget "that nest of hysterical Scotsmen up there and do some pictures". *There Was A Man* already seemed very much in the past tense. I wrote to Gerry, but got a reply from Tom:

> "Dear John – I understand from Gerry that you have finally withdrawn from the Burns project. I accept this as a professional decision . . . on the whole I think your decision the safest – even the wisest.
> All the best with the films."

I understand that Tom then offered the script to Bill Simpson.

The scene now is the Connaught Hotel, London, and the year 1964. A casting conference is taking place in one of the suites of the hotel for a film to be made of Thomas Hardy's *Far From the Madding Crowd*. Preliminary casting had been going on for weeks but now the final stages had been reached. I was one of two actors being considered for the part of the young farmer, Gabriel Oak. This role had third billing behind Julie Christie and Peter Finch and alongside Terence Stamp. In other words, this was quite an important interview. But I was as confident as one can be in such circumstances. I had been strongly recommended by the film's casting director, Stuart Lyons, and I was already known to some of the other executives as a coming film name. I was assured that this final interview was only a formality. I hoped so, for I had ordered a new car, a Renault 16, on the strength of the large fee I might earn in the coming months, and only hoped that the arrival today of the American producer, Joseph Janni, wouldn't upset the apple cart.

It had come down to a decision between me and one other actor who was the choice of director, John Schlesinger. I understand that voting got very close, so close in fact that they couldn't make up their minds. I was brought into the room again. The producer smiled in his kindly American way.

"We sure got a problem here with you two guys. But just as a matter of interest, where do you come from, John?"

"Glasgow," I said.

"And where's that again?" went on the producer.

"North of London," I replied lightly.

"Five hundred miles north," added Stuart Lyons for the benefit of the producer.

"That's a helluva way from Wessex," said the latter, going on. "Where does the other guy from come?"

"Buxton — I think," somebody said.

"Where the hell's that?" asked the Big Boss.

"Well," said my fellow Scot, Stuart, "it's a lot nearer Wessex!" And that's how my film fate was decided. I lost the part to the other actor on a matter of geography. Or perhaps, one might say, an accident of birth? There may have been other reasons, for the other actor was Alan Bates!

I was, needless to say, quite shattered, but I remember my only concern was for the new car about to be delivered to my home next day. As the big producer took me to the lift, his arm about my shoulder, he drawled, "Well you see, John, you're Scotch."

"So I am," I muttered. Outside in the street I found myself facing the famous Farm Street Church. I paid a brief and grumpy visit.

"Well, so be it," I sighed to myself. As one door closes, the others slam tight shut! I rose from my knees remembering an old saying of my mother's — "What's for ye will no' go by ye!"

It was a very downcast actor who stood on Paddington Station
waiting for the next train back to Maidenhead. I had already rung my
agent, but how was I to tell my wife? I hadn't even told her about the
new car! My eye was suddenly caught by a British Rail Transport
Commission poster, looking a little bit yellowed and apologetic, which
showed the figure of Robert Burns standing looking off, surrounded
by characters from his life and works. It must have been left over from
'59 Centenary Year. What was it doing here in Paddington? Probably
put up in error by a West Country railwayman with Scottish
connections. Suddenly it made me think again about Burns, about
Tom Wright, about Gerry Slevin, about that idea I had for that
one-man show. I stared hard at the central figure again, his hands
behind his back. Dammit, I even looked like him. What the hell – I'll do it!
I've nothing to lose, except money of course and a bit of time. But I now
had that time.

Yes. Why not? It could be really exciting. I was so lost in thought in
front of the poster, I nearly missed my train. I had to sprint for it. On the
journey home I could only hear that slow American voice, over and over
again. "You see John, you're Scotch." Well, I'll be bloody Scotch! And
what could be more Scottish than Burns? And what could be a greater
challenge for any actor than a one-man show? One-man shows were not
at all numerous then. Only Emlyn Williams, Hal Holbrook and Micheal
Macliammoir as Oscar Wilde were in any way known to the general
public. Why had I never gone ahead with it? Because of other work. But
perhaps, deep down, I was scared.

By the time I reached Maidenhead, I was hot with excitement. *Far
From the Madding Crowd* was far from my thoughts now. I couldn't wait to
tell Sheila.

"Well?" I'd hardly got in the door.

"Hi, darling," I said.

"How did it go?" She was just like a wife.

"Well –" I began.

"You didn't get it," she said.

"How did you know?"

"We'd have heard you at the end of the Avenue if you had." Just like a
wife.

"Listen darling," I said, "I've had an idea."

"Oh-oh," retorted Sheila, "that generally means trouble."

"Remember that Burns thing I was going to do?"

"I knew it, you didn't get it."

"Oh, come on darling, it's a good idea. The time might be just right for
it now."

"The Tom and Gerry show!" she went on derisively.

"It won't be for ever – just the time I would've been on the film anyway."

There was a pause. I went to her.

"That means you'll have to go back to Scotland?" she said quietly.

"Probably, at least till we get started. What do you think?"

"I think you're mad." I drew her warmly to me. A joyous surge of inexplicable confidence coursed right through my bones. I would write to Tom tonight. This was it, I thought. I could feel it. But all I said was, "By the way, we're getting a new car tomorrow."

Tom replied at once:

> "Thanks for your letter. I have my irate sister working on the script again . . . I know you must have a great fear of the whole thing, and sympathise. No use in saying 'Don't worry'. We've a lot of worrying to do yet."

I spent most of the year in theatre, while Sheila moved us to a bigger house in Maidenhead. In a removal, the best place to be is away. I was in Scotland. I did *Battle Royal*, a new comedy, for the Citizens, and big Iain encouraged me to rewrite to my heart's content. Like me, he held that a play is not a play until it is performed. It is only a rehearsal script. Fortunately it was a great success. I stayed on to do John Arden's *Armstrong's Last Good-Night*. No chance of rewrites here. It was not a great success. I returned to "Highways", our new house, and to a spell on *Emergency Ward 10* at Elstree with Richard Ainley – one of the old school of actors. I love old actors.

Then, out of the blue, John Calder the publisher invited me to Ledlanet House to take part in his Festival, in something called, *A Happening With Robert Burns*. Leonard Maguire was to play Shakespeare and we were to improvise a mock trial, where I was to defend as Burns and Leonard would prosecute as Shakespeare. I had great fun in that few weeks with Leonard and with the other artists, singers and musicians who were at Ledlanet that summer – Geraint Evans, Thomas Hemsley, Isobel Black. I got to know Isobel quite well. She used to organise late-night singsongs after the shows in what came to be known as Cairney's Cottage in the grounds. But she was scared off by the mice. They didn't bother Geraint Evans as he sat in an old rocking-chair crooning softly. He said he didn't like to sing out after midnight. Meanwhile, *There Was A Man* was still simmering . . . still waiting.

It was John Calder who supplied the vital Edinburgh connection. He knew printer John Martin, who knew Richard Demarco, who knew Tom Mitchell, who owned a property at St James' Court in the High Street. Somehow they'd been given the idea that it might make an intimate theatre on the traverse principle, that is, with the audience on either side of the playing area. The man behind the idea had run a paperback book shop in Edinburgh and his name was Jim Haynes. Jim was a long, laconic, charming ex-GI, with a love of life and people and a propensity for attracting attractive young ladies. Jim had been told of our problems in finding a home for *There Was A Man*. He offered the new Traverse Theatre. "Come on, you guys, let's go," he drawled. We went.

The Traverse Theatre in Edinburgh is now world-famous, but in 1965 was little more than a cheeky assertion to apathetic Edinburgh that theatre was a vital and necessary element in the arts and was closely linked to all of them – music, painting, poetry, dance – and to every aspect of the written and spoken word. This was not the kind of theatre Edinburgh normally preferred. Its douce citizens in the main liked their theatre at a remove – behind velvet curtains and seen only as a nicely framed picture from the comfort of the dress circle. No, Edinburgh is not a theatre town. Yet everything about it is theatrical; its Castle, its Gardens, the Royal Mile, Holyroodhouse, Arthur's Seat.

But thirty years ago its newest theatre was no more than three small rooms knocked into one on the first floor of a rickety old tenement up a narrow close off the top end of the High Street. Yet what a lovely intimacy it provided. It was just like being in a room with friends. No setting could have been more apt for the first night of one of the longest ever solo theatrical performances. For that's what Tom, Gerry and I had hacked, chiselled and polished over the preceding weeks until it was now a very long performing script. It was made all the longer by the fact that on the first night I dried stone dead in the middle of Act One. Luckily, only God and stage management could tell – it was a one-man show remember – so I just sat down with my back to the stone wall, and chatted to the audience as Robert Burns till something approximate to the script came back to me and I resumed as per text. I had learned the first lesson of going solo – an audience never knows! Bingo Maver in the *Scotsman* next morning suggested that perhaps I was a little overtired by the solo exertion. I wasn't. I was exhausted.

The atmosphere on that memorable (well, almost memorable) first night on Monday 25th January 1965 was unique. Winston Churchill had died the day before but we hardly noticed. All the talk in the papers and on TV was about the funeral, and nobody mentioned the handful of people huddled in the Traverse obsessed by an opening night, but the rest of the world was still happening, I think, despite our preoccupation. Lay people might not understand how much of a monastery theatre is. We are its monks – or monkeys.

Our first night, however, appears to have been unique to more than just us. Several times in my travels around the world since then, I have met with people who were there, and who remembered it clearly. Considering that the place only seated a hundred, it was remarkable that on that particular first night the audience contained so many foreigners. For instance, there was a Russian there. He was studying at Edinburgh University. And in 1977, during my week in Moscow (of which more later), he bore down on me after my performance, flourishing the original Traverse programme, pointing to my photo, saying over and over again, "You! You! You!" I had to agree. Similarly, there was a lady in Canada, who wrote to me regularly on the anniversary till she died, a schoolmaster in London, a doctor in Seattle, a baker from Kincardine-on-Forth – all members of the "TWAM Club" – those who attended the first night of *There Was A Man* at the Traverse Theatre in Edinburgh. I don't remember if Jim Haynes actually saw the show that night, but afterwards, at the bar, he gave me one of his bear hugs – "Great stuff, man!" he said. All the Wilson family from their Myron hotel, where I was staying, came and their actress daughter, Jan, said it was just marvellous. Ricky Demarco was telling everyone in a three-mile earshot that it was out of this world and insisted on having his photograph taken with me – or do I mean mine with him? Gerry thought it was "not bad for a first try". He had spotted my big dry though. I don't remember Tom saying anything. My dear old father-in-law nearly broke my hand with his handclasp. "Yon was braw," he said simply. But his eyes were shining. When I finally got to bed, I couldn't stop shaking. First-night nerves had finally caught up with me. I couldn't sleep and had a bath about four in the morning.

By the end of the first week, *TWAM* had become the talk of the town. Since seating capacity was so limited, tickets were scarce and very much in demand. I was pestered continually on all sides, and couldn't really cope with continual requests from all the new friends I seemed to have made. Jim Haynes (or more likely Sheila Colvin, the very efficient secretary and house manager) had banned all complimentaries and professional seats, which was right in the circumstances. It was suggested by the agent, Robin Richardson, that I extend the run. As is the normal practice, I said I would discuss it with the cast! Jim and I had originally agreed to do a trial night, and hopefully it might run a week. Now it had run a month, and I had only a few weeks left before I was due to do a television film with John Gregson at Elstree. So we extended it as far as my commitments would allow, and scooped in the resulting bookings. Had it not been for the Elstree film we would probably have transferred to a larger theatre, and then no doubt we would have toured it, but we were in a limited run situation and we would have to make the best of it. Still the ticket touting went on.

To satisfy all my family connections, I bought the whole theatre out for one night, and divided the tickets between the Cairney family and the Cowan family (my in-laws). It was something of an Old Firm event, since the Cairneys and the Coyles from Glasgow made up the Celtic end as it were, and the Cowans and the Cross's from Fife might be described as the Rangers. They were as staunchly Protestant as the other lot were Catholic and, true to the football tradition, they were segregated on the night – Catholics to the left, and Protestants to the right. This posed a problem for my Swann cousins from Ballieston, who came through on the Glasgow bus, and were decidedly not Catholic. Ideally, they should have sat centre stage with me, but they disposed themselves on either side, and sat where they could.

I don't know how many relatives were there exactly, as most of the stairs were used as well. All I know is it was a packed house, with both sets of relatives staring at each other in the house lights, each aunty guessing who the other aunty was, every uncle with arms folded defiantly, staring straight ahead. Some had of course met before, but the family situation was slightly abnormal in that Sheila and I had virtually eloped to Glasgow eleven years before, so that the two families hadn't even had the opportunity of formal wedding day introductions. That didn't prevent their hurling playful insults at each other, much to the amusement of stage management and my embarrassment in the tiny dressing-room under the stage. Apparently, each group had hired buses through one organising aunt on each side. I had nothing to do with the allocation of tickets, not wishing to excite any jealousies by showing any preference. I merely gave a block of tickets to each of the organising aunties and left them to it. My mother wasn't there she was in America, where she had been since my father's death, otherwise, no doubt, she would have had something to say. I now wonder, had my parents been alive, if I would have done such a thing. All I know is that when the blackout faded and the spotlight discovered me on stage between these two family factions, I found myself hardly able to talk, because of an unexpected lump that rose in my throat.

Here were the people in the world who knew me most, if not best, but there were old ladies here who had wiped my nose when I was a little boy in Parkhead, and there were at least two who had changed my nappies. There were great hulking men whom I remembered as intimidating

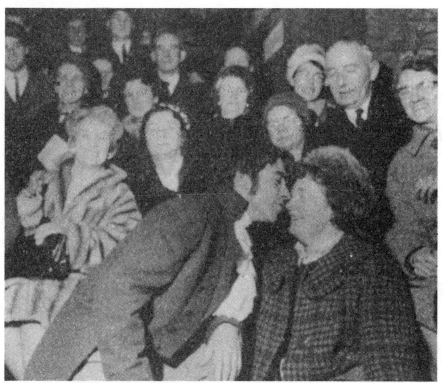

Kissing cousins – John kisses his cousin Margaret at the family performance of There Was A Man, *1965.*
(Photograph: Scottish Daily Mail*)*

uncles, and there were gangling young men who were once my playmates in the street. On the other side, my wife's parents, sisters and brother. No blood ties but, nonetheless, a concern for me and a connection with me. I stood that night, in the spotlight, pincered by this emotional pressure and wondered how I could begin. I was either going to cry or burst out laughing. It wasn't until I heard Auntie Jeannie from Baillieston mutter audibly to my dear Aunt Sarah, "My, he looks awful thin", that I woke to the moment and began to play.

I don't think it was a great performance. I found I couldn't be as intimate with the audience as I normally was. As I advanced to one young man, he would either give me a wink, or turn away muttering, "Oh, for Christ's sake!" Other times, it would be the comments, with no attempt whatsoever to be discreet, like – "Here, is he no' awfy like oor Mary?" Mary was my mother. Yes, there are definite barriers in playing to one's own family. How could I expect them to take me seriously? During one particularly crucial moment dealing with Burns' intended emigration to Jamaica, I distinctly heard one female voice on my side of the family enquire of her neighbour – "That reminds me, hiv ye heard how Mary's gettin' oan in America?"

There was no doubt *There Was A Man* made a sensational impact on its first appearance but, in true Scottish fashion, this didn't seem to please everybody, particularly our playwright, Tom. Now that his property was splendidly proved he was determined to make the most of it, but I had the feeling he could never forgive me for making a success of it. That Scottish admiration for failure again. At any rate, he still seemed to think that Bill Simpson would have made a better Burns. Failing that, David McKail. David had sent me a copy of Hogg's *Confessions of a Justified Sinner* as a first-night present so that I might better understand Burns' Protestant soul! There was also Victor Carin as a likely Burns. Or Brian Cox? Anybody, in fact, rather than John Cairney. Certainly the original project had been my idea, but it was now his play, and it was Gerry's production. I was merely the hired hand. One would have thought the three of us could have gone ahead from this first triumph to even greater heights together, but no, we must preserve the Caledonian gift for internecine quarrel. It has been ever thus in Scottish history – which Stevenson rightly called "nothing more than a long story of brawls".

Tom simply saw the piece as a conventional play, to be presented as such. I saw it as a skilled compilation, which relied more than usually on the similar skills and personality of the player. Different players would play it in different ways and with different results, as indeed was later found. I didn't deny Tom his status or his good work. I only wanted to indicate the actor's (any actor's) contribution and to emphasise Burns' part in the enterprise. However one sees it, it is not a wholly original piece of writing and that's the difference between *There Was A Man* and *The Three Sisters*. This is not to derogate the writer's work or talent but only to define its classification and to know what we are talking about. The fact that we had a quality compilation on our hands is only due to the fact that Tom was a quality writer. We should have been happy with that but, alas, we could not agree on anything it seemed, so I thought – to hell with it. I've made my point – proved that a one-man show about Robert Burns can work. If necessary, I'll create my own script, for I saw now, as my own Burns studies had progressed, how much of a compilation it was.

I say this again without detracting in the least from the poetic skill Tom showed in linking the various Burns extracts. The rehearsal script was heavily overwritten, as it should be, and most of the rehearsal time was taken over in cutting and shaping it for performance. The Burns works were the original marble. Tom took it away and rough-hewed it into an acceptable rehearsal shape. Gerry and I then worked on it from a theatrical point of view with a finer chisel, and the playing script of *There Was A Man* was the result. But technically and legally that script now belonged to the author, and he could dispose of it as he willed. As a matter of fact, he sold it almost at once to the BBC for a televised version, and it was by no means certain that I would play Burns. I was sure Tom would rather I didn't just to confirm his view that the play was the thing. So I was quite prepared never to play in *There Was A Man* again.

I returned to London and to films to play a deaf-and-dumb mortuary attendant in *Study in Terror* at Shepperton with John Neville. Not having any lines, I didn't have cuts or rewrites to worry about. It was sheer luxury and pure cinema. I couldn't lose, and was even noticed by Dilys Powell in one of the posh *Sundays*. I had plenty of time on the set, time to think, and I couldn't help feeling that if *There Was A Man* had failed, we would all still have been great friends. We would have been bonded in glorious defeat instead of being divided by a brilliant victory. How ironic. How sad. How Scottish. "Never again," I said. "No more Scotland for me." I had another kind of family to think of. And I turned again to making money and not enemies.

It was Gerry who persuaded me. I had come up to Glasgow to do a play in the *Glaister* series for STV and we met at Celtic Park. He told me that the Traverse wanted to put the Burns on at the Edinburgh Festival.

"So?" I said.

"Not at the Traverse this time but a bigger venue – get some loot in at the door."

"So?"

"And they're wondering about who could play Burns," went on Gerry wanly.

"What about Jerry Lewis?" I replied.

"Let's go back to the game," he said.

I had dinner that night with him and Helen at their Bellshill home. (Celtic must have won.) We drank a lot of wine and did a lot of talking. Eventually Gerry said, "Look, this thing's a lot bigger than you and Tom – and your wee personality problems. There's a lot of mileage in Burns for both of you, there's also a lot of bucks if you both play your cards right. It's your meal-ticket, man. You could be playing it till you're fifty."

"Don't be daft," I said. "Burns died at thirty-seven."

"Ay, but we've got penicillin," grinned Gerry. "I rang Tom. We're seeing him tomorrow at the Ivanhoe. Come on, I'll drive you back to your hotel."

It was an odd feeling coming back to it. It was still warm, as it were, from January. And it was difficult relearning lines I had so recently learned. Nonetheless, the Traverse run had taught me many things about the text, and further cuts were made and some adjustments to the sound tape, although Frank's excellent music was retained. The stage management team, Rita Guinacault and her friend, Lillian Nielson, the original stage manager, were re-engaged. Lillian would also dress me (Hal Duncan having gone on to higher things). We tried out at the old Rep in Dundee, and we were a hit, a palpable hit. It was standing-room only by midweek. I was beginning to sniff that sweet smell of success that Olivier says is like seaweed. I hoped it wasn't the pier at Broughty Ferry. I knew we must go to Edinburgh. But before that we'd to be approved by the University whose premises in Blackfriars Street the company was renting.

Mr Michael Westcott made a point of seeing the show to make sure that it was "worthy of the University connection". I am glad to say that both he and his delightful old mother approved. *TWAM* opened at Morton House as part of the Edinburgh Festival Fringe. I was asked to do some matinées, as the demand was there, but refused. This was the kind of show one could only do once in a day. Larry Adler did the late-night cabaret to follow. A feature of his programme was the harmonica obligato he gave to my speaking of "My Love is Like a Red Red Rose". Or was it the other way round? Larry couldn't do the last week because he was replacing Elizabeth Seal at the Lyceum. At my suggestion, Matt McGinn, that dear, late little Glasgow genius, was brought in to do his own kind of thing at 11 p.m. All I can say is it wasn't anything like Larry Adler. It wasn't to everyone's taste in Edinburgh. I remember taking a local newspaperman outside because he was giving Matt a hard time. I punched him so hard I nearly broke my fingers. I wondered how John Wayne did it so effortlessly!

The Edinburgh lightning struck yet again, and *There Was A Man* sold out from the first week. A Mrs Pat Fuller from London Productions in Geneva saw one of the performances and invited me to go for a week to Geneva and take part in their Festival of Solo Theatre. She also offered continuing dates in Paris, Brussels, Warsaw, Leningrad and Moscow, as part of a continental tour. I was more than happy to accept and terms were agreed for October and November. Pharic McLaren also confirmed that he would like me to do the television version for BBC, despite Tom's misgivings. Another BBC man, Peter Graham Scott, saw the show, and he asked if I might be interested in a new series he was planning about a secondary school? I wasn't sure. Too much was happening at once.

Dundee asked me to go back after the Festival. So did Ledlanet. The Sol Hurok office wrote from New York offering the Henry Miller Theatre for the next January. Jimmy Logan also wanted the piece for his Metropole Theatre in Glasgow. His father, Jack Short, had seen the show in Edinburgh and had reported that I was "drawing the town". What a lovely phrase that is. In fact, everybody in Scotland, except Perth and Ayr, now seemed to want the Burns. Suddenly, *There Was A Man* was all the rage and I was being asked to do everything at once. It's always the way for actors – either feast or famine. When you're up you're on top of the world and feel you can do everything, but when you're down nobody wants to know and you feel you can't do anything. But then I could see *TWAM* lasting at least until 1966 – perhaps '67? Even '68. How was I to know that I was in the process of changing my whole life?

When the Festival was over, we returned for a special performance at Ledlanet. I had several surprises. The play was performed on a platform space before the stairs in the big hall of Ledlanet House. We began in a blackout and when the lights slowly came up there was I sitting in a chair in the middle of the platform as if I had suddenly materialised. It was a good surprise start, provided nobody heard me tip-toe up the steps and across the carpet in the pitch black. I rehearsed not bumping into the chairs. But I was the one who got a surprise when the lights went up and there was Sheila sitting right opposite me, and John Calder grinning away at the side. He had arranged that she fly up that day – as my own very special surprise. She certainly was. She looked really lovely, and the performance was entirely for her. I felt like a bullfighter offering the bull's ears!

As it happened, "God was there", in Sarah Bernhardt's phrase. It turned out to be one of the rare, great shows and when the blackout came down at the end and I made my way up the stairs, I could hear my boots creak in the absolute silence. I was glad Sheila was there too.

When the end of the week came, dear John Calder had his usual cash-flow problem and offered me my fee in abstract paintings. I took two – a Pulsford and an Alistair Park. I only have to glance at them today to remember a very beautiful young wife and that extraordinary Ledlanet silence.

I asked Sheila to join me in Geneva. No children. No pets. Just the three of us – her, me and Robert Burns. It would be our honeymoon, I said. We had never had one in 1954 – unless you call a twice-nightly Saturday at Greenock Empire in Roddy McMillan's *All In Good Faith* a honeymoon occasion? She agreed on condition she didn't have to see the show again.

In Geneva, we were the guests of the delightful Mrs Pat Fuller and her partner, Marie-Antoinette. On the very first morning, on the stairway of the hotel, we bumped into Michael Macliammoir, the very individual Irish actor, who was here to do his justly famous Oscar Wilde. He barely acknowledged me but had eyes only for Sheila. I stood by patiently while they had a long discussion about Max Factor make-up.

Everyone at the Théâtre St Pierre spoke French. This might have led to problems back-stage but we discovered that, given some good will, a few well placed francs and a smile, a kind of theatrical *lingua franca* emerged and things were quickly sorted out. My own French was strictly sixth-form, but I managed to read the advance pieces in the Swiss press. "Qui est John Cairney?" was one of the headlines. C'est moi! I was very nervous about the performance especially as I heard that Sir Charles Chaplin was out front. This was my first time with Burns in a totally foreign environment and it was a very odd experience. I mistimed a lot of the laughs, but I got a better kind of silence. I don't think it was altogether due to the language barrier. There was an uncanny and intense dynamic in it, and the death scene never went better. So much so, that when I faded into the final blackout and the last chords of "Auld Lang Syne" melted away there wasn't a sound – not even a solitary handclap. Just like Ledlanet. It's when the moment for applause passes. No one wants to break the silence, and the audience doesn't want to applaud. It is not at all embarrassing. Well, that's what happened that summer night, but I never saw Charlie Chaplin. There was a man in a wheelchair – but he was asleep most of the time.

After the show they gave me a reception in one of the big houses. That morning a very haughty voice rang me at the theatre to ask if I had any special preferences in the way of food or drink for the evening. I told her that the matter of my after-show eating had a very low priority at that moment, but if the show were a flop I'd just have a plate of cornflakes and go straight to bed with a book. On the other hand, if it went well, I would be so high that a plate of cornflakes could still suffice, except that I wouldn't go to bed right away – and certainly not with a book. But I explained that my wife Sheila was at that very moment at the hotel and would be happy to answer any further questions.

After the performance I got changed as quickly as I could and with no back-stage visitors I was ready in five minutes. Rita, who was the stage-director for *TWAM*, gave me a bundle of notes and instructed me to give two to each outstretched hand that I met on the way down the iron spiral staircase to the stage-door. She had gauged things perfectly, and I arrived on the street empty-handed. I made my way to the big house as I had been directed and as I mounted the steps to the very imposing front door I could hear the sounds of the string trio inside and the babble, or "babel", of excited foreign voices. "Ceci la vie pour moi, sans dout," I said to myself, as I pulled on the bell. "Listen to all those people in there – and all for me!" The big door was opened no more than an inch.

"Oui?" said a man's voice in the aperture. I didn't know what to say.
"Er – is this the house –"

"Moment," said the voice, and the door closed again. Perhaps I've got the wrong house, I thought, and suddenly I felt very alone standing there in the portico. "Sheila, where are you?" I screamed inwardly. I was already coming down to earth after that wonderful theatre "silence". The door opened again, wide this time, and I found myself blinking in a light which burst on me like a No. 1 flood. Framed in the doorway, like Mrs Danvers in *Rebecca*, stood a formidable woman in a white overall.

"Yes?" The voice was glacial, but I recognised the tone as that of the housekeeper, who had rung me at the theatre.
"I'm John Cairney."
"So?"
I was now at something of a loss. "Er – I'm the actor –"
"Ah, yes, the actor – M. Burns, n'est-ce pas?"
"Oui – er – yes."
"Follow me please."
I did. I didn't dare not. I followed her ramrod figure into the vestibule and straight across the hall and along a corridor and through a door and down some steps until she opened another door – and I was in the kitchen! "Mrs Danvers" indicated the long wooden table imperiously –

"Le Corn Flakes!" she said. And sure enough, laid out at one end, on a starched, white cloth, there was a bowl and a packet and a jug of milk with a large silver spoon on a linen place-cover. This was my supper.

"Bon appétit," she said curtly, and was gone. Other people working in the kitchen ignored me completely as I took my seat at the table. So this was the actor's place – in the kitchen. Some reception! Still, I was hungry, so what the hell.

I was on my second bowlful when a tall and strikingly handsome man came in.

"There you are – what *are* you doing in the kitchen? People are waiting you know."

This was Brian Aherne, a British actor and sometime Hollywood star, then a doyen of the English set in Switzerland. He was as charming as he looked and acted, and was very kind about the show.

"Not my cup of tea, all that haggis and stuff, but I must say, it wasn't like that at all. Good show old man. Now come on, let's have you upstairs." The he stopped suddenly. "Good Lord," he said.

"What's up?" I inquired, wondering if the milk had dribbled down my chin.

"You can't go up like that." He waved a slim hand at the denim suit I was wearing over a black polo-necked jersey.

"Oh!" I said.

"It's a black tie job, you know," he said sympathetically.

"Oh!" I said again.

"Pity you hadn't a kilt," he mused.

"No, it isn't," I said quickly. He puckered his brow, then –

"I've got it! Your costume!"

"What?"

"Wear your costume – you know, all that flashy stuff in the second act – lace cuffs and all that."

"But it's at the theatre."

"Then we'll just have to get it, old chum, shan't we?"

The next half-hour was traumatic – back through the streets at a run, fractured French chats with the stage-doorman, who luckily was still there. His reason for working late was far too young for him as far as I could see, but I persuaded both to let me have my dressing-room back for ten minutes so that I might change. I returned to "my" reception in a worse state than Burns when he first arrived in Edinburgh. I could feel sweat on my brow and at the small of my back as I stood once again at the main door. This time the door was opened wide – they were waiting for me – but standing inside was a flunkey, dressed almost identically except that I had riding-boots on instead of buckled shoes. We bowed gravely to each other before I was whipped upstairs by Brian and Pat Fuller, who brought me in front of an old lady.

"Have you met the Queen of Spain?" was the first question I was asked.

"Of course," I said. "Hasn't everybody?"

But it *was* the Queen of Spain! I bowed again before hurrying in the direction of Sheila, who had her own circle of admirers around her.

"Where have you been?" she hissed between smiling, clenched teeth.

"In the kitchen," I answered between large gulps of excellent champagne.

"You were supposed to come back to the hotel, idiot."

"Was I?"

"Of course – and change into your dinner jacket."

"Oh!" I had a feeling this was not my night.

"And what are you doing in that silly costume?" It was difficult to explain while holding a tray which had suddenly been thrust into my hands. People were loading it with empty glasses. It suddenly dawned on me that they thought I was one of the waiters. I started to get the giggles, and might have dropped the tray, which was now quite full, but I was rescued by Marie-Antoinette, who plonked the tray on a chair and dragged me off to meet some of the Russians.

"After all, you want to go to Moscow don't you?" she said.

That girl never stopped working. I could feel Sheila's eyes boring into my sodden back. I had the feeling there would be an inquest later.

I was amazed that the Russians knew more about Burns than I did, and was even more astonished by their drinking capacity. I was glad I had that second bowl of cornflakes. Then Brian reappeared to take me to meet Charlie Chaplin. I was absolutely thrilled, but by the time we had made our way through the throng again, nodding right and left and smiling like damned villains, shaking hands here and spilling a few drinks there, a good half-hour had passed, and the alcove where the Chaplin party had waited was now empty. I was heartbroken.

"Tough luck old son, but the old boy's getting on – aren't we all? – He needs his beauty sleep."

I couldn't hide my disappointment. "It was hardly worth while dressing up for," I said, taking a glass of champagne from a passing flunkey, who bowed to me. I bowed to him, and I'm sure he winked.

Before we left Switzerland, we were asked to put on a special performance for combined girls' schools at Vevey. "Isn't that where Charlie Chaplin lives?" I asked. They said he might take a box. I hoped so. We arrived at the school selected for the performance to find in the building the most exquisite miniature theatre. I loved its red velvet curtains and the old-fashioned floats. They wanted the whole performance but we settled on the first two acts. It was just as well. There was a constant twitter of girlish whispers throughout. It was like playing in a very posh aviary, and a few of the things I overheard caused me to blush like a girl myself. Some of these girls were finished already. However, they were attentive enough and I think I was coping. Although I could see no sign of the Chaplin party in any of the little boxes. They said he would come. Never mind, I bashed on until I had to go through the audience at the end of Act Two, murmuring fervently to a little tea-table, and the tea-cup on it:

> Ae fond kiss
> And then we sever
> Ae fareweel
> And then forever –

The scene was a very slow, lingering, dying fall to the act, and paced to the gentle rhythm of one of Burns' most beautiful and poignant love songs.

> Deep in heart-wrung tears
> I'll pledge thee
> Warring sighs and groans
> I'll wage thee –

I then started to hear sighs all round me. Was I being sent up? With some trepidation, I stepped off the stage to go through the audience as usual. Even though it was a miniature theatre, it was still a long way to the exit.

> I'll ne'er blame my partial fancy
> Naething could resist my Nancy.
> But to see her was to love her
> Love but her and love forever –

Fair young hands were now fluttering round my middle and nether parts like impudent butterflies. I was glad I was wearing a long black coat.

> Had we never loved sae kindly
> Had we never loved sae blindly –

"Grab him!" shrilled a very refined voice. Somebody screamed. I think it was me! I ran "blindly" for the door – all pretence lost . . .

> Never loved or never parted –
> We had ne'er been broken-hearted
> Ae fond kiss –

I gathered my cloak around me, fending off those delightful fingers, and sprinted for the exit –

    And then we sever –

I made it in some confusion and from the other side of the door pandemonium had broken out. I kept running till I reached the car!

I've never been back to Vevey since. They told me later that Sir Charles Chaplin had indeed been there and might have been interested in seeing me at his home afterwards – but it was obviously not to be.

    Ae fareweel – alas . . ..

When I did return to Switzerland a few years later on a film, he was dead.

The Cairney family now had two cars. Sheila's was a Renault and I had a little black Volkswagen. I got it as a gift for opening a garage in Dunfermline.

I had to put on my Burns costume and arrive by train at the railway station, where I was met by a little delegation. I then mounted a horse and rode through the town with the little delegation running after me most of the way to the Volkswagen garage, where I dismounted, declared the garage open and drove away in a brand new car. It was a good morning's work. I drove on to Glasgow, where I was rehearsing at Jimmy Logan's Metropole Theatre, as Gerry Slevin was now Director of Productions there. I must confess I was Scottishly uneasy about getting a new car so effortlessly but the garage people seemed happy enough. They had got the publicity, the photographs, the local interest, but deep down I felt just a tiny bit guilty.

God must have agreed, for I only had the vehicle a few days when I drove from the Metropole one evening out to Ruchazie to pick up my Uncle Hugh and Aunt Cathie and their son Hugh-John and take them to Ibrox to see Rangers play Hibernian. I don't know why, we were Celtic supporters. Anyway, it was pelting down with rain and I thought I'd take a traffic-free route through Carntyne. Since the car was so new to me, I hadn't quite got the hang of the de-misters, so visibility was poor. Coming to a crossroads in the middle of the housing scheme, I asked Uncle Hughie in the passenger seat if the road was clear on the left. My Uncle Hughie was a lovely big man but he was not known for decisiveness.

"Well –" he muttered, – then BANG – CR-RUNCH – WHEE-EE – the car spun like a top and the next thing I knew I was lying face down in the middle of the road about two feet from the wheels of a Corporation bus which had just screeched to an emergency halt. Uncle Hugh was sitting on the pavement staring up at the bus. I think if it had been going his way he would have taken it. Aunt Cathie was screaming from the car, "His face – his face – my God his face!" From where I was lying I could see nothing wrong with Uncle Hugh's face, and Hugh-John looked absolutely fascinated by the events as any nine-year-old boy would. But it was *my* face she was worried about! I hadn't a scratch. I felt more the injury to my dignity rather than to my person, and was reassuring the bus driver that I was fine I hurried to my car where it lay nestled against a Ford Escort, as if in an embrace.

The driver of same, an Englishman, was hopping up and down saying, "Look at my car! Look at my car!" But I had only eyes for my own and, to my amazement, it didn't seem to have a scratch on it. But when I got round to the passenger side I found the door was missing! Eventually, after much placating of the Englishman, and exchanging of numbers, etcetera, we agreed not to call the police, and since, thankfully, an ambulance wasn't needed, he with a dented front bumper, and me with my doorless Volkswagen, continued on our different ways. Believe it or not, the engine was still running as I got into the driver's seat. Uncle Hugh, now looking decidedly thoughtful, had used our ties to fasten the door to the stanchion, remembering first to replace Auntie Cathie and Hugh-John in the back seat. Without even thinking about it, we drove on to Ibrox.

We arrived only a little late to find the car park attendant terribly solicitous about parking our car.

"You'll no' want to scratch your new car." Then when he saw the other side, "Still, in your case, I don't suppose it would make any difference." I don't remember much about the match. Oddly enough, I felt better about the Volkswagen after that. It was now truly mine. I had gained it by lending my name and new Burns fame to a garage for a day. But I earned it by that crash in Carntyne. Which I may say is the only car crash I've ever had – so far – in 33 years of driving. And I got it going to see Rangers. Serves me right!

It was the same "car-crash" Uncle Hughie who retailed a conversation he heard behind him on the first night between two male Metropole Monday-night regulars. A few minutes after my entrance, one of them asked the other, "Is it just him?"

"Looks like it," was the reply.

"Hell's teeth," went on the first. "Nae lassies?"

"Doesnae seem so."

"No' even an accordionist?" the first one persisted.

"I cannae see any."

"Oh, hell!"

At the end of the first act, being young and fit and eager to please, I used to whip the scarf round my neck, pull down the bonnet on my head, and take a running jump over the orchestra into the centre aisle, and run off all the way to Edinburgh. It made a good exit and an effective end to the act. But as quickly as I jumped, and as fast as I ran, I still didn't beat those two Metropole regulars, who were ahead of me at the door on the way to the bar. As I ran, they started running, so it looked as if I was chasing them out. When I resumed for Part Two in my long black cloak, standing sombrely centre stage, I used to wait until there was absolute silence before I intimated that I had now arrived in Edinburgh. But as the lights came up and the silence came down, all I heard was a voice from the stalls – "Christ, it's him again!"

It was during the Metropole run in Glasgow that I was visited officially by the Burns Federation. I understand that they had been initially outraged at my making theatrical capital out of their subject, and in fact demanded a royalty from me for each performance. I was quick to point out that Robert was not only in the public domain; he was a world literary figure and didn't belong entirely to Kilmarnock No. 0 or Greenock No. 1 or whatever Burns Club claims pre-eminence. I reminded them that one of my principal advisers at the very conception of the project was that kind and learned Edinburgh solicitor, John McVie, a pivot of the Federation. And the more adventurous Burns authorities, like Jock Thomson, Sam Gaw, editor James Mackay, not to mention scholars like Professor David Daiches, were all for anything that would propagate the Robert Burns story and bring him to a wider audience than that available at arcane suppers every January. Now they had come complete with chains and badges and Burns tartan ties to sit in judgement on me.

Afterwards, even when we'd killed the first bottle, I had the strong feeling that I had let them down a little because I wasn't a Freemason.

I was hardly home again in Maidenhead when Barry Krost rang and dropped a bombshell. The BBC wanted me for the lead of *This Man Craig* but it was to start right away with filming in Glasgow.

"But I have Burns dates –"

"Forget them darling," cooed Barry. "This is big-time and not just a bit of haggis-bashing for the natives."

"Just a minute – " I started to say, but Barry was quicker.

"I know you're famous up in Scotland and all that, but this is London, this is where the real action is for real money darling."

"But Barry –"

"Have you signed anything with them up there?"

"No, I –"

"Good. Right, this is what you gotta do . . .".

I did the *Craig* series – for two years. But somehow Burns went marching on. The television version of *TWAM* came out on Burns Night 1966. It was the first time ever that the life of Robert Burns had been shown to a national audience. It was also the longest solo performance ever given on television until that time – a continuous, unbroken hour.

The only trouble was that I had been living for more than a year with the full two-and-a-half-hour, three-act script in my head, and now I had the more difficult business of unlearning instead of relearning. I also had a camera script to deal with. I found myself chasing the red camera lights, trying all the time to keep up with them. Ideally, the cameras should follow the actor. At least, that's how it is in rehearsals, but once the camera script is printed it becomes the Bible. And sacrosanct. This is all the more acute when one is the only actor in the cast. You get all the notes! The trick is, whenever the load is heavy, to play it lightly, to float with it occasionally. If you try to make every syllable count, none does, and the audience switches off. They can't take a relentless battering. We all need corners to hide in occasionally. But it's hard to hide in an exposed studio with cameras everywhere.

Now here was I, only months after renouncing Burns and all his works, living him again for BBC guineas. How horrified I was to see the bright scarlet ground-cloth that designer Helen Rae had provided. It made me feel quite shabby. Actors prefer green. I can also remember a very high crane shot for "Holy Willie's Prayer", which was only one of the many effective camera angles used by ex-Citizens actor, now director, Ian McNaughten. But perhaps the best memory was the comment made by the young English assistant stage manager, Kate McCall. Kate had hardly heard of Robert Burns, but told me that she loved coming to rehearsals each day in the old church hall at Byres Road, just to hear all those lovely words spoken. Her special memory of rehearsals is of "Burns" standing in the haze of his own cigar smoke, the makeshift set filtered in the sunlight from the stained-glass windows, and "My Love is Like a Red, Red Rose" being spoken to guitar accompaniment.

> And I will come again, my love,
> Though it were ten thousand miles . . .

Between *Craig* seasons, Liam Hood, an old friend from College, then Head of Drama at STV, asked me to read "Tam o' Shanter" as a voice-over while Phil McCall did all the dirty work. The sight of little Phil on a horse was unforgettable. He looked every inch the wee Glasgow insurance man that he once was! He would have looked just as uneasy on a clothes-horse! Even the bottle of brandy I got for him didn't seem to help. It only made him drunk. Still, so was Tam.

Liam and I found we got on well in the studio, even though I was only narrator.

"Ever thought of making a film on Burns?" he asked me one day in the canteen.

"Who hasn't?" I replied.

"Has there ever been one?" he went on.

"MGM made a short with Count John McCormack before the war, and the Russians did something about Burns with a choir," I told him.

"Sounds exciting stuff," said Liam.

"There's always talk of a Burns film," I continued. "Denis Morgan, Dirk Bogarde, Sean Connery, Albert Finney — even Engelbert Humperdinck have all been touted as possible Burnses in a film."

"Not John Cairney?" quipped Liam.

"Yes — once," I said. "Somebody put my name up for it in a letter to the old *Picturegoer*."

"Probably wrote it yersel'" put in Phil.

It was out of this very casual conversation that Liam got the idea of making a life of Burns as a serial for television — not as a solo — but as a full-blown, dramatised story of his life in all the locations and with full supporting cast — especially all the girls.

"But who's going to write it?" I asked, remembering my previous troubles.

"I don't know yet, old son," answered Liam. "We'll find someone."

"Why not write it yourself?" said Phil. "Ye'll only rewrite it anyway."

"But I've never written a script," I said.

"Think about it," said Liam.

I said that I would.

Another summer holiday brought me back to Burns for the Festival of 1967. What intrigued me this time was that it was a season of matinées only. Robin Hall and Jimmie McGregor were already booked for the evening slot and Julie Felix, the American folk-singer, was the late-night attraction. I could have all the matinées at 2.30, except Sunday and Monday — well, who wants Mondays? The arrangement suited me perfectly. I could have slow mornings for letters and business calls. I was staying with John and Dorrie Martin at their lovely flat in Saxe-Coburg Place. In the afternoons I would work then have a meal in the Bella

Napoli and see a show. I had a great Festival. The crowds turned up as before but there was one afternoon in particular . . ..

I often found while declaiming some of the more familiar bits of Burns that members of the audience would join in – some not even aware that they were doing so. Well, during one of these Festival matinées a rather well-dressed farmer figure in the middle of the stalls, distinguished by the mellow clink of bottles he seemed to have in every pocket, not only joined with me but was away ahead of me at times, and I could hear that he was upsetting some of the audience around him. He didn't bother me so much for I could see that he was friendly and genial and did know his Burns – but there was no doubt he was quietly wrecking the show and I knew I could never manage the end if he kept up this constant droning commentary. Yes, he knew his Burns, but I knew my script. I waited until the right lines came up, moved off the stage and down among the audience, saying:

> Oh ye who are sae guid yersel'
> Sae pious and sae holy
> Ye've nocht to do but mark and tell
> Ye're neighbour's faults and folly.

I began to move up the aisle:

> Hear me, ye venerable core
> As Counsel for poor mortals
> That frequent pass douce Wisdom's doors
> For glaikit Folly's portals.

I reached the heckler, by now in full flow, and said to the ladies beside him:

> Ye high, exalted, virtuous dames
> Tied up in Godly laces,
> Before ye gie poor Frailty names –

Indicating our farmer friend:

> Suppose – a change of places?

On this, I beckoned him to come out – and he did, as meek as a lamb. "Right, Rabbie – anything you say Rabbie." I put my arms round his shoulder inhaling at least half the contents of his bulky pockets, and together we walked up the aisle towards the rear exit.

> A weel-lov'd lad, convenience snug,
> A treacherous inclination –

By this time he was beaming seraphically at me.

40

Well – let me whisper in yer lug –

"Aye Rabbie?" And as he leaned closer –

Ye're aiblins nae temptation!

And with that I pushed him through the door with a hefty assist from my riding-boot. He shot through into the foyer, where he was grabbed by two attendants. I turned back towards the audience:

> Then gently scan yer brither Man
> Still gentler sister Woman
> Tho' they may gang a-kennin' wrang
> To step aside is human.

The audience rose to their feet in a laughing ovation which carried me back on to the stage, with the text remaining unerringly apposite. You must remember I had not changed a word of my rehearsed script. I merely gave it another focus, and when things were quiet again and he had stopped banging at the door I went on:

> One point must still be greatly dark
> The moving – why they do it?
> And just as lamely can ye mark
> How far perhaps they rue it –

More applause:

> Who made the heart – 'tis He alone
> Decidedly can try us
> He knows each chord its various tone
> Each spring its various bias –

Someone shouted "How true – how true." But the moment had passed. It was time to finish it. I raised my hand.

> Then at the balance, let's be mute
> We never can adjust it
> What's done we partly may compute
> We know not what's resisted . . .

And I was back to the action of the play.

   This incident was reported at length in some of the papers the next day – although I'm not sure how they heard, but it didn't do the box office any harm for the rest of the run. I received many letters about it, asking how much I had made up the lines, and even the suspicion that it was a plant. I had always hoped that I would have heard from the little man himself, but I don't suppose he remembered a thing the next day about his walk up the aisle with "Robert Burns". However, I did receive one letter which intrigued me. Benno Schotz, the Queen's Sculptor in Scotland, was there that day with his wife, Millie, and he loved every minute of it – especially the drunk. He said he would like to meet me if I were ever in Glasgow. He might be interested in doing my head one day if I were interested? I picked up the phone right away.

Benno was the Queen's Sculptor in Scotland and a redoubtable and remarkable man in every respect. He had come to Glasgow from Estonia in 1914 to be an engineer but stayed to become a formidable artist. He became Head of Sculpture at the School of Art, but when I first knew him he was long retired and had set up in his comfortable studio in Kirklee, Glasgow, as a portraitist in bronze. As I mentioned, he and Millie had seen the Burns performance in Edinburgh where I had become involved with the drunk, and this had so tickled him that it gave him the idea of doing a Burns head. Naturally, this appealed to me enormously and during my frequent Glasgow stays I would steal any free time I could to visit him at Kirklee Road and sit by the stove in his studio. He would then uncover the clay from its hessian sacking and start pounding into my "head" on the stand in front of him, glancing up at me only now and again to see if I were still there – or if I had fallen asleep. Not that one could sleep in such an energy-presence.

Benno was proudly Jewish, and consequently articulate on most matters artistic and realistic. I would notice a bust of Golda Meir, and would be given a brief recapitulation of the past and present state of Israel – his special interest being the Hebrew University where he went once a year to lecture.

"You must do your Burns there, I will arrange this."

"Yes, Benno."

Then I would see a figure of a goalkeeper in full flight. It was John Thompson. He was killed in a Rangers and Celtic match before the war.

"Did you ever see him?"

"I was only eight before the war, Benno."

"You still had eyes, didn't you? I was eight when I was in Estonia, and I saw many things. Yes, I could tell you."

"Go on," I would say.

"No, no, there are some things a man should only remember for himself. Everything that happens does not make a story. But I will tell you about John Thompson. He was a poet in motion. This is why I should do his figure in bronze. Besides, the Celtic people pay me to do it. So I make Thompson. He was so young, and agile and graceful, and I try to capture this – and his strength. Strong hands – to hold the ball – hands like a sculptor. Hands like mine."

42

John with his Benno Schotz head in his hands, 1969.
(Photograph: Hugh Thomson*)*

And he held two clay-spattered hands above the shapeless mound that was to become me – or rather me as Robert Burns. Or was it Burns as me? Benno would decide.

He had dealt with actors before. He had made a wonderful bust of Duncan Macrae as Harry McGog in Bridie's *Gog and Magog* and I could see the long, lanky image staring down at me. Like every Scottish actor of my generation, John Duncan Grant Macrae was my hero and mentor. Like all the actors of his time, he had begun as an amateur in Glasgow but after the war gave up teaching to become, with Alastair Sim and Roddy McMillan, one of that trio of Scottish actors who might be said to have a genuine spark of genius.

"Macrae was always an amateur," said Benno, when I spoke of the great comic actor. "That was his strength. He never knew what he should be doing, or what he was supposed to be doing, so he did what he liked in his own way, and it worked for him. But he was a whale among the sprats," he said. "What was wanted he should go among the big fish."

"He acted with Olivier," I put in defensively.

"So he acted with Olivier – I have worked with Epstein – what did I learn? That I wasn't Epstein, I was Schotz. The artist must learn who he is, not worry about who he is not. All that Duncan Macrae wanted was a theatre to play with and he looked to his friend James Bridie to give him it."

"Did you know Bridie?" I asked.

"Nobody knew Bridie – least of all Bridie. He was a Scottish playwright, but he was always in London. He pretended to be an amateur playwright and a professional doctor. Actually he was the other way about. I wouldn't like to have been sick and Mavor was the only doctor."

It was hard to imagine Benno sick.

"The artist can only be professional, because only then can he give all his time, all his life to his work. He needs commitment or he will get nothing done. He doesn't work for posterity, or for history – he works for himself. For his own satisfaction, and for enough money to get bread."

"And wine," I added.

"You talk like a Papist."

"You talk like a Jew," I would counter.

"Quite so," he would retort with a laugh. "With all the wisdom of the centuries." And so we would go on, his mind darting as nimbly as his fingers. I could see my "nose" begin to take shape.

"What did Macrae talk about, Benno?"

"Himself, like all actors. It's the only subject they know."

"Was it Plato who said 'Know thyself?'

"No, no," shouted Benno. "I did, five minutes ago. Now, what were we talking about before I interrupted myself?"

"I was asking what Macrae did when he sat here."

"He learnt his lines from a book. I think he was shy of me," said the sculptor.

"All actors are shy," I ventured.

"The good ones are." How perceptive this sharp old man was. Yet he wasn't old – I think he was the youngest man I've ever known. Alive in the moment, and living for his work. Always was now for Benno.

Sometimes he would work away in silence, and then I would find myself caught by that steely stare. He had the most remarkable eyes – eyes one couldn't hide from.

"Why are you shy of me," he would suddenly say, "when you can stand up so calm before hundreds of people?"

"They're looking at me – not through me. Anyway, it's not me they're seeing. I'm just pretending. Lying, if you like."

"Ah, yes," he put in quickly, "but you get at truth sometimes, eh?"

"Sometimes – by accident perhaps."

"That is the difference between us – I do not work by accident. I see what is happening under my hand and I decide. This clay will always be clay, even when it becomes a bronze, but what it will suggest to people who will see it a hundred years from now will be YOU – not the likeness of you, but the 'You-ness' of you. And by then you will be dust. This is something eh?" It certainly was.

"I thought it was to suggest Robert Burns, not me?" I offered.

"It will do both," he said. "That is my lie." And he disappeared behind his mound of clay.

He had also made a real poet's head – Hugh MacDiarmid – perhaps a genius like himself.

"Christopher?" he chortled. "Yes, yes, we had many discussions in my old studio in West Campbell Street. I tried to tell him about his precious Communism, but he only changed the subject and drank my whisky." I could imagine those two wily old foxes sniffing round a topic before one or the other pounced for the kill.

"The trouble with Grieve – I never call him by his stage name – was that he was also bad-tempered with the world. I used to tell him he must have an ulcer. He should go like me to the Kingston Clinic now and again for a clean-out. You can't do good work if your stomach's full of acids. The good artist doesn't only work from his imagination – he works from the soles of his feet, from his thighs, and from his diaphragm. Art is a physical matter. To be an artist is to be strong." Benno was in his seventies then and he made me feel feeble. I was never tired in our sessions – even if I was sitting in one of the several real Rennie Mackintosh chairs he had picked up years ago for shillings. He knew Mackintosh too. "He was good, yes, but his own worst enemy. But he left for London when I came to Glasgow."

And I remembered that Benno had been in my city for nearly 60 years. The hands were now working confidently and speedily on the clay and a head was already emerging. "Yes. I remember Glasgow in the First World War. Do you know when my brother and I first came to Glasgow, we were so poor we went for our summer holiday to a farm in the Byres Road. I will tell you about it . . .".

I tried to see as much as I could of Benno, especially after Millie died. We would often lunch at the Arts Club, or at the Ubiquitous Chip or at some fish place he would find. Sometimes, I drove him to Edinburgh for his Kingston Clinic visits. He phoned me on the morning of his 92nd birthday – "It is not much fun being old," he said. He died soon after.

If 1967 was what could be called "a good year", 1968 was a palpable "annus mirabilis". It began promisingly with a chat with my old pal, Jimmy Logan, on BBC radio on a programme called *Late Night Extra*, hosted by an unknown Dublin bank clerk – Terry Wogan. He was as disarming then as he is now, though when Jimmy and I went on about Lauder, Burns, Hogmanay, Haggis, Rangers and Celtic and other Scottish clichés, young Terry grew untypically agitated. We learned later he was afraid he'd miss the late boat train to Holyhead, as he had to work in the bank the next day .

However, he must have made it, for I was invited back again on Burns Night, and got into an argument on the phone-in with a lady, who described herself as an "Ex-Fan" of mine. She hated all Scots in general and Robbie Burns in particular, and had gone right off me now that I had shown my true colours and gone "all Scotch". She had preferred me as Bramwell Brontë or Edgar Allan Poe. I explained that I had to "go all Scotch", as she called it, to play Robert Burns, and that some people in Scotland thought that I hadn't been Scottish enough.

"Who was he anyway?" persisted my former fan.

"He was a famous Scottish poet, wasn't he?" interpolated Terry helpfully.

"What did he write that English people would know?" was the retort.

"Didn't he write Old Lang Zyne?" said Terry.

"Oh," said the listener, "I thought that that was one of Harry Lauder's songs."

"He also wrote some wonderful love poetry," I said.

"Oh, my hubby writes poetry," answered our unimpressionable caller. "He writes me a verse on my birthday and every anniversary."

"Does he now?" murmured Terry, then alertly he interposed,

"John – or should I call you Robbie Burns –"

"Please don't."

"Fine – perhaps you'd like to give a little love poem to Mrs – " I made a face. "Sure, I knew you would now. After all, wasn't she the great fan – once upon a time?"

I could hear the lady on my headphones trying to get in, but Terry skilfully faded her down, and nodded to me. "A love poem," he said gently, "by Robert Burns, read for Mrs – tonight by Rob – John Cairney. Quiet now for a bit o' real poetry."

He gave me a smile and a wink. I took a breath, allowed a beat, and began, almost in a whisper:

> O, my love is like a red, red rose
> That's newly sprung in June,
> My love is like a melody
> That's sweetly played in tune . . .

I heard music being softly fed in.

> As fair art thou, my bonnie lass,
> Sae deep in love am I
> And I will love thee still my dear,
> Till a' the seas gang dry . . .

I let the music swell and recede, then I resumed:

> Till a' the seas gang dry, my dear,
> And the rocks melt wi' the sun,
> And I will love thee still my dear,
> While the sands of life shall run

More music, then –

> Fare thee weel, my only love,
> And fare thee weel awhile,
> And I will come again, my love,
> Tho' it were ten thousand mile.

The music faded. There was a pause, then Terry concluded, "Thank you John. And listen, Mrs –, if your husband could write stuff like that, sure it's his birthday we'd be celebratin' tonight, and not Robbie Burns'." And he quickly faded her out. "That'll be enough of her," he said. I've liked Terry Wogan ever since.

This Man Craig had finished in the spring of 1967 and it was intended that it should resume in the autumn for a third season – but nobody had asked me. I didn't want to play that earnest Scots schoolmaster for yet another year, even it were for aggregate fee, allowances and repeats of nearly £1,000 a week. This of course was the principal inducement, but I would only get half of it anyway after tax. They couldn't understand an actor who was not seduced by money. Not that I was stupidly altruistic, far from it, but I knew the grind involved in a weekly series, however successful, and I thought there were pleasanter ways of making a living than the factory acting of the serials. Besides, I still had latent Burns plans, and if I didn't move now I would be too old to do anything about it. Or worse, I would get used to money and fame and start to need it. I still had dreams of a Burns film – I mean a real, super-duper, wide-screen technicolor beauty telling the Burns story in a sweeping, soaring, romantic way that could tell the world about the man. And I could play him – I knew I could. And perhaps we would let Alan Bates play brother Gilbert. Julie Christie could be Jean, Peter Finch, Gavin Hamilton, and Terence Stamp, Bob Ainslie. Whaur's yer Thomas Hardy noo? Oh yes, I had my dreams. Meantime, I had to get clear of *Craig*.

I suggested to David Attenborough over a bacon and egg breakfast at Television Centre that *Craig* be "transferred" on a special exchange to America, and a young American actor could take my place in the series, but this posed Equity problems, and he said bluntly if I didn't play *Craig* they would drop the series. I thought of my colleagues and all the guest stars and all the children featured and I realised I would not be very popular with my peers were I to cause the end of the show altogether. My wife, being sensible and realistic, would have preferred me to have continued *Craig*, taking advantage of the series to build up a name and then go into good theatre at Stratford for instance, cushioned by the BBC earnings. She still wanted me to be a "real" actor. My agent, being greedy and realistic, thought that I should go for the money and keep on running! Poor little Barry, it bled his Jewish soul to see such a fat commission being lost – and for what? A bloody incomprehensible Scotch poet who was randy for anything in a skirt and deservedly died of drink. Besides, he shrewdly pointed out that colour was coming and cassette recording – a whole new world of residuals was looming up and I could make a fortune from repeats and overseas sales.

All this was good sense, but it was accounting sense and, who knows, I could be crushed to death by a blackboard or assassinated by the pupils any day in the playground! Life was too short and I had to make that Burns film before I was forty. I didn't have long!

"For Jesus' sake," expostulated Barry, seeing I was quite determined. I used to wonder why Barry Krost invoked Christ so often — "Because darling," he would say, "Jesus was a good Jewish boy like me before he got mixed up with you Christian sods! And if you wanna get crucified go and do your Burns then — and I hope you get your Scotch bollocks roasted for it!"

So with his blessing ringing in my ears, I withdrew from *Craig* for good, moved the family to a four-acre, walled gentleman's mini- estate near Bray in Berkshire, didn't buy a Rolls-Royce, but swopped the Renault for a Saab and drove to Scotland, ostensibly to have talks with STV about the proposed Burns serial and do some location research, but really it was to get out of the house removal again and be away during all the confusion of packing and unpacking. This was our fifth house, and our largest so far — it was no place for a man at such a time. So, like the professional coward I had become, I pointed the new car north, switched on Radio Three and headed for Scotland again — and Robert Burns.

I had never been so happy. I was fit and healthy, solvent, very contentedly married to a beautiful and witty woman, had four lovely daughters (and hopes yet for a son!) and I was doing what I wanted to do in my my own time and on my own terms. It was a rare and real and heady freedom, and I was sure it would last for ever. Ah well!

M4 – M1 – M6 – Carlisle – where Burns had stayed on the night of 31st May 1787 at the Malt Shovel. Apparently in the morning it was found that his horse had strayed on to the landlord's private grazing and the landlord, who was also the Mayor of Carlisle, charged the poet an extra four pounds on his lodging, or else the horse would be impounded. Burns paid up grudgingly, but with the following lines:

> Was e'er puir poet sae befitted,
> The maister drunk, the horse committed.
> Puir harmless beast, tak thee no care,
> Thou'lt be a mare when he's nae "mair".

Crossed into Scotland over the ugly iron bridge at Gretna and turned left towards the Solway. Visited the Brow Well — an inconspicuous sort of place where Burns had "taken the waters" as instructed by his mad Dr Maxwell and so effectively committed suicide. Imagine anyone afflicted with rheumatoid arthritis being advised to plunge twice a day up to the neck in freezing sea-water! As Burns said ruefully, "How many of us die from doctors' guesses?"

With the Solway on my left I was reminded that Burns, with the help of a company of His Majesty's Dragoons, took possession of the French schooner *Rosamond* and brought it into Dumfries harbour as a prize of war. Then, being Burns, spoiled it all by buying the ship's guns and returning them to the Republican revolutionists with his poet's compliments! From being hailed as a hero he was almost transported as a traitor. Yes, Burns, could be a man worth writing about.

Dumfries was, and is, probably always has been, smug and bourgeois. The first house that Burns had there in the Wee Vennel was almost a ruin, kept intact only by the efforts of the shopkeeper who lived below it. Yet it was in that little room he wrote "My Love is Like a Red, Red Rose". His other house in what is now Burns Street is a much grander affair, but it now looks and feels like the museum it is. The English Curator was reluctant to let me look round because I had arrived outside official opening hours. I'm sure he did so only because he recognised me. I found the bedroom a very moving place and made a note of the bed recess where he died on the morning of 21st July 1796. It all seemed so small. Was Burns smaller than I imagined him?

The Globe Inn, however, was just as I had imagined it and the landlady, Ma Brown, was just that kind of cheerful wee body who might have delighted Burns himself. I was allowed to sleep in Burns' room that night, in the very bed where he had lain with Anna Park. But no ghosts came. Perhaps they were as put off by the blue nylon sheets. I didn't sleep much. Next morning, I saw the theatre in Shakespeare Street where Burns himself had attended. It was now run by an amateur Guild of Players. I made a note to see them about playing the Burns show there.

Drove on to Ellisland Farm. Was well received by the present tenants even though they admitted they didn't like Burns. He gave them too many visitors. Walked by the banks of the Nith where he wrote "Tam o' Shanter". Couldn't find the tree where he was supposed to have kept a charcoal pencil and writing-paper, but for the fun of it I recited "Tam" to myself and the wind. Still "dried" in some parts! This was the place he had been happiest. I could almost feel it. I was now very much in a Burns mood and in the heart of the Burns country.

I was seeing all the places I had read so much about and relating the locations to the people and the incidents. The TV script was almost writing itself and I was on to my third notebook. Dalrymple and the dancing-classes, the Gavin Hamilton place at Coilston, Mount Oliphant, the first farm, still gaunt and remote. It reminded me of the Brontës. A young girl answered the door to me, but I wasn't asked in. Lochlea was much more comfortable and they showed me the huge boulder Burns was supposed to have levered with a long pole out of one of the "wet-bottomed" fields. Mauchline was very much of today and I was disappointed in Poosie Nancie's Tavern which was more prepared for bus parties than Burns' Jolly Beggars. Mossgiel was now a flourishing and

Recovering after a hard night's work, Dundee Rep., 1965.
(Photograph: D. C. Thomson)

efficient farm and the present owners were kind enough to give me tea. They were also looking forward to seeing themselves on the television. I tried to explain that it wasn't that kind of programme.

At last to Alloway and the Victorian relic that is now the original cottage. It looked exactly as it does on the cake-tins and souvenir mementos – the outline of a building, filleted inside and with no suggestion at all of the smoky hovel it had really been 200 years before. Still, I suppose that's the inevitable fate of famous houses – to become more and more unlived-in as the years go by. I enjoyed a good browse among the book and papers in the adjacent museum but I couldn't get rid of the feeling that this was Burns mummified and fossilised. I was glad to get into the open air – or should I say Ayr?

This little seaside town has always been one of my favourite places. As boys, my brother Jim and I were taken there for the two weeks of every Glasgow Fair Holiday to stay with Mrs McPherson in George Street – neither alas no more. I took a walk along the prom and breathed in the Atlantic. Funny, Burns lived so near the sea, yet hardly mentions it. Looked out at Ailsa Craig, or Paddy's Milestone, and wondered if Burns could have shifted that with his long pole! Had a drink in the "Tam o' Shanter" pub but was driven out by autograph hunters – "It's no' for me, ye understand . . .".

At Tarbolton, saw the Bachelors Club – "where every fellow desirous of becoming a member . . . must be a professed admirer of one or more of the opposite sex!" That's my Burns. I was a little put off by the man who showed me round, railing against this fellow Cairney who had set himself up as Robert Burns. He didn't think it was right that anybody should pretend to be Burns – nobody was worthy enough. But, after all, he was only pretending, I tried to put in. "Ach," he said, "you're English. You widnae understand." I drove away quickly in case I disillusioned him further.

> Ye banks and braes o' bonnie Doon
> How can ye bloom sae fresh and fair?

Despite all the so-called improvement and Philistine progress one could see on every hand, the Burns country of Burns' time can still be glimpsed here and there if you have eyes to see it. Copses of trees on a hill, stones whitening a stream, the wind whispering in the fields – these are timeless images and they must have been seen by him then much as they were by me now. I must have been a menace on the road as I meandered through Ayrshire in my Burns reverie. But ideas were coming thick and fast. I couldn't wait to get them down on paper.

In Irvine I saw the Glasgow Vennel and the site of the heckling shop and made a note it could make a good location. At the Burns Club I tried on a coat actually worn by Burns. It fitted like a glove. I didn't dare try on his boots – just in case they didn't fit! Drove on to Greenock. The Mary Campbell sequence, however doubtful, would have to have a part, but I could find nothing in the town that gave me any fresh ideas, although I did meet some of the people from the Arts Guild who were keen that I should bring the Burns stage show to Greenock some time. I said I would and they said they wouldn't charge me much! It seemed I had to pay them! Up through Paisley to Glasgow on the route Burns would have ridden on horseback. Now here I was doing the same thing by horsepower. The roads may have been made easier, the inns now had TV in every room, telegraph wires abounded and houses were more and better, but I bet the people haven't changed all that much in 200 years. People don't. They were as friendly and obliging, dour and taciturn, as beautiful or ugly or tall or fat. In other words, as wide a variety of differences as there could be in any given group of people anywhere. And being Scottish, however great our xenophobia, makes very little difference. Nationality is rather a fallacy. Patriotism is certainly not enough. People are people are people.

And this I was finding out as I moved around my own country, knocking on doors and asking questions. For two months I was a one-man Burns survey and I was finding out just as much about Scotland and the Scots as I did about our National Bard. I stayed at the Lorne Hotel in Glasgow while I had discussions with Controller Francis Essex and Director Liam Hood about the Burns serial. They wanted to film in October in the Burns country with studio scenes in Glasgow in November and December, so that it might go out on Burns Night '68. This was a tall order. Six episodes meant six hours of material to be written from scratch and worked into camera scripts in six months.

"No trouble old man," smiled Liam. "It's all in your head just bursting to get out."

"Maybe so," I said, "but it comes out through two slow fingers at the typewriter I'm afraid."

"Give you time to think," added Francis.

We clinched the deal while standing at the urinal of the Circle lavatory at the Theatre Royal which was the old STV headquarters in Glasgow. We were hardly in a position to shake hands on it, but they washed their hands of me in a sense and left me to get on with it.

It was arranged I meet Liam in the Lundin Links Hotel in Fife, while I was on holiday there with the family in July to hand over the first drafts for camera preparation. Meantime, tried to find the site of the Black Bull Inn in Argyle Street where Burns stayed while in Glasgow, but had no luck and carried on to Stirling. I stayed with Sir William Murray at Ochtertyre House. Visited Harvieston where Burns had proposed to Peggy Chalmers and got turned down flat. However, it was here he won a horse race with a drunken Highlander at the price of being thrown and breaking an ankle. Sir William had something of the same idea by challenging me to race him up to Aberdeen – me in my Saab, and he in his brand new red Lotus – but his lovely blonde girlfriend talked him out of it. Just as well, or the Burns serial might never have been written. Endearing and impulsive, Sir William was the perpetual wee spoiled boy, ever excited by his latest new toy, and I could never make up my mind which it was at that time – the car, the blonde or the little theatre-cum-cinema he had just had built at Ochtertyre. Later I was to play the Burns there and never get paid. He had some less endearing traits, but later, poor man, just as impulsively, he blew his brains out.

Through Perth via Balmoral to Aberdeen. Was delighted to be pointed on to Cairney Junction near Keith, where some of my own forebears had come from. Saw Clochnahill where Burns' father, William Burnes, had grown up. Tried to find links with Neil Gow, the fiddler, whom Burns had met in these parts, and also the lovely lass "who had made the bed for me", but no luck and I came south again. Through Kincardineshire to Montrose and Arbroath, where Burns had met his Burness lawyer cousins and taken a trip on a fishing-boat. I didn't fancy going to sea so carried on to Dundee and into Fife at St Andrews. Saw Alex Paterson at the Byre Theatre. Arranged a Burns show for the following year and pressed on to my in-laws in Kirkcaldy.

Willie Cowan, or Bill, as his wife Betty called him, was a squat, brawny Fifer with piercing grey eyes, a handsome head and the remains of a pleasant tenor voice. He had a vehement love of education, good music and Socialism, which every miner seems to have – well, Scottish miners anyway. Some of the Cairneys had been miners in Lanarkshire between the wars and they seemed to have the same passion for music and the arts, or in the Cairney case, for books, Maybe it is that theirs is such a bestial occupation that they only want to live for fresh air, sports and choirs when they come to the surface. Yes, I like miners. And I certainly liked Willie Cowan, even though it was hardly mutual to begin with. I was everything he detested – Glaswegian, theatrical (which to him meant emasculated), and worst of all, I was a Papist. "Ye're ower intelligent to be a Catholic, man," he kept saying. But we loved the same woman, his oldest daughter Sheila, and we both adored his four granddaughters, so we agreed to differ about the ultimate intentions of the Pope and Freemasonry, and got down to working on what we agreed on. One of these items was Robert Burns, whom like many Scots old Willie could quote by the yard. He was always delighted when he caught me out on a line or a fact. There are thousands who have this encyclopaedic knowledge of Burns, but absolutely no understanding of the man or his work. Old Cowan, however, had the heart as well as the facts – oh yes, he certainly had heart. And remember, it was he who had given me my first Burns book, when he heard I was rehearsing for that little Burns sketch on television with Jimmy Logan years before. If I were going to play Burns in any form, then by God I'd better play it right! I used to tease him about the fact that the foreword for the book was written by Sir Patrick Dolan, who had been born like me in Buchanan Street, Baillieston, and was also, as well as being a past-President of the Burns Federation, a Lord Provost of Glasgow – and a Catholic!

"The exception that proves the rule," would snort Willie and pour me another beer, then he would go on with something like, "Did ye ken that Burns was a confirmed spiritualist – oh aye – ye ken 'The Vision' o' coorse . . .".

"But, surely, you don't think –"

And the debate would go on into the night.

Next morning, hung-over but enlightened, I crossed over the new Forth Bridge into Edinburgh and my usual hotel room at the Mount Royal. Next day it was a quick tour of the Burns places – Lady Stair's Close, Baxter's Close, St Cecilia's Hall, Smith Square, Clarinda's house (now gone, alas), and a thoughtful reunion with my other Burns mentor, John McVie, who was failing fast. He asked me not to sensationalise the poet – "He does that well enough himself don't you think?" he would say with a twinkle. I was suddenly aware I had a responsibility as well as a deadline. There were so many Burns ideals to so many different kinds of Scots. I couldn't please them all so I may as well please myself. I didn't stay too long in the Capital. I was as uncomfortable there as Robert himself in 1786. Perhaps west coasters do not take kindly to east winds?

At any rate I moved down into the Borders – via Biggar, the Home Hotel at Eyemouth (where Burns was made an Arch-Mason), Jedburgh, Duns, Melrose – drinking it all in, in every sense, as I travelled along by the banks of the Tweed, until I turned towards Moffat and the A74 and turned left towards England, Maidenhead and my four acres at Braywick. It was time to put it all down in six hourly episodes.

We had a big new house in its own grounds with small pool, stables and tennis courts, and a study for me with its own balcony. I had interesting work to do and time to do it in. I was following my own path and positively skipping along it. It would be hard to go back to being a hired hand on the open market, which is all the freelance actor is, however successful. Perhaps the best of the year, however, was the fact that Celtic became the first British team to win the European Cup! In the next two years, with the help of players Craig, McNeil and Wallace, I helped them to win BBC's *Television Quizball* -- twice! Yet, through it all, I was living two quite separate lives.

At home in Braywick Cottage I was the perfectly contented husband, father and property owner, quite happy to act as labourer to the contractors I was employing almost permanently on the house alterations that were to turn the early Victorian dower house into a show-place. Between barrow-loads, I worked on the garden with the old gardener I had inherited, or helped mend the fences. What I know I didn't do was swim or play tennis or just lie back in the hammock that was slung between two gigantic Wellingtonian pines at the edge of the front lawn. I did, however, drive the children to their convent school in Windsor and always walked Jane in her pram around Bray. I also washed most of the dishes before putting them into the dishwasher and occasionally I took Sheila into the cinema in Maidenhead.

My other life was in Glasgow in a little flat I had in Hyndland Road. This too was a working life, but it was another kind of work. This work was more like a hobby, yet it was what I did for a good living. I did get the scripts written in time, the whole series was cast with some of the finest performers in Scotland – Leonard Maguire as the father, William Burness, David McKail as Davie Sillar, Roy Hanlon as Jock Richmond, Paul Kermack as William Creech, Bryden Murdoch as Bob Ainslie, Donald Douglas as the Earl of Glencairn, Ewan Roberts as Gavin Hamilton, Paul Young as John Lewars, Jimmy Gibson as Holy Willie, Roddy McMillan as Willie Smellie and John Laurie as Reverend Auld. The girls too – and what girls! Collette O'Neil as Jean, June Andrews as Bella, Kara Wilson as Mary Campbell, June Alcorn as Nancy McLehose, Isobel Garner as Anna Park, Anne Kidd as Marie Riddell, Morag Hood as Jessie Lewars and Nell Brennan as Bess Panton. Ah yes, young Helen Brennan.

It was a wonderful company. Most were dear friends but some were dearer than others. For instance, I never really hit it off with my leading lady Collette. Perhaps it was my fault. We were too like each other – in background and temperament. Perhaps she never really trusted me. I understand I got her so agitated that after the serial she went straight back to London and got pregnant – by her husband of course – or maybe it was the effect of playing Jean Armour? Kara Wilson was Highland-attractive and properly mysterious. Even then she was being wooed by fellow-student, Tom Conti. June Alcorn I had known on *Craig*.

Anne Kidd was, and still is, lovely and became a real friend. Due to a location mix-up in hotel bookings, we first met when I gave up my bed to her at the Dumfries hotel and was chivalrously rewarded by being taken home to Glenalmond at the weekend to meet her wonderful parents. Anne was the very best type of Scottish girl who just happened to be an actress. I wonder if she ever married? Lucky man if she did. Morag Hood was Liam's little sister and perfect casting for the sweet and gentle Jessie Lewars. It was hardly nepotism, she was so obviously good as her subsequent career proved.

By the back end of the year, we were all hard at work telling the Robert Burns story for television. Or my version of it. It was a marvellous experience, though not without its problems. Because I was so unusually central to the production, not only as the leading actor but as writer and co-producer in a sense, I kept getting in the technicians' hair and up the actors' noses. Whether they liked it or not, I kept interrupting with comments and suggestions and corrections, but only because I was so immersed in the whole thing, and had been for so long. I had lived the story we had to tell and, to my mind, there was only one way to tell it. This was not to usurp Liam's place as director. It was the only way I knew then.

Anyway, Liam didn't seem to mind, as he knew only too well how closely he and I had worked on the project beforehand, and on every spare moment during actual production. Sadly, he was already growing increasingly tired with the multiple sclerosis that was so tragically to kill him only a few years later. I don't think he really needed the strain of me at that particular time. Dear Liam, bless his memory, we had always got on well. We worked in different ways towards the same end and I think we made a good team. I have never really worked effectively on television since he died. I got on the same way with Jimmy MacTaggart and Pharic McLaren at the BBC and with James Crampsey and Eddie Fraser on radio, Tyrone Guthrie and Callum Mill in theatre. All of them, except Callum, now dead. I must watch who I work with in future!

However, at that time, few others outside the STV production office knew how closely I had worked with Liam in the pre-planning and preparation of cameras. The whole thing, including outside locations, was done on television cameras, and not film. This gave it a good overall uniformity of texture, but posed a lot of technical problems on the way. Consequently, much time and temper was lost and both actors and technicians kept protesting and standing on their dignities. But I didn't have time to be dignified – especially on location. I still shiver at the memory of the sea-bathing sequence. It killed Burns, and pretty damn near killed Cairney.

For convenience this was done at Irvine harbour, but it was the middle of November and I had to clamber over rocks in breeches and riding-boots, and walk into the icy water till it was up to my chin, and I stood staring numbly at the camera in the launch above me. Apparently the pressmen present had a sweepstake as to whether I would go in, and if I did, how long I would last! But "Dr Greasepaint", as ever, takes care of mad actors in pursuit of their calling, and I emerged after an hour and a total immersion at one point, quite intact. Indeed, I felt quite heroic – that is until I got into the limousine that was taking me to a house nearby for a bath and a change and breakfast. As soon as I settled in the back seat wrapped in a huge STV towel, I almost screamed with the pain in all my fingers and toes and in that other more private extremity. They told me later I had frostbite! Which I made even worse, by climbing into a steaming bath – and catapulting straight out again, to be reassured by a very cold shower. A very large neat brandy eventually saved the day and all my members!

The same medicine did the trick again in Dumfries. I was being filmed as the dying Burns, slowly making his way in the street to his front door. It was also – courtesy of the Dumfries Fire Brigade – "raining" heavily and by the third or fourth take I was freezing and soaking. Remembering Irvine, however, I said loudly, and hopefully, "God, I could do with a large brandy!" Well, by some electrical freak, that expostulation was heard on every TV set in the Dumfries area, and dear John Laurie, visiting home with his two sisters, jumped up from his chair saying, "That's young Cairney – I'd ken that voice anywhere!"

"That's right, he's making a film down at Burns' house," said one of the sisters. "That's what I heard too," said the other. They kept a shop in the town. Within minutes, dear old John was by my side in that street and I have the happiest memory yet of our drinking a whole bottle of brandy (his) in the snuggery of the Globe Tavern that night. Ask and you shall receive! Especially when a sound boom picks up the local TV signal!

At that time, though, I could have asked for anything in Scotland. For more than two years now I had been coming into their homes through their TV sets and they had made me more than welcome. We had shared moments together in the privacy of their imagination, and they were never to let me forget that over the years. A genuine friendship developed and it's got damn all to do with selling, or promotion or publicity. This is real celebrity, but it's got to be earned. The public tells you these things. Not just by letter and applause, but by the way they remember. Every actor, if he's lucky, has his time and this was mine. There is indeed a tide in one's affairs – and it swept me recklessly along with it.

The first of the four TV solos, 1966.
(Photograph: Radio Times*)*

I was so confident and certain, I forgot how unconfident and uncertain other people are who work in the performing arts. I should have been calm and considerate and available to all of them, but instead I was impatient, rude and intolerant. Rehearsals in the studio were often noisy to say the least. I was reported to every union that was, but it made little difference. The *Craig* experience now stood me in good stead. I knew now how to cut a lot of corners, and play a few technical tricks. This seemed to upset a lot of people who were not used to having their bluff called, but we had eight weeks to put six hours in the can and there was no time to waste.

On one occasion, one of the union officials asked for a meeting "at my convenience" to discuss my directorial tendencies. I agreed to meet him next day in the Circle lavatory – but he never turned up and I heard no more about it. However tactless and unthinking I may have appeared, they all knew, even the most pompous and self-important of the union men, that my first loyalty was to the job in hand and to make it as good as any cast and crew could. I was less worried about my personal glory than perhaps they thought. I had written the damn thing and was well paid for doing so. I also knew I had a good part, but I knew too that I could only be as good as everyone around me. Television, like film, is a team sport and it only needs one poor player for everyone to lose the game.

But we didn't lose. In fact we won handsomely, and when it eventually went out on the screens (to Scotland only) it is fair to say it stopped the traffic in the streets. I'm sure many will remember it yet. Alas, it can never be repeated. It was "wiped" by a well-meaning junior technician, over-zealous in his tidying of the STV vaults. Perhaps, one day, Scottish Television will do it again with a new director, a new Burns, a new cast, on film this time, and in glorious colour. Will Scotland take it to their hearts again? I think they will. It's a good story and we all live in a story, as I said at the very start of this book. Besides, Scottish Television own the script for another 30 years. It would be a shame if they did not get full value for their investment.

I registered Shanter Productions as a trading name for my own theatrical company, and as a first venture decided on a short season with *There Was A Man*. I had always rather liked the idea of being an actor-manager, even if it were only myself in a one-man show, so a deal was struck with Tom and Gerry, and though they trusted me to set up matters in a businesslike way, they both sent me lawyers' letters to make sure I did.

I was to open at the Theatre Royal, Dumfries, and after a season there do a Scottish tour before bringing the piece to London. Discussion was already under way with several managements including John Calder, Peter Bridge and my old mate Tony Marriott, author of *No Sex, Please. We're British* and producer of my first Burns LP in 1968. One way and another, prospects were very good for a West End season by the end of the year if all continued to go well.

Fortunately, it did. Especially in Burns' own theatre in Dumfries, the very building where he had been given a free pass to see Mr Sutherland's company. I wonder what he would have made of the éclat our show caused. I was virtually the age he was when he died there, but I was having a ball; toasted by the town, reassured by standing room only every night, and enjoying my days on the farm I'd rented at Dunscore from the charming Mrs MacEntegart, the artist-widow of an Air Marshall.

My mother had by now returned from America, a little bewildered and not all that pleased to find that her elder son had become quite famous. The first time she had noticed it was when I went to collect her at the airport and she was suddenly aware of the nudges, winks, pointing fingers and open stares. I don't think she liked it. Now she was installed on the farm with Lena, an old family friend, and the three Cairney girls, Jennifer, Alison and Lesley. Sheila once again had stayed behind to look after the builders and little Jane. So, by day, the Cairneys had a country holiday and by night daddy went out to work – which was also a kind of holiday.

It's easy to go to work every night in a success. There's a wonderful and permanent buzz about the theatre which is contagious. I had reduced stage management to the minimum, and relied for the most part on a small-part actor and part-time journalist called Elliot Williams, who was something of a character, and a well-known figure in Annan and around the south-west. He had developed from being a nuisance into something like my very best friend; also manager, press agent, front-of-house supervisor and general factotum. He could do none of these things well, but he managed the sum of them so engagingly that I forgot to get angry with him and was glad of his loyalty and affection.

When I first met him he was an extra in Tony Guthrie's 1959 production of *The Thrie Estaites* at the Edinburgh Festival, in which I played the young king (my present Edinburgh bank manager, Graham Buchanan, was the boy page!). Elliot and I had kept in touch, mostly when he had to borrow money. But there was one night when he phoned me up at my home in the middle of the night to say that he was going to commit suicide.

"For goodness' sake man," I spluttered. "What's happened?"

"My cat's died," he said solemnly.

I talked him out of it. Now this was the man who was my minder and professional companion. He was good in certain situations – like dispensing dressing-room hospitality and defusing pomposity. It was hard to be serious around Elliot. He knew his theatre for all his eccentricities, and he could count the house to the nearest penny. He was a good man to have on your side.

On that first Scottish tour I played three dates in Arran – Brodick, Whiting Bay and the local golf club, where I was the guest of Professor Alan Gemmell (of *Gardeners' Question Time* fame). But I was looked after generally by the redoubtable Bess MacMillan, the local hairdresser and impresario. She worked on the sensible principle that if they were to see this much-talked-about *There Was A Man* it was easier for one (me) to come over on the ferry to Arran than it was for her to organise bus parties and block bookings to bring Arran over to Dumfries or Glasgow. So she wrote to me and said just that. I was completely won over and, besides, I'd never been to Arran.

The dressing-room, in Brodick I think, is just under street level, and sitting at the mirror getting ready for the performance, I was aware of the feet I could see at the window to my side. I could also hear their voices very clearly – perhaps too clearly. But then if we eavesdrop, we deserve to hear whatever we hear. In this case I could judge by the high heels and the shapely ankles that this was a couple of young girls, with an old couple in front of them and a pair of young boys behind them. It's interesting to conjecture on identity when all you can see of the person are their shoes and six inches of leg! Anyway, one young girl was saying to the other, "What time does it start?"

"Seven-thirty, I suppose," replied her companion.

"And d'you know when it finishes?"

"I dunno," said her pal.

Then I saw the sensible shoes in front of her slightly swivel, and an older woman's voice told them,

"About half-past ten, I think."

"My," went on the first young voice, "That's a long picture."

"What'ye mean – picture?" asked the friend.

"It's a film, isn't it?" There was some laughter.

"Don't be silly, it's John Cairney doin' his Burns thing – ye know, like on the telly. We saw it remember?"

"Ye mean – alive – in person?"

"I hope so. At least that's what we've been queuing up for."

"Ach then, it's you that's silly. John Cairney would never come to Arran."

Much to my delight and surprise, Sheila agreed to come up and leave the children with their gran in Glasgow and join me in Arran. Tony Marriott may have had something to do with it – or, more probably, Heulwyn his Welsh wife. However it happened it was wonderful, and some very precious hours were stolen on that wonderful Scottish island. Why couldn't we do this more often? I suddenly realised what a marvellous marriage I had.

Coming back on the ferry we met Peggy Macrae, widow of Duncan, standing on the quay at Fairlie waiting to catch the boat to her beloved Millport. She nearly missed it because we talked so long. She looked small and wistful and was obviously missing her wonderful husband.

"How are you managing, Peggy?"

"I'm not," she answered candidly. "Listen, did you ever think of playing *Gog and Magog*, John?"

We waved her off, and never saw her again. She died not long after, less than a year after husband. When there's no will, there's no way. Sheila and I were very quiet on the drive back to the children in Glasgow. But as she took them south, I went north.

Dundee is a little Glasgow. Maybe that's why I like the place. It was always lucky for Burns and me. It had been the first commercial theatre to take the show after the Traverse, and it had me back at every opportunity. I played all the Burns performances in the former kirk at Lochlee Road, where you could see some of the audience "keeking" around the various pillars – but it still had a good theatre feeling nevertheless.

Backstage seemed to be entirely populated by bonnie Dundee girls whose collective accent would have delighted McGonagall. I remember the Angus twins who appointed themselves my dressers and personal assistants – and always made sure two of them were there! And sweet little Mary, the usherette, whose mother was persuaded to give me a room in their council house across the road on the late technical rehearsal nights, and who was mortally offended when I offered to pay. Once again, good, ordinary people impinging their decent standards on our whirligig world of theatre.

The Lyceum in Edinburgh, with the Citizens in Glasgow and His Majesty's in Aberdeen, are my three very favourite theatres. It was the Lyceum, however, that gave me the first sight of long queues at the box office. *There Was A Man* was the first of many happy productions I was involved in there – under Clive Perry, Bill Bryden, and Richard Eyre – in the decade that was to follow. Yes, I loved that theatre. The only drawback was that it was in Edinburgh!

I returned to Jimmy Logan's Metropole Theatre with a Gala Night in aid of the National Research Trust for Speech, sponsored by Jack Hawkins and the Gift of Speech Campaign. I was glad to do so for such a cause. I had always been conscious of my own rather idiosyncratic voice and in my student days had to work like the devil on its high-pitched, mono-tonal, town-husky whine.

James Crampsey, then Head of Drama, came to the Drama College to give a talk on Broadcasting Techniques. "In Radio," he said, "we deal mainly with the voice beautiful and the voice odd . . .".

At the end of his lecture, he invited questions. I rose at once. "Speaking as a Voice Odd" I said. Now that odd voice was carrying me through two and a half hours of use a night, non-stop; not to mention all the rattling-on I do afterwards and the nervous prattle before. I never stop talking. I can never get away from my voice. Nor can you from yours. The voice matters.

Many years ago, I attended a stage lunch in London and heard Jack Hawkins speak through a hole in his throat by pounding his ribs with his arms. I knew then that my vocal problems were trivial. Nevertheless, even now, I have to work on my voice, otherwise the old, throaty, proletarian tonelessness will reassert itself. I'm not sure whether an immediately recognisable voice in a performer is a good thing. My recording manager at HMV, Norman Newall, was convinced that it was. "Your voice could be nobody else's," he said. Who would want it? Tony Guthrie on the other hand held the view that the voice was the actor's first instrument and should be trained and ready to play all parts like a trumpet. Mine, I'm afraid, is a city saxophone – and the city of Glasgow at that!

My first memory of bringing Burns to Aberdeen was driving on the road from Stonehaven towards Aberdeen and seeing at the end of a long, straight stretch an advertising billboard which I gradually made out to be for His Majesty's Theatre. As I drove towards it, I saw my own name looming larger and larger till it was in the largest print I had ever seen. It made me laugh out loud. Apart from the sheer vanity of it, there must be something in us all that makes us want to write our names on walls – and to have that instinct fully satisfied for ever is to see one's name on a hoarding in letters as big as one's self. You could have your names in lights of course. I was to have that later, but they were so very much smaller. But I've never been so thrilled as I was on that Sunday afternoon in 1968. Then again, I've never had sole star billing since either.

The first thing I saw from my hotel window in Aberdeen next morning were white footsteps painted from the base of the Burns statue on Union Terrace and leading towards the stage door of His Majesty's Theatre! Was this an Aberdeen joke? I knew I was going to enjoy my week there,

"The face I sold for almost twenty years".
(Photograph: Dennis Straughan, The Scotsman*)*

and I did. I had the whole fabulous old theatre to play with and Aberdeen responded by helping me establish a house attendance record – more than a thousand people for a one-man show – and every one of them could hear and see perfectly, thanks to the classical acoustic qualities of that old-fashioned interior. It was real theatre in every sense of the word and in James Donald it had a matching custodian. His pride in it rubbed off on his staff – just as Jimmy Logan's with his Metropole people. This in turn rubs off on the patrons, who give the benefit of it to the performers. It's a simple process many modern theatre managements ignore.

Reviews for the Burns were good and the town responded, especially the girls' schools. I hadn't seen so many in one place since that eventful night in Vevey. But what was so different about these lovely Northern maidens was that they were so well behaved compared to the Amazons of the finishing schools! Except perhaps for the smokers. I don't know why but these young girls of nearly twenty years ago dearly loved their cigarettes. I suppose they thought they'd never be noticed sitting in the dark of the stalls or the circle, but I could see them from the stage light up like so many little glow-worms, and then gradually the pall of smoke mantled over them like a canopy. Sometimes I thought I was playing in a working men's club. But otherwise they were wonderful audiences and many of them were pretty enough to be quite distracting. Audiences should remember the effect they have on the performer. It is often more powerful than any effect he might have on them.

I must have had some effect because something happened in Aberdeen that had never happened to me before. Some of the schoolgirls organised a public petition to bring Burns back! Yes, no less than 269 young ladies signed their names to a demand that I should bring my Burns show back to Aberdeen. And James Donald had to take them seriously.

"Can you extend another week?" he asked.

"'fraid not, we're due in Inverness."

"Well, next month then?"

"Sorry – we're due to open in London."

"OK," said James, "Next year then?"

"Done!" said I, and we shook hands on it.

Yet it wasn't *my* show as everybody called it. Legally it was Tom Wright's, technically it was the property of whatever company was touring it at the time – Traverse, Festival, Shanter or Talus of London – but morally I felt way deep down it was really my baby, and as far as the public was concerned there was no doubt about it. It was Cairney's Burns. They didn't really care who wrote it, or directed it, or presented it, they only wanted to know who was in it. The public goes to the theatre to see actors. They always have done, always will. Fashionable writers may engross the intelligentsia, fashionable directors may excite the critics, but people go to live theatre to see people. As far as the public in Scotland was concerned I was Robert Burns and that was that. I worked really hard to sell that image in the few years I was totally involved in the character. What has been difficult since, is trying to lose it.

I played Burns actively from 1965 till 1969, then in a restricted manner until 1981, and since, hardly at all. Even when I do the one-man Burns Suppers today it is only to talk about him rather than perform him. Yet still the legend persists, and I am thought of only as Burns. I should be pleased to have maintained an identity for so long. But in a way, as I have created him, he has killed me. I am a Frankenstein to a Burns monster, who was killed off a long time ago but just refuses to die. In 1965, Gerry Slevin had said I could play the part till I was 40. Last week I had my most recent invitation to play the part again. I shall be 58 next birthday! But in 1968, I was 38.

> My heart's in the highlands
> My heart is not here
> My heart's in the highlands
> A-chasing the deer.

Inverness is quite a small town really yet it has all the grace of a capital city – the capital of the highlands. I bought a kilt there, and in a tartan I was entitled to wear too. Here was I, six parts Irish, but the two parts Scots that is mine gave me my name and an entitlement to the Ancient Gordon, by virtue of CAIRNIE which is the variant of our family name. My father was right, he had always said that the lesser Scots element in us would always outweigh the greater Irish! He told us we had come from somewhere in the north-east, and here I was, learning from Arthur Varley, a Londoner, but Kilt Maker to the Highland Brigade, that the Cairney family came in fact from a place called Cairney, north of Aberdeen, in the land of the Leslies, who were a sept of the Gordon family. So, the man who played Robert Burns could have a faint and distant connection with Lord Byron!

It was in Inverness, and thanks to John Worth, the theatre manager, that I played *There Was A Man* twice nightly on one occasion. Normally, I found the two-and-a-half-hour programme arduous enough without thinking of about-turning within a couple of hours and starting again in costumes still wet with perspiration from a matinée. However, I had reckoned without John Worth. John was a theatre man through and through. A brilliant pianist, he had come north with a touring show which got itself stranded in Inverness just after the war – the second of course, although John has been so long in Inverness that it might have been the Boer War! Anyway, John and the producer of the show found themselves sitting at Inverness station with a hamper of props and a pile of scenery. They hadn't the money to return south nor could they find anyone to buy their equipment, so John, ever-enterprising, moved the lot into a local hotel and put on a show called *Highland Delight* or something like that, with local singers and instrumentalists, till he was able to move into the Empire eventually as resident manager. The Empire, alas, is now demolished, and John himself is a bit shaky, but he continues to survive even yet as an agent, impresario and accompanist – and because he is still the resilient enthusiast, God bless him. He has kept the same digs he first had because his landlady gives him limitless credit through the lean times and joins him in a wee dram when things improve. "Not to worry" is his motto and the slogan that has carried this charming little man through 40 struggling years of theatre. Yes, John had charm, and he was never ashamed to use it.

Which is why I ended up one Saturday afternoon playing to half a house instead of watching the local football match. John had said in his nasal Lancastrian drawl that this family had made a special trip to see the show from Golspie in the north, you see, and couldn't wait to see the evening performance because of their long car trip home. So I agreed to a matinée. It was in the contract. I was actually supposed to do two matinées (Wednesday and Saturday at 2.30), according to the old Esher Standard Equity agreement, but in the case of the one-man show, managements could use their discretion and they generally waived the matinées, especially when the nights were doing so well. But not our John. He would have at least his half-a-pound of flesh!

The family he was talking about did indeed attend – occupying most of the front row. I started, intending to play it very cool indeed, but as always the thing caught me up and, by the middle of Act Two, I was lost in the world of Robert Burns. And so indeed were the Golspie lot – like something out of the Giles cartoons strung along the front row – from grannie to the toddlers – and all more or less attentive. There was much shushing and hissing and "Listen to the nice man now", but somehow we all got to the end together and I hurried to my dressing-room for a gallon of milk, an apple and a bar of chocolate – and to listen to the football results on my little Roberts radio. When I came out again at 7.30, with my first-act shirt newly ironed and feeling all warm on me, would you believe that the Golspie-Giles clan were still there? Yes. Minus the youngsters, there they were again in the front row beaming at me. A couple of the younger girls waved. They told me later that they had so enjoyed themselves, that they had decided to stay over another night and see it all

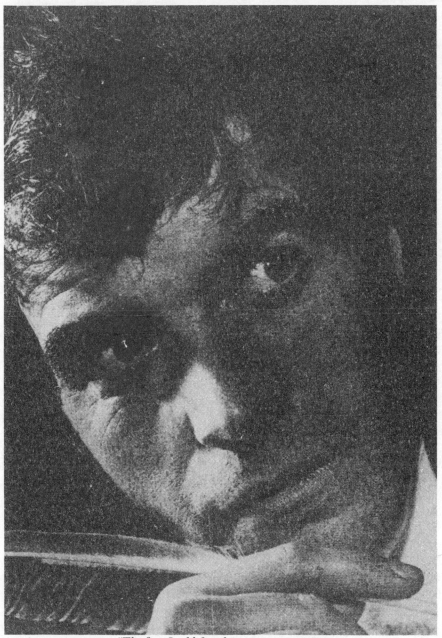

"The face I sold for almost twenty years".
(Photograph: Dennis Straughan, The Scotsman*)*

over again. "After all," said the father, "ye'll never come back to Golspie." And I never have. Yet.

It was in Inverness that I made the acquaintance of another Highland family, the Grants. Hugh Grant had been the assistant-manager of the Caledonian Hotel when I first came to Inverness, and I gather he had not been unduly impressed by the news that he was to have Robert Burns as guest. You must understand the Highlander's natural apathy to the Lowlander's patron saint. However, when he learned that I liked football he thawed somewhat and gave me the full benefit of his grave Highland courtesy and charm. His wife Joan was very different. She was a woman. And what a woman. Vivacious, curvaceous, audacious and flirtatious. When they changed hotels in the area, I used to change with them. A good hotel manager is like a good bank manager – one never lets the matter of a mere building interfere in a good relationship. Besides, I enjoyed Joan's company – and I've enjoyed it at all five of the establishments Hugh has been involved in when I've brought my various shows to Inverness. McGonagall, Stevenson, Novello, Robert Service, it's all one to the Grants, for they know it's just John Cairney underneath them all.

I am, I suppose, a commercial traveller in the Spoken Word, but how many other gentlemen of the road adopt and are adopted by a family in nearly every town they visit in the course of their work? The Grants in Inverness remind me of the Brennans in Glasgow, the Waughs in Edinburgh, the Knights in Aberdeen, the Brotherwoods in Carlisle, the Braids in Ayr, the Equis in Hamilton, Lanarkshire and the McVicars in Hamilton, Ontario, the Prestons in Toronto, the Evanses in Winnipeg, the Morrises in Calgary, the McLeods in Vancouver, the Turnbows in Texas, the Palmerlees in san Francisco, the Joneses in Cleveland, the Murrays in Sydney, the Overtons in Auckland, the Vinnells in Christchurch etc. – with apologies to any I may have forgotten.

None of these is family in the consanguineous sense, they are not relatives, nor are they involved with me professionally. They are friends, and each couple in its way has shown a family kindness to me when the Burns odyssey brought me to their doors. They took me in, they warmed me in their hospitality and they refreshed me by their concern. And what have I given them? Only the passing memory of a performance, the ephemeral blessing of a transient, and of course, my gratitude. If I ever forgot to mention it, I'm doing so now. I'm not sure why they all did it. I'm not exactly God's gift as a guest. No actor is. Perhaps they recognised, that for all the hubris that surrounded me in my high days of public glory, I was a genuine one-man show, in that I was a solitary, a loner, and but for all of them I should have been very lonely. Over the years I saw quite a bit

70

of these friends. They were my alter-family. The only pity was I saw so little of my own. But some are born alone, some achieve loneliness and others have it thrust upon them! But not for much longer. The out-of-London tour, as it were, was now over, and I was due at my next date which was the Arts Theatre, Great Newport Street, London.

It was during the Metropole week that Tony Marriott had come up from London with Denis "Slim" Ramsden, the actor-director. I knew Tony, of course, but this time he was representing Talus Productions in London. Would I be interested in playing a limited season at the Arts Theatre in London – with "Slim" directing?

"For the benefit of Sassenach audiences," he said with a laugh.

"Why don't I go in during Sir Peter Daubeny's foreign season with the Moscow Arts Theatre?" I asked drily. I was only half-joking.

"Well?" said Tony. "It'll get you home for a change." I hesitated for 30 seconds.

"Where do I sign?"

I opened at the Arts Theatre, London, before only a little more people than I had left at home in Maidenhead! As I said to that first audience, "It is rare indeed that the cast of a one-man show almost outnumbers the audience!" Luckily for us all involved, what was lacking in numbers was more than made up for in perceptivity. Most of the London critics were there. And they saw that it was good! For the most part, the notices were kind to everyone concerned. I was agreeably surprised. First of all because I was so very, very nervous. Despite the acclaim the show had received at the Festival and all round Scotland, I was terribly aware that this was the Capital, this was London, this was it.

I know now how wrong an attitude this is, but such a sense of provincialism must be deeply ingrained in most of us north of Regents Park for me to have felt so tremulous about appearing before the London critics. All I know is that when I started through the sparse audience on that first night, I felt very lonely, and my voice when it did come out seemed to be floating six feet above my head. I was in no contact at all with my limbs and my hands felt as if they were on fork-lifts, but I went through the ingrained motions and just prayed that I would soon come down to earth again. Each of my fingers was about six inches thick as I attempted to casually undo the buttons of my jacket. I was on automatic pilot, going through the robot moves, following myself about that little stage, hearing the words coming hollowly from somewhere behind me. It was an eerie sensation. It wasn't really until the start of the second act that my voice and I were reunited, and that I felt that I was free at last of that numbing stage-fright.

And I had another reason for dreading the notices. I was standing centre-stage, after the first interval, looking exactly like an advert for Sandeman's port in my tricorne hat and long black cloak, as the spot came up slowly to discover me. It also revealed about half-a-dozen stooped and suited figures making their way along the front-row stalls as if they were in the trenches. The audience and I paused to watch and eventually all were seated and looking up at me with flushed and shining faces. I then spoke my first line of the act, "I arrived in Edinburgh – " I should then have continued, "on a borrowed pony." Instead I substituted, "before some of the critics returned from the bar!" Sir Harold Hobson, who had not been among the latecomers, laughed loudest from his seat at the end of the second row. However, that didn't prevent his calling me "James Cairney" in **This** *Was A Man* in an otherwise favourable *Sunday Times* review. This vital London opening was the first, and last, time on the stage I suffered really badly from first-night nerves. Every actor on every first night has the usual dry voice, thumping heart and fluttering tummy, but not before or since have I felt so bad as I did on the night of Wednesday 13th November 1968 at the London Arts Theatre.

Unlike the oldest profession, where half the pleasure for the participant is anticipatory, in the second-oldest profession all the pleasure is retrospective! I was especially aware of this by the end of that momentous evening when the final reception was as thunderous as 50 people can make it, but I was well satisfied. I had got through it and was still alive – what else mattered?

I don't remember anything of afterwards except that I joined Tony Marriott in his car to go to the restaurant booked for a first-night supper party. I've no idea where, it wasn't the Ivy or the Caprice or the Café Royal. Perhaps it was a Wimpy Bar somewhere. All I know is that we were cruising round Leicester Square looking for a place to park, when Tony was stopped by a policeman for some very minor reason, like going slowly down the wrong side of the street. Tony, like any good producer on a first night, had been celebrating our success, or drowning his sorrows – either way, he was feeling no pain. And even a policeman would have seen this. As a result, dear old Tony was in trouble, but to my delight, the policeman was a Scotsman.

"Leave this to me, Tony," I said grandly.

"Officer," I said in my most Caledonian manner, "I have just finished playing Robert Burns at the Arts Theatre – "

"I'm delighted to hear that you've finished, sir. If there's one thing I canna stand it's Robbie Burns. I'm from Oban myself!"

Trust me to land a "teuchter"!

My advocacy helped Tony not at all and in fact may have led to his being charged with being drunk in charge of an actor in addition to his other offences. And, at the end of it all, would you believe that that Philistinic copper had the nerve to ask me to sign an autograph for his mother in Oban? I declined on the grounds of manual incompetence and Tony and I slouched away in the general direction of Soho.

During the two weeks of the run audiences grew and grew till there was only standing room left by the last night. Which reminds me, I was given a standing ovation on the last night, but perhaps that was only because half the audience was standing already? At any rate, Talus Productions made enough to pay Tony's fine and travel us all – actor, director, stage director, stage manager, wardrobe assistant, company manager, secretary, publicity officer two redundant musicians (a musicians' union requirement!) and a hamper of costumes and props to the Theatre Royal, Newcastle, where we were to play the week before the pantomime. It's astonishing the number of people needed to put on a one-man show in the commercial theatre.

Newcastle vies with Aberdeen as my most favourite theatrical town outside Glasgow, but on that occasion I was not at all keen to go north. The Arts fortnight had just caught alight and a transfer to another theatre in the West End, like the Fortune, was on the cards. Broadway interest had resumed and I was becoming in demand for a lot of interview and magazine programmes both on radio and television. There was talk of its being filmed. In short, we were just taking off, when we were taken off. Unfortunately we had the previous booking in Newcastle, and of course we had to honour it. A pity, for it prevented a real build-up with the Burns in London and all the fringe benefits that accrue therefrom, but alas it was not to be and we all took the M1 to where it joins the A1 and the Great North Road.

Newcastle was memorable for visits to St James' Park to see the famous United and for my first meeting with Glasgow-born, Jewish playwright, Cecil P. Taylor, who was living then in a caravan just outside the city and writing his soon-to-be-recognised plays in a wooden shed at the bottom of his garden. I liked him at once, and his young wife, Liz, as much and we promised to meet again as soon as our respective commitments allowed. After all, we both had the same agent, and Barry soon saw that our paths crossed again.

This was the final week of *There Was A Man*. Yes, this was to be the end, at least as far as I was concerned, but not at all with the bang that had heralded its Traverse run and saw its eventual triumph at the Arts, but with a whimper. It faded in the north-east in what could only be described as an anti-climax. The week had been as good as ever in terms of audience, the Geordies were lovely about it, but suddenly I was tired. And jaded. It had been non-stop since '64 and I badly needed a rest. And a change. Not only from Burns, but from the relentless round of driving-seat to dressing-room, to restaurant to hotel room, and back to the driving-seat again. Tour offers poured in but I didn't want to know. Returning to London was also considered, but it was almost Christmas and we couldn't get a theatre until the spring, and that seemed a whole year away. Yes, I needed a rest.

Resting is often considered by non-theatre people to be only the actor's euphemism for unemployment, but there comes a time when it is the only thing one can do. The body, the mind and the soul all tell you to stop and, if you don't, they will stop anyway, and that way every kind of trouble lies, as I had already found. Besides, actors go on working frantically because they are certain that it's never going to last and much hay is made while that sun is shining. But I now had quite a bit of hay in the barn. I could afford to come in from the fields for a bit. My accountant, Stanley Aarons, quietly suggested that a year without working would be a very welcome tax buffer. I didn't really understand what he meant, but it was with a real feeling of relief that Sunday morning when instead of carrying on north to Scotland for yet another tour, I turned the wheel south, to home, and encapsulated with Mahler on the motorway, let my mind drift on to other things, other people, other places . . . I was out of work but I was not out of pocket – thanks to Robert Burns. But Robert Burns was dead – long live John Cairney!

I used my new leisure to tout a possible Burns film. The Arts run had reawakened interest in that area, and a man called John Hayman gave me lunch at World Film Services to talk about it – but who would write the script? Barry suggested I combine with Cecil Taylor. Why not? I hope his suggestion was entirely altruistic and not influenced by the prospect of a double commission? I agreed to talk to Cecil about it. Meantime, two other nice Jewish boys, Cyril Ornadel and Hal Shaper, had written a musical called *Tam o' Shanter* in which they hoped Albert Finney might star as Robert Burns. Now that I had jumped off the Burns bandwagon everyone else seemed to be jumping on. An American company sent me a script called *Great Scot!* about Burns which had actually been presented off Broadway, but not far enough off in my opinion. I couldn't believe that such a great hero, and such a great story, could be so traduced and reduced to sub-college show level. I sketched out my own first ideas for a Burns musical and sent it off to Robin Richardson at Traverse Festival Productions in Edinburgh – but he lost it. Or so he said. I had called it "The Various

Man" – which was a quote from Burns. Now I can't remember quote nor script, and a full-scale Burns musical has still to be done. It's amazing that with such a natural subject and nearly 400 tunes to choose from no one has yet put it on. Perhaps I shall yet – who knows? Now that I had time, I began courting my wife again, playing with the children, messing about in the garden and dabbling in home decorating. I even thought of writing a book. What I did do, however, was to build a brick wall all round Braywick Cottage. That must have had a deep Freudian significance, but I enjoyed the therapy of labouring to the bricklayers. True to form, I dropped a few. All this time, I was in constant contact with Cecil in the north and a film script was gradually growing under his hand in the woodshed. I had written as a guide for Cecil a very long, very detailed account of the life of Burns in basic film terms, and also gave him my STV scripts on the subject. He was now writing his own version and I had to comment at each stage. I now realise that, whether I liked it or not, after nearly a decade of involvement, I was becoming something of a Burns authority. I had a vague notion of perhaps doing a post-graduate degree on the aspects of Burns in theatrical performance. The idea appealed as I was certain I was an academic manqué, but perhaps this wasn't the ideal time. But one day . . .

Sheila and I celebrated our 15th wedding anniversary with a luxury weekend at the Royal Garden Hotel at Hyde Park. She made me promise that I wouldn't mention the name Burns all the time we were there. I didn't. I was only too glad to be reminded that I had such a wife. I knew the pianist in the hotel orchestra, Sid Haddon, from my earlier recording days with Sammy San at Abbey Road, and Sid got the band to come forward and ring our table with violins. Very romantic. No, they didn't play any Burns songs. They probably didn't know any. But they did play "Please", "Deep Purple" and "Those Were The Days My Friend" – I thought they'd never end. I had almost forgotten there had been other days – forgotten I had been an up-and-coming young actor before all this Burns bonanza. But I had promised not to talk about Robert Burns – for the weekend at least. We sat up so late we didn't really have enough time to enjoy the luxury penthouse. I went round switching on televisions and trying the telephone in the loo just to make sure I got my money's worth.

Next day we looked in shops in the King's Road, saw Ginger Rogers at Drury Lane that night, but left before the end to come back to Knightsbridge on the top deck of a red bus. Next morning we heard Mass at Brompton Oratory and after a winey lunch in Chelsea meandered along the M4 towards our four little girls. It had been an idyllic time. We should do it more often. Not long afterwards, Sheila mentioned very casually that she was pregnant again. On second thoughts perhaps we shouldn't do it too often. On the other hand, this could be the boy?

It was. Jonathan William Thomas Cairney was born on St David's Day – 1st March 1970 at the Taplow Hospital – and I was there!

Cecil and I met in a Bond Street café to discuss the Burns film script. I was so disappointed in what I had read of it. Cecil was a self-evident writer of real talent (as he later proved with a whole stream of plays), but there was something not quite right about the film treatment. I couldn't put my finger on it, but the story had been distorted somehow. I tried to explain to Cecil that I found the character of Burns as written quite unlikeable. "I don't like the bugger, either," said Cecil. Perhaps that explains it. John Hayman of World Film Services hated the script so much that he cancelled the production forthwith. Well, so much for film stardom. I seem fated to be denied it. Still, Cyril and I got £3,000 each. And I hadn't wanted to earn anything. But I didn't say "no" to it. Instead I did some more building and conversion work around the property and pondered lazily on what I might do next. I was in no real hurry. I would wait and see what happened.

Robin Crichton phoned from Nine Mile Burn in Midlothian. He had just opened Scotland's first-ever film studio and he wondered if I might be interested in using it as a base for my intended Burns film? I explained that the film was no longer on, even though Columbia had been very keen and plans had already been made to film it in Yugoslavia. But all that had now been scrapped. The script had put them off, although it was true that the Americans were already pulling out of productions in Europe because of the situation in Cambodia and Vietnam and the consequent increase in overseas taxation for US companies working abroad. Robin didn't seem unduly fazed by all this.

"Let's make our own Burns film," he said jauntily.

"Can you afford it?" I asked.

"Of course not," he replied. "But if you're willing to come up here and work out an hour's script, and play it with amateurs in a sequence of stills taken by students rather than shooting it on film, then I think we might be able to make something."

"Do I get paid?" I then asked.

"Don't be silly," he promptly replied. "But you might not be able to afford to work like this again, so we might as well do it while we can – and while I've got these film students. Let's have a go anyway. We'll pay you something. At least enough to pay for all those Hamlet cigars."

"I'm giving up smoking."

"Good, that's a saving already on the budget."

I liked Robin. Even more, I liked his family. Even more still, I liked his stylish wife Trish – and I just loved her home-made soup.

"You can live with us and we might even give you a little bit of say in the production. I think you could do with the experience."

That did it, and so it was agreed. Sometime next year perhaps – just as long as we did it. It could be worked round my other commitments. It was a kind of Burns film after all, I suppose. It could be the beginning of something. Or the end? Well, well, so Burns was dead? If he were he was still not lying down! If I had fallen out of the London frying-pan it would seem I had stumbled into the Edinburgh saucepan! "Oh no, not Burns again?" said Sheila.

In that same year we decided to return to live in Scotland. It was the "Friendly Games" that did it. We sat in our, by now, very comfortable sitting-room at Braywick Cottage watching the 1970 Commonwealth Games being relayed from Edinburgh. Perhaps it was the colour, or the crowds, or the very Scottishness of it all, but suddenly Sheila was homesick – for the first time since we came to London in 1954. It was all very unexpected but it was real enough. The children were dumbfounded and I understand there were many long anxious union meetings in the playroom, and Jennifer, as their shop steward, made a good case for not disrupting their education at the Brigidine Convent, or losing them their life-long friends, or making them give up their ponies. But Sheila and her mother had found a ruin in Pittenweem, Fife, which bore the title, "My Lord of Kellie's Ludging" and now as Kellie Lodging was to become Cairney's Castle!

I had gone native – a Scotsman once again. And an in-comer Fifer at that. Pittenweem reminded me of a Breton village. It was nearly as fast and incomprehensible, but at least we had a whole new magnificent house and the Anglo-Scots family Cairney in England became a Scoto-English family in Scotland. The reaction of the locals was mixed to say the least.

On one hand they were delighted that we had restored an imposing edifice to the centre of the village High Street and they were intrigued by the superficial gloss which passing celebrity had given this intrusive familial group, but our very theatricality was a barrier and there was also in some quarters an out-and-out resentment of our ability to buy such a place. I suppose it's the way people resent pop stars buying huge, rolling estates. While the vast majority of Scots made me very welcome again in my own country – I was one of the runners-up to

Tom Jones in a *Scottish Daily Express* poll to find Scotland's Dream Man!
– some were not so sure.

The times they were a-changing. By now Shanter Productions had
an office in Edinburgh, a nurse-cum-secretary, the 18-year-old Monica
Barry. She came to me with an interesting sister and two delightful
brothers, and together with a gallant and handsome architect called
Colin Campbell (who had an admirable weakness for pretty women),
we tried to interest the City Fathers of Edinburgh in creating the
Scottish Centre for the Performing Arts at the old Tron Kirk in the
High Street. After much "politicking", a meeting of the Provost's
Committee decided that public money could not be entrusted to an
actor and the scheme was dropped. I paid all the fees involved, gave up
the project and decided that for me there was no business but show
business! My sabbatical was over. It was time to get back to serious work
and, of course, it had to be Burns.

My old college pal, Andy Stewart, asked me to join him in a Burns
Night to be held in the Massey Hall in Toronto. I was to do the first half
and Andy would do the second and we would join up for the Finale. I
couldn't resist this very first chance to fly the Atlantic and, besides, they
had promised me a weekend in New York at the end of the
engagement if receipts went over the 80% mark. The contact dealing
with all arrangements was an ex-Coatbridge man by the name of Peter
Glen, whose only ambition was to sing tenor, and he organised all
kinds of shows solely for the purpose of exercising his not
inconsiderable voice. Actually, he was a John McCormack sound-alike,
but for the purposes of this particular show he would do his Robert
Wilson. He and his associates had read of my Burns doings in the
Sunday Mail and thought I might just draw the Scottish Torontonians.
And if I didn't, Andy certainly would.

When I stepped on to the landing-strip that served as a stage in the
old and vast Massey Hall that January night in my well-worn Burns
costume, I heard a woman's voice say clearly, "Who's this guy?" I
stopped in my tracks and told her that I had no idea who she was
either, but if she would allow me I would introduce myself: "My name
is Robert Burns. It is a name that has made a little noise in my own
country . . ." and I was into my Burns "spiel". The interruption had
given me a wonderful start and eased the tension at once. I was able, as
far as I could in the huge auditorium, to talk to the audience as Burns,
using as much of his material as was fitting to the occasion, so that in
less than an hour I had more or less covered his life, got a few laughs,
cued the songs for Peter and even had the dancers on at one point. I
finished with "Tam o' Shanter" and it almost finished me. I wasn't

using a microphone, and by the time I removed my steaming shirt in the dressing-room, my voice had gone completely. I must have been more nervous than I thought.

In a way it was a relief, for I didn't need to say anything to the wave of strangers that swamped the dressing-room during the interval, but Peter and his "MacMafia" soon cleared the place, and while Andy had the packed house roaring in the second half, I was already in the restaurant next door tucking into the inevitable minestrone, spaghetti and Chianti. Miraculously my voice, or most of it, came back just in time for the Finale. I skipped coffee and, very casually, strolled on in my dinner jacket to the strains of "Auld Lang Syne", this time to a microphone centre stage. I was adjusting it to my height (Andy's no giant), when another female voice was heard out front. It was explaining, "He must be the manager. It'll be an announcement". I was still the stranger it would seem.

Toronto was a quaint, unexpected, green-timbered, red-roofed, not yet sky-scrapered Toronto then, from what I could see of it, for most of it was under four feet of snow. I didn't mind. I was snug in a comfortable hotel room opposite the CBC building and only came out to be wined and dined by various newspapers and theatre people.

I did a radio interview with Peter Gorsky which was scheduled for five minutes and lasted the whole afternoon. We disagreed on so many things, it had to be interesting for listeners. At any rate, he ignored the other guests in the outside studio and persisted with me and Robert Burns till the end of his air-time. Similarly, when I was with Bruno Gerusi the next morning we hit it off so well, he asked me to stay for lunch – which he would cook! Actors never refuse a meal. It was during Bruno's programme that he came up with the idea of my doing a show on stage as myself rather than Burns. I said I would be happy to do it if someone ever asked me, and not five minutes later a man came on the line to the programme and offered me the use of the Eaton Auditorium – now alas, like the Massey Hall, no longer with us – for a programme to be called *An Evening with John Cairney*.

"But nobody knows me here," I protested. "I mean they thought I was the manager of the Massey Hall."

"Listen cookie," said Bruno in his friendliest manner, "'you're on my programme. They know you in Toronto – what night can you do it?"

"Friday, I suppose. I leave for New York on Saturday morning."

"OK, Friday it is."

And there and then on the air, he announced to most of Eastern Canada that this unknown Scottish actor would be performing his own thing at the Eaton Auditorium on Friday night beginning at — ? I glanced at Peter, who was with me. "Eight o'clock," he whispered.

"Eight o'clock," I said.

Bruno continued, "Eaton Auditorium, eight o'clock. And it'll cost you — ?" Another look from Bruno. Another glance at Peter, and he said, "Three — er — FIVE dollars."

"Five dollars," I repeated.

"Any advance on five dollars?" said Bruno wryly, And so it was arranged.

To everyone's amazement, except Bruno's, a good audience did turn up at the Eaton Auditorium after the store had closed for the day. This was one of the most famous department stores in the city, but its founders in their wisdom had created a theatre out of the centre space made by the shop floors, and a thriving letting-space it turned out to be. What a pity more large commercial enterprises don't provide such a beneficial and profitable utility within their premises. I had a really lovely night there, "in conversation" with the audience. And, of course, Peter got to sing and I got to meet Sheila's Aunt Isobel who lived in Toronto and happened to hear Bruno's show on her car radio.

Radio is first-class in Canada. With such vast spaces to cover, it is the ideal medium. It is hard to remember that Glasgow was nearer Toronto than Vancouver was. Bill McNeill pointed this out when I did my coast-to-coast interview with him in a programme called *Open Air*, which is exactly what good wireless should be of course. I couldn't get over that a five-minute exchange on the radio could help fill a theatre. Perhaps it was only that the Burns had allowed me to make a mark, and that I was as much a novelty in Toronto in 1971, as he was in Edinburgh in 1786. Whatever it was, it let me go back to Peter Glen's apartment and share out a lot of dollars with him on the sitting-room table while we listened to his extensive John McCormack record collection and Kathleen, his charming colleen of a wife, made us mince and potatoes. I might've been back in my gran's in Baillieston. Next day, they took me to the bus and I crossed the border into the United States with a light heart but a heavy wallet!

I made my way in a trance out of 42nd St bus terminus. I couldn't believe I was actually in New York, but I was and I loved it. Uncannily, thanks to a boyhood of inveterate film-going, its streets were as familiar to me as Glasgow's, and I felt immediately at home in them. For me, the United States was still United Artists!

I took a subway to Brooklyn (which I wouldn't do nowadays) and found myself standing on the steps of the main door of a brownstone tenement, that was nothing like what I had known in Parkhead. I had last seen my Aunt Sadie just before the war when she came to Ireland to join our family on a holiday there. Now, opening the door to me, was a taller, better-dressed version of my mother, who yelled, "JOHN!" and threw her arms about me. Thus, and typically, was I welcomed to America. Her daughters, my cousins, Virginia and Betty Ann, were now married and living in their own homes. But with Aunt Sadie at that time was another cousin from Glasgow, Margaret, who was about twenty, and other various Glaswegians, mostly footballers in transit, who occupied several bedrooms. Later that day, Margaret took me uptown to to see the sights and climb the Empire State Building, and that night I took them both to a Broadway Theatre – to see "1776", still running as a hit in New York as well as in London. This was the play I refused the year before, not thinking it had any chance of succeeding! So much for my theatre taste. But if I had done the play in London, I couldn't have done the *Burns* in Toronto, and if I hadn't been in Toronto, I wouldn't have been able to be sitting here in Sardi's with my cousin and aunt, gaping at the celebrities. Yes, New York , New York is a wonderful town!

I was unexpectedly called back across the St Lawrence by Andy Stewart. He had agreed to do a special show at the Mohawk Auditorium in Hamilton for the Hamilton Rangers Supporters Club in aid of the Ibrox Disaster Fund, and asked if I would join him again to do something like our Massey Hall success – he and I, choir and dancers – but no Peter Glen. I was glad to stay on for such a good cause. The Ibrox Disaster had been a terrible thing, and in the Four Seasons Hotel I wrote out a kind of soliloquy in memory of the poor Rangers fans who were crushed to death on the stairway after a Rangers and Celtic Ne'erday game. I wrote it out on the hotel stationery just as it came into my mind:

> Speaking as a Celtic supporter,
> I would have reached out both my hands
> Across that green, dividing pitch
> And held you back,
> Held you up.
> Put my arms about you
> And embraced you
> But all the fears
> Of too many years
> Held back my helping hands

From you,
Blood-red, Death-white, True-blue,
Across the park that day . . .

I can't remember now how the rest of it went, but it was about two or three pages of longhand that tried to put into words, sincerely and honestly, how all of us who loved football and Glasgow felt when we heard the news of that awful event. I asked Andy, himself a poet and a Rangers supporter, if he thought it would be in order and in good taste at such a time if I were to recite the lines at the end of my section. He read it through and said, "Sure. They'll love it."

I completed my Burns segment, and had arranged with stage management to finish in a spot centre stage. I would then take the pages from my pocket and read them. At the end of the piece, about five minutes later, I would back slowly out of the spot to the centre aperture in the curtain behind me. This is always a tricky business, backing to an exit, but if I made it as the light slowly dimmed at centre, it would make a nice end to the act and a fitting conclusion to the memorial soliloquy. My only real worry was failing to reverse into the curtain opening, and being enveloped in yards of heavy scarlet velour. When the moment came, I finished the "Tam o' Shanter", but didn't exit as usual on the applause. I waited until the last handclap died. The audience went very quiet thinking I was going to make some kind of announcement, and with some trepidation, I started with the first line, "Speaking as a Celtic supporter . . ." There was no reaction whatsoever. The audience seemed stunned. I proceeded very quietly, line by line, to the end. I was able to make the opening behind me without any problems and the lights dimmed to absolute silence. And then such a cheering broke out. Andy pushed me on again, and I seemed to spend half the interval taking bows.

After the show, Andy and I were guests of the McVicars family and with them attended a party given at a local politician's house. Like everyone else, he was a Scotsman. In fact, I never heard a single Canadian voice the whole night. One particular man who endeared himself to me was a printer formerly from Shieldhall in Glasgow, who said to me in his still pure guttural Glaswegian,

"See that poem you did. Aboot the Cel'ic supporter an' that."

"Yes?" I said.

"Rat wis great, so it wis."

"Thank you very much," I said.

"Wisn't it?" he said to his mate, who stood smiling beside him, never saying a word. "This is my pal."

"How do you do?" I said. But the pal just nodded amiably. "Here do you know whit, John?" continued Shieldhall. "You don't mind if I call you John?"

"That's my name," I said, a little pompously.

"Aye, that's what I thought. Aye. Is it true you're a Celtic man, then?"

"I was brought up in Parkhead," I told him. "It was either Celtic or Strathclyde Juniors."

"So you're a Tim?"

"Eh?" I said.

"A Cath'lic." I could see he was reluctant even to say the word.

"Yes, I am," I said simply. There was a pause.

"I've never talked to a Cath'lic afore," said Shieldhall. He nodded to his mate. "Neither has he."

"That can't be true," I said.

"Straight up," he said. "There werena' many Cath'lics in Shieldhall. At least no' up oor close."

"Is that right?" I said.

"Aye, it's funny that."

"What's funny?" I said.

"You know – I mean, you bein' a . . ."

"A Catholic?" I said, and then I put on my "Shakespeare'" voice – "Hath not a Catholic eyes? Hath not a Catholic hands, organs, dimensions, senses, affections, passions?" His eyes were popping out of his head by this time. "Fed with the same food, hurt with the same weapons, subject to the same diseases, healed by the same means, warmed and cooled by the same winter and summer as a Protestant is?"

I stopped. His mouth was hanging open. A little crowd had gathered round us. I carried on with my mock-Shylock, making it up where I didn't remember it. I was enjoying the little circle we had created. Like any ham, I always respond to an audience.

"If you prick us do we not bleed? If you tickle us, do we not laugh? If you poison us, do we not die? And if you wrong us, shall we not revenge?"

I broke off here – loudly. Enough was enough. There was some mock applause, and I raised my glass to the group. The buzz of conversation resumed.

"What wis all that aboot?" enquired Shieldhall, mildly.

"Shakespeare," I said.

"Oh, aye. I thought you wrote that an' a'." He gave a small laugh and went on. "When did ye write it by the way – the disaster thing?"

"Yesterday."

"Zat a fact' – here, my pal an' me, we'd like copies, sure we wid." He turned to his friend, who nodded again in agreement, then he turned back to me. "I don't suppose . . ." he began.

"Here it is," I said, bringing the three pages out of my pocket, spelling mistakes, crossings-out and all. He took it uncertainly.

"Kinna read it?"

"Of course."

"I mean noo."

"Help yourself."

He took it into a corner, peering at it closely. I was left staring at his mute mate, but before we might have entered into any meaningful dialogue, I was dragged off by someone else to meet someone else. It was that kind of party.

I never saw little Shieldhall again the rest of the evening and, to tell you the truth, I forgot all about him, and his silent friend, and the scribbled manuscript. Although it's not like me not to keep copies of everything I write. That is my sort of vanity. Anyway, you never know when it might come in useful.

Andy and I, and Jimmy Warren, his likeable tour manager, spent a few days with our hosts, Bill and Chris McVicars, doing a couple of radio spots as well, much to the consternation of the smooth Canadian disc jockeys, who, for once, couldn't get a word in. And then it was time to go home from Toronto airport. I was on the Prestwick plane and Andy went the opposite way to Winnipeg.

It was while waiting for the boarding call with the McVicars and Peter Glen, who had suddenly turned up as well, that two men appeared, one of them waving a large brown envelope.

"Hallaw there, John!" It was Shieldhall and his pal. "We wis told you wis here. Never thought we'd see you among a' rese people."

"What's this?" I said, examining the envelope. It was folded over and inside were a few pages of what looked like typescript.

"It's your poem. Mind, the thing you done at Hamilton forra club – aboot the disaster."

And so it was, printed out beautifully on two sheets of paper. The Memorial Soliloquy.

"We're printers, see, the pal and I here, and we done that up for ye as a wee memento, like. You know, a souvenir, frae the Hamilton Rangers Supporters Club."

I was enormously touched, and we all adjourned happily to the nearest bar for an appropriate "Old Firm" celebration – and I missed the boarding call. Panic all round, but thanks to Peter Glen, who

Burns in the Americas, 1975.

knew a man who knew a man who was at school with him, I was hurried out to the plane in a luggage-puller. I was hauled aboard up a ladder by very impatient stewards who were not impressed by my small repertoire of football songs, and was strapped into my seat like a soggy parcel by an unimpressed stewardess.

I woke as we were circling Prestwick. I remembered nothing whatsoever about the flight. It's the only way to travel by air, I swear it. I staggered through Customs exciting only pitying glances, and fell into the airport bus for Glasgow, still bemused by all the events of a very busy couple of weeks in North America. I was halfway to St Enoch Square before I realised I didn't have Shieldhall's envelope with my "Disaster" poem. I had left it either in that airport bar or in my seat on the plane. Perhaps even on that luggage car? Who knows? It was lost forever. I'll never drink again!

I was unable to trace Shieldhall or his pal either. Nobody seemed to know them. Had I dreamed them up? The last I saw of them were hands waving above a blur of figures at a barrier before the sliding doors closed behind me. I've never seen them since that day. Perhaps if they read this in Ontario, they might get in touch with me again? Unless of course, they are still uncertain about talking to a Catholic?

The Matteo family asked me to do "your Burns", as they called it, in barter exchange for the amount of credit I had run up in spaghetti and Chianti over my many Glasgow visits to their Parkhead restaurant. I had taken to signing my name on my bills, since having officially opened the "Duke of Touraine" myself in suitable ceremony when the brothers Tony and Robert, with delectable sister Linda, had refurbished their parents' former café as the first up-market eating place in the East End. In fact it had now become a very "in" sort of place indeed and for their Burns Night they decided it would be black tie only. Some of the regulars thought that someone had died. Ties were rare enough in Parkhead, and black ties meant only one thing . . . The restaurant held no more than fifty, but a hundred crowded in that night. Archie McPherson, Jack House, Jimmy Black and Jimmy Copeland were among those who squeezed in.

I did a perspiring hour, on that memorable first night, mostly standing on my chair, looking through the screen of cigar smoke to where every street trader, car dealer, market operator, butcher, baker and Candleriggs faker – not to mention various high-ranking policemen in plain clothes, or should I say, black ties, sat sardined to make one of the best audiences I have ever played the Burns to. Like most rich audiences, and these men had money, they were difficult to please but, like most ordinary men, they were highly sentimental and therefore easy to reach.

What was begun that night soon extended to a kind of tradition of Cairney evenings at the Duke of Touraine. The old "Duke" became quite a cult place and drew its audience widely from all over Glasgow and beyond. Rough men, beautiful women, excellent food, good wines, first-rate service, Glasgow humour, pathos and bathos, there had never been a place quite like it. Nor has there been since. It was raucous but it was genuine, and it generated an atmosphere something like what eighteenth-century theatre must have been, or the very early days of the working-class Old Vic. I had some truly wonderful nights there in the decade of its prime and in no time at all I had earned a lifetime supply of spaghetti and Chianti. I could now even afford a good Bardolino.

Bobby Cawley was, and still is, a businessman and entrepreneur in Dumbarton. He was typical of the go-getting entrepreneurial "Duke" patrons. He had just started a gents' outfitters in Dumbarton called "This Man Craig's" – would I open it, for a fee of course, and as much clothing as I could wear. I was delighted to oblige. This did much to soften the blow of losing the part of Alan Breck in a film of *Kidnapped* to Michael Caine. I drove to the shop myself that morning, and couldn't get in for girls. In the shop, in the street outside, they were everywhere, but Bobby was kicking himself – "I should've made it a Ladies shop," he said.

While I was in Scotland I heard that another theatre friend, Maurice Roeves, had made a great success as Robert Burns on BBC Television in January and actually was now playing *There Was A Man* at the Edinburgh Festival. A few nights later I found myself sitting among no more than twenty people in the Demarco Gallery watching Maurice play an excellent Robert Burns in the same *There Was A Man* by Tom Wright, which had served me so well seven years before. Maurice told me afterwards that he had seen me in the audience and it had really put him off. His was a very different performance from mine. He said he had set out to do everything different from me. He was very much the ploughman and not so much the poet, but Maurice is too good an actor to be dull and I enjoyed it. But he hadn't drawn the houses. I wonder why.

"Because you've killed it for us son," said Maurice genially. "Whether we like it or not – and we don't like it – you're a helluva act to follow. We can knock our pans out here, but as far as Joe Public is concerned, there's only one Robert Burns, and it's not me, I can tell you. I should have stayed with James Joyce. Never mind, it's great to see you again. Let's have a drink."

We were on our third round at least in the World's End pub across the road in the Royal Mile, when I pulled out an envelope from my pocket, containing most of the fee Bobby had given me a few days before. I counted out ten tenners, and gave them to Maurice.

"What's this?" he said. He couldn't understand why I was giving him a hundred pounds in cash. I explained that twenty years before when I was a student in Glasgow, at the same College as he had gone to later, Sir Alec Guiness had attended a student show and left a hundred pounds to be given to a student called John Cairney, should he graduate successfully in two years' time. I was given that hundred pounds. Only the previous summer, I tried to return it to Sir Alec at the London theatre where he was playing. He refused to take it, saying that if I could afford to give away a hundred pounds, I should give it to a young actor who I thought deserved it, just as he had given it to me in 1951.

"And what makes you think I deserved it?" said Maurice, taking a huge gulp of his beer.

"After tonight, Maurice," I said, raising my glass to him, "you more than deserved it."

"But what's it supposed to be for?"

"To help the young actor get started, to help him buy a wardrobe, to let him survive the tough days at the start of his career, to allow him, perhaps, to pick and choose."

And here were the two of us, two Scottish actors (although Maurice is more of a Geordie), two products of the same Glasgow school, none of us having really known a day out of work since we left, and here were we both now recipients of a cash award from one of Britain's greatest actors.

"All you have to do," I said, "is to pass it on. That's Sir Alec's rule."

"Right," said Maurice, "let's have a wee dram for Sir Alec."

"You mean a wee dram on Sir Alec." And we raised another toast.

"What gave him the idea, I wonder," mused Maurice.

"He had a tough start himself," I said, "and I think John Gielgud helped him out in the same sort of way.

"Right," said Maurice, "let's have a wee dram for Sir John Gielgud."

"I wonder who gave him a start. Probably one of the Terry family,"

I said. "And so it goes on all the way back to Macready, Kemble, Kean, Garrick, Burbage perhaps."

"Let's have a drink to them all," cried Maurice. And we did – till the pub threw us out around 2 a.m.

We then adjourned to the North British Hotel and continued the session there. By the time dawn came, I don't think Maurice had enough left of his hundred to pay for his taxi. I wonder who he gave his hundred to? Whoever it was, I'm sure he'll never enjoy it as much as Maurice and I did on our very special Burns Night at the Edinburgh Festival of 1972.

I agreed to return to the Lyceum for Bill Bryden's *Willie Rough* in an all-star Scottish cast, Roddy McMillan, Fulton Mackay, Archie Duncan et al, and also to play the Laurence Olivier part as Archie Rice in John Osborne's *The Entertainer* for Dundee Rep. There was about six weeks between, so I recorded a Scottish version of *The Taming of the Shrew* for BBC in Glasgow and had a month to spare. This was when John Worth, still surviving in Inverness, came up with the idea of a West Highland and Northern tour with this new intimate *Evening with Robert Burns* along the lines I had done at the Brunton Theatre in Musselburgh. I had recently bought a brand new Range-Rover and this gave me an opportunity to try it out. In a tour that took me from the Harbour Arts in Irvine to Solsgirth House in Kirkintilloch, the Murray Hall in East Kilbride, the Howden Theatre in Livingston, the Meadowhead Hotel in West Calder, the Cramond Inn, Edinburgh, the Ollerton Hotel in Kirkcaldy, the Arts Centre in Glenrothes the Baddenoch Hotel in Aviemore, the Town Hall in Inverness, the Gordon Hotel at Invergordon and the hotel at Nairn where Charlie Chaplin had stayed. It was all something of topographical swim.

As a result it was a very tired actor who reported for rehearsals of *The Entertainer* at Dundee. These weren't helped by the fact that I had to learn to tap dance. I'm afraid mine was more of a soft-shoe shuffle. However, the production was held to be successful and while I was in the run, the BBC rang again to ask me to fly down to London and do a special *Jackanory* which the children themselves had written, and make an appearance in *The Persuaders* with Roger Moore and Tony Curtis. I returned to the north-east to pick up dates in the tour which I had not completed around the Inverness area, where I resumed acquaintance with the Grants and the Farquhars. Then south again to Coupar Angus, and Broughty Ferry, before going on to Perth and the Lovat Hotel, where I completed another Burns Evening.

Afterwards, I went upstairs to change out of the dinner jacket and remove what I thought was yet another sodden shirt, to find that, in fact, it wasn't sweat, it was blood! I was haemorrhaging badly. I can't recall very much of the subsequent events. All I know is that I was in the Range-Rover, semi-dressed with my overnight bag hastily repacked (by someone), racing from Perth to Pittenweem. I must have arrived about three o'clock in the morning. I drove the car through the opening at the rear of the property, straight down the back lawn to the steps of the terrace outside the bedroom, and sat in the car, clinging to the wheel, and sounding the horn. The driving-seat was warm with what I knew was blood and I was afraid to move. Sheila came out in her nightdress, lights went on all around me, and I remember nothing more.

I woke to find myself lying in bed shaking all over, looking up into the face of Doctor Kennedy, the local doctor. He was trying to tell me that my body, or part of it, had broken down. I had been doing far too much for far too long and my body was now saying, "Enough". I must rest now, completely, or become dangerously sick. I was physically and mentally exhausted. I tried to tell him that I was in the middle of a tour. "Forget it," he said curtly. "I've arranged for a specialist to call here tomorrow."

Dr Wilfrid Sircus, known behind his back as Bill, was a lithe, alert, Jewish doctor of international fame and gruff kindliness. He had a sparse, laconic manner which hid a deep concern. He was also quite literally weighty, as I found when I woke to find his nose was no more than two inches from mine, and his voice was telling me that I was "a very sick, young man". (I was 42 at the time.) No one ever quite explained those terrible reverberating shivers that shook my whole frame. Not that I was all that interested in my symptoms. I was appalled and angry and ashamed to be so suddenly struck down.

Dr Sircus arranged that I go into the Drumsheugh Nursing Home at once. I have little recollection of that time, apart from the flowers surrounding the bed in my private room and the trivial and pointless geisha attentions from an au pair girl of indeterminate foreignness, who came wafting in and out from time to time to do nothing. As I became more and more aware, I found I could hear all the street noises and, even more clearly, voices in the corridor outside, especially two males who had a very brief discussion in the late part of the day. The first voice said,

"I think he's going to make it."

"Looks like it."

"Nothing in it for us, then."

"True. Might as well get back."

I learned later from Miss Sweden/Denmark or Germany that they were "two Press gentlemen who have waited for two days". Waiting for what, I thought? For me to die? I was out of that nursing home the next day.

I left the flowers for the girl in the cause of European unity, and reported to the BBC in Glasgow to begin a series called *Scotch on the Rocks*, in which I appeared with Bill Simpson, Iain Cuthbertson and my "hundred pounds a night" man, Maurice Roeves. In my role as the Communist spy I had to play opposite a very autocratic young lady called Maria Aitken. One of the first scenes shot was a supposedly nude bedroom interlude between Maria and myself, pictures of which naturally landed up in the *Daily Record* and the *Sunday Mail*. It was really quite controversial for her to be so nude within the august portals of the BBC at Queen Margaret Drive, but as everyone on the floor knew, she kept her jeans on, and I, too, was modestly trousered. But I had underestimated the recent effects of the medicinal steroids and I had put on noticeable weight.

"You look like a pear," said Maria languidly, as I lifted up the sheets to get in beside her.

"Do I?" I replied. "But then you're like a peach," I said sweetly, but with malice in my heart.

We then had to go on location on Glasgow Green, and I, as the political agitator, had to address the crowd. One very unexpected result of this was that I was formally invited by the Scottish National Party to stand as a candidate for them in the forthcoming elections. A case of life imitating art? But that night after a long cold day out of doors, I collapsed again and next day was driven back to Edinburgh, this time not to the Nursing Home, but to a room in the Western General. The first face I saw when I came to was that of my old mother, tight-lipped, in her headscarf and maroon coat, sitting on the edge of the chair at my bedside.

"It's cancer, isn't it?"

"Oh, mother," I croaked

"It must be, or they wouldnae have you in here again."

"They like me, mother," I tried to joke.

"Aye, sure," she said. "They havenae you to live with."

It took the staff and doctors quite some time to reassure her that I had acute ulcerative colitis, due to physical strain, mental stress and unwise eating habits.

"And what about the drinking?" my mother said. She'd never been sure about wine.

"Oh, they don't mind the Ribena, mother," I said.

91

I had started in a private room, then in a small ward, and over the next few weeks dwindled down by degrees, till I occupied the end bed in Ward D1, and once again came under the stern, but benevolent, rule of Dr Sircus. The days were very long, and some of the nights even longer. I became very depressed in the night noise of the ward and the real and sometimes fatal sickness all around me. At one time, I felt it would be no great loss if I went myself. I had merely to let go and the enveloping fatigue would take over.

Late one night in the ward I suddenly found myself looking down on myself from the ceiling. Yes, I was outside looking in, and I wasn't the most beautiful thing I had ever seen. I hadn't realised I looked so much like a Pakistani – and I don't mean to insult my Indian brothers – but I was fat Pakistani, bloated on steroids with weeks of growth on my chin. For some reason I had decided not to shave. I don't know why. I just didn't want to. The nurses were very upset. Like most women, they regarded being unshaven as being unclean, whereas I know I am positively scrubbed in my stubble. Daily shaving is only yet another of our pointless social mores. Sorry, I digress. I was telling you of how I found myself abruptly airborne – looking down on myself with beard, wet face, matted hair and totally unlike what I thought I looked like. I got such a fright, that I yelled at the top of my voice – and there I was looking *up* at the night nurse who had me by the arms, crooning soothingly, "There, there, Mr Cairney, you were having a wee dream."

BUPA was a complete waste of time.

I didn't get my insurance money or my private room, so I withdrew all my insurance money from everywhere, at a great loss, and bought the house beside Kellie Lodging with the unexpected capital received, albeit minus penalty clauses, cancellation fees, severance charges and everything else that could be crammed into small print. Still, I now had an empty house to play with, which had once belonged to John Smith, the clockmaker. I had an idea away at the back of my mind that it could form part of the Cairney Hotel a long time in the future. Then I could have my own Burns Supper!

Meantime, all the little Cairneys had to eat, which meant that Daddy had to take every crust offered to him out of hospital hours, as it were. Hence my nocturnal trips to the Gartwhinzean, the Meadowhead, the Elm Tree Inn or anywhere else who would give me cash in hand for a Burns Hour after dinner. I was an unashamed theatre hooker, hustling the dates under cover of night! I would tip the driver at the end of the "raid" and keep the balance to give to Sheila with my dirty washing next time she visited.

Every day I tried to walk as much as I could. Out to the newsagent in the morning to buy the *Glasgow Herald*, out in the afternoon in ever-increasing circles until one day I walked all the way to Princes Street. All the time looking about – street-walking can be a pleasure – looking into everybody's windows; all those lives, all those concerns and preoccupations – back again to the ward for a bath and Radio 4, then another night of reading. I wasn't a great one for the ward chat or the usual flirtation with the nurses. I was enjoying being shy again.

Nights are long in a hospital, and they are never quiet. There's always someone snoring, talking in their sleep, calling out, coughing, crying. I was always glad when it was first light and I used to watch for the dawn every morning behind the blinds. I was always wakened by the birdsong. I would lie and try to disentangle the various whistle strains from the general chorus, wonder which bird was which. Suddenly, I found myself, with my head on the pillow, looking right and directly into the bright, beady eyes of a sparrow. (I think it was a sparrow – I am no ornithologist.) It had popped in under the raised window, and was now jerking and swivelling its little head swiftly right and left in timid curiosity. I found myself at one moment looking right into its piercing gaze and, for no more than a heart-beat, I thought I could read pity in that little, fleeting glance. It then returned its darting looks to the ward, and with a shiver of feathers, seemed to say, "Don't fancy it much here", and, just as suddenly, with a whirr and a cheep it was gone. I rose up on my elbow to watch it fly, but it was already out of sight. I was jealous of that little bird. It belonged to the big, free world outside – and so did I. I wasn't born sick, I had merely become sick, but now I was sick no longer. I was nevertheless on the hospital conveyor belt – it had to run its course. I was part of the syndrome.

Luckily for me, an emergency occurred – of the social variety, not the medical. A very distinguished consultant was visiting his peers at the hospital, and the Scottish doctors had a wish to give a dinner to their esteemed colleague, but they were at a loss about entertainment. Then one of the young doctors remembered my occasional exploits from Ward D1. The upshot was that my dinner jacket came to me this time by courtesy of Monica (her doctor father and doctor brother were to be at the dinner), and I gave the company a brief Burns excerpt which concluded with a very vigorous "Tam o' Shanter". Deliberately so, in order to impress my fitness on all concerned. The very distinguished visitor was very kind as we sipped a glass of wine afterwards and politely enquired where I had come from that day – Glasgow or London? "Oh no," I said, "I've just nipped up from Ward D1".

I was discharged the next day.

One of the first things I did when I got out into the world again was to lay a wreath at Burns Statue in Ayr in a special ceremony organised by the Burns Federation. I was giving a show that night in the Beach Pavilion, so it was also a matter of good public relations. I remembered the Pavilion as a place for dancing when I was a boy on holiday in Ayr before the war, but for this event they had created a theatre space in the ballroom area and it drew a packed audience, among whom was the then Secretary of State for Scotland, Mr Willie Ross (now Lord Marnock), who reminded me in some ways of my Uncle Eddie. We had met before at an STV Burns Supper, but this was the first time I had a real chat with him. I found him highly knowledgeable about Burns and most unlike a politician. I reminded him of Burns' comment to Alan Cunningham regarding politicians in 1793: "Politics is the science wherewith, by means of nefarious cunning and hypocritical pretence, we govern civil polities for the emolument of ourselves and our adherents." Willie nodded. "I know politicians like that," he said, "but most of them are Tories!"

Miss Burns, the manageress of the Pickwick Hotel in Ayr, was undoubtedly a Tory, but that didn't prevent her being a most considerate and tactful hostess to me in my frequent visits to Burns' own town. I was able to sign the account ("You have a trusting face," she said), and she gave me the corner room with bath en suite ("That way you'll be out of the way"), and in no time the Pickwick was yet another home from home. My only complaint was that they couldn't supply my normal Hamlet cigars and they weren't too delighted when Cairney and his Burns friends took up most of the residents' lounge before dinner. But I explained that the Burns in question was Miss Burns, not Robert, and we were forgiven.

It was in the Pickwick that I had the first idea for a comprehensive Burns Festival in Ayr some day. If Jedburgh has Scott, Hawarth has the Brontës, the West Country has Hardy, why can't Ayrshire have Burns?

It was festival time for me that year – the Livingston Festival, the Johnstone Festival, the Coatbridge Festival. Who needed the Edinburgh Festival? However, an evening at the Falkirk Festival brought me a little nearer home and a special night arranged at the Kelty Co-op Hall was virtually on the family doorstep. Kelty was

Cowan country. My father-in-law, Willie Cowan, and his brother, John (father of soprano, Rhona Cowan), were still well-known figures in the community, and Sheila had many memories there of early schooldays; Careira's, the Italian ice-cream shop, Ella Ford, her first elocution teacher, and so on. I had offered to do a show there to honour these connections and to acknowledge their memories but, at the last minute, Sheila was not so sure. She was retreating more and more from the whirl of my touring activities and the constant demands of my professional life. She preferred the company of her children, and created the solid base on which their lives were founded. She was their security, mine too.

Perhaps we should have had another child, a Katie or a Tom? But by then drastic action had been taken in that respect, and it appeared to be irreversible.

So, too, was the tide that was gradually sweeping me up again as the normal frantic work-pattern resumed. I seemed to be enveloped in a non-stop carousel of one-night stands. My world was spinning and it took all my strength just to stay on. When I did get home at weekends, it was harder and harder to slip back into the family unit. I was kept somehow on the outer rim of things with the dog and the cat. I knew my place. As head of the house I couldn't even decide when we had tea. We were growing imperceptibly apart in our interests and priorities. It wasn't at all like this in Maidenhead. I was beginning to wish we'd never moved back to Scotland. Perhaps little Alison had been right after all in not wanting to move to "rotten old Scotland".

The only things my dear wife and I really had in common were the deep love we had for our five children and the growing concern for the rising costs of our superb house. It had been designed by us as our final domicile with every possible mod con – the best that money could buy. Everything we had learned from all our previous houses had gone into this Pittenweem pile. It was our "ideal home" in every sense of the word, and after it I had no more domestic ambitions. But now that I was concentrating so much on my own touring, with earnings drastically reduced from the former film and TV level, and with oil, electricity and gas prices beginning to rise, not to mention the spiralling rates, the cost of keeping up with Kellie Lodging was turning into something of a handicap hurdle; we no longer cleared one thing and another continually presented itself. I think Sheila was just beginning to get a little worried. That illness of mine had taken something out of both of us.

My main worry, however, was trying to chase up an audience for the Kelty Co-operative Hall. After all, why should they pay to see me when they could see me for nothing any time pushing a trolley in the supermarket? Yet less than ten years previously while I was playing *This Man Craig* on television the crowds had stopped the traffic in the street when I came to open the extension to their library in the company of local MP Willie Hamilton. Of course, Willie may have been the draw, but all I know is that I couldn't get out of my father-in-law's car as we drew up at the appointed place. Crowds of housewives and young girls totally surrounded the vehicle, and once again I felt that old stab of fear when in the centre of a crowd. An epicentre really, for any crowd has a demonic power and you never know when it might spill over and run amok. But I forgot it was Willie Cowan's car, and a new one at that. Before we knew it, he was out of that driver's seat and laying about him vigorously, not clearing a path for me, but making sure the women didn't scratch his car! Now where were those same women?

Perhaps dear old W.C. had dealt so heftily with them they were scared to come out in case they got bruised again? *An Evening with John Cairney* in the Kelty Co-operative Hall was not one of the great evenings. The audience was small and self-conscious and though I tried to establish an early rapport with them, the family weight was perhaps too much. What surprised me though was their appreciation of my singing, which with me is always a matter of pot-luck. I must have struck a lucky patch that night. Or should I say pitch? Of course, I was in mining country, and they have a bias towards music. I ended a very long evening by reading some of my own verse. Sheila's presence weighed so much on me psychologically that it would be fairer to say it was more an Evening with Sheila Cairney than John Cairney.

I think the whole thing was too close for comfort. Yet I never felt like this on the Traverse family night with *There Was A Man* or at the Coatbridge Festival with my mother there? But then Sheila wasn't at either show. Perhaps I was too near her – or too distant? We had always had this family joke that daddy was like the gas cooker – a "big blaw" on the outside rings, that is, to the world, and a "wee peep" in the oven, that is, in the home. Sheila always had the capacity to reduce my "gas" to a wee peep. After Kelty, I was almost relieved when the next date took me away again – even if it was only to Glenrothes, just a few miles up the M90.

June was busting out all over with students of the Napier College of

Science and Technology in Edinburgh, armed with cameras of all kinds, chasing me round most of Midlothian under the direction of Robin Crichton. He had finally got his team together and a Burns film was now being made as a clever montage of stills and graphics with voice and music-over. This was interesting for me in that it allowed a first feel towards what might be a later feature film, and gave me the added pleasure of living en famille with the Crichtons in their home at Nine Mile Burn, when it wasn't a film studio. Another happy feature of the production was that the Cairney girls joined up with the Crichton girls to form most of the Burns family when young, and with some neighbours and friends hurriedly dragooned into costume, provided half the village of Mauchline between 1760 and 1785. It was what one might call a very tight production. But at least it gave a proper family feel to the whole event and allowed me the pleasure of my children's company on shooting days. Unfortunately they had their mother's horror of the public scene and showed no great liking for the cinematic life. Many would think this a good thing.

Filming, whether for motion or still camera, is more routine than romantic. Hours of standing or sitting about, then hurried preparation for a moment of panic. And all happening, seemingly, in a miasma of ill-organisation and haphazard chaos. Of course, this is not so and any good production, however apparently rambling and amorphous, is in fact a tight, well-planned operation, almost military in its exactness. At least it's supposed to be. But since it depends so much on variable ingredients – the actor, the weather, mechanical function – it is occasionally subject to last-minute change and the consequent muddle. Filming, indeed, could be best summed up by Winston Churchill's description of his pet bull. "Even if he does lead a life of unparalleled dreariness, it is punctuated by moments of intense excitement." That's filming!

The further, and not the least pleasure for me of course, as Burns, was the happy succession of lovely girls Robin had engaged for the story. Not all of them were professional actresses. One of the loveliest, Catherine King-Clark, was a student at the Edinburgh School of Art, and was training to be a sculptor. Her own shape was inspiration enough! She really was very lovely and when she and I and Robin were ensconced in the Globe Inn bedroom it was so very easy to see how Burns made his second illegitimate child in such happy circumstances.

> Yestreen I had a pint o' wine
> A place where body saw na',

> Yestreen lay on this breast o' mine,
> The gowden locks o' Anna.

Catherine knew nothing about Burns whatsoever, but said that since I seemed to know everything there was to know, there was no point in learning. Her mother owned the Tick Tock Boutique in Dumfries, but was encouraged to stay away from the actual shooting as her daughter was called upon to be a little more revealing in the seduction scene than perhaps a good mother thinks a good daughter should. Not that Catherine as Anna Park did anything she might have been ashamed of – but what the camera saw . . .

> The kirk and state may join and tell
> Tae dae sic things I maunna,
> Well the kirk and state may gae tae Hell
> And I'll go to my Anna!

This is where the public have a misconception, if that's the word, about filming and actors in it, in what are thought of as daring scenes. Actually, there is nothing more puritanical, or more unassisting to the libido, than the cold, technical sight of a mostly male unit, in regulation anoraks, clustered apathetically around a camera, even if you do have a beautiful girl in your arms looking up soulfully into your eyes. Nine times out of ten she has had garlic for lunch, and more often than not you have cramp in your leg. No, filming's not always fun. But then it's not always miserable either. So for the sake of my art, and Robert Burns, for a couple of weeks I fondled, kissed and cuddled with one nubile female after another. Men can think what they like but then God does not punish us for our thoughts!

I'm surprised, however, that a bolt did not come down from the blue when I stood in a leafy, yellow-dappled glade, in the heat of the day somewhere in Lothian, feeling the sun on my back, the grass at my feet, the flowers all around me, kissing the sweet lips of "Jean Armour", otherwise Edinburgh actress, Maureen Jack. It is right that a man should enjoy his work!

> Of a' the airts the wind can blaw
> I dearly like the west
> For there the bonnie lassie lives
> The lassie I lo'e best;
> There's wild-woods grow, and rivers row
> And mony a hill between
> But day and night my fancy's flight
> Is ever wi' my Jean.

Maureen was married to a doctor, but there was nothing clinical about her. She was a natural, uncomplicated, forthright person, with one particularly irresistible attribute – her car. It was a vintage, pre-war open tourer, which she drove with panache and flair and would not sell to me under any circumstances. My still-memory of this lovely girl is of her auburn hair streaming out from under a headscarf as she sat at the wheel of this car and passed me on the road. She made me think of Isadora Duncan, but remember what happened to her? I was in a Triumph Stag myself, which was in a sense a gift from my daughter, Jennifer. I had loaned her money to make a deposit on a flat in Glasgow, when she was at University there. Like all fathers, I regarded any money loaned to daughters as good money lost. To my surprise, however, thanks to her nightly efforts as a waitress in the Ubiquitous Chip, she repaid me every penny. On an impulse, I traded in the car I had and with the balance suddenly to hand, bought the Stag. In such a car, I could easily have overtaken Maureen on the way back to Edinburgh, but much better to follow behind and admire her number-plates. Better still, draw up at some delightful roadside pub and have a beer, perhaps, a chat. This was the acceptable face of filming.

> I see her in the dewy flowers
> I see her sweet and fair
> I hear her in the tunefu' birds
> I hear her charm the air
> There's not a bonnie flow'r that springs
> By fountain, shaw or green;
> There's not a bonnie bird that sings,
> But minds me o' my Jean.

The hour-long script was soon in the can, and I believe was sold to Continental television as *The Robert Burns Story*. It was not a real film, but it was an experience.

I came to love the Crichton family, and I suppose I was a bit in love with the girls in the film – especially Maureen. Who wouldn't have been? But at least something about Burns had been put on screen at last. At least it was a start. One day someone will do the deserved big-screen treatment of his story. They must, and what a picture that will be. But I wonder if they will capture the innocence we all felt that summer month at Nine Mile Burn. I doubt it.

But now it was time for me to report to Richard Eyre at the Lyceum to play Bothwell in *The Burning* by Stewart Conn, and in the cast was to be a new friend and very good actor, Derek Anders. He was in digs with Betty Waugh and her daughter Annette, who was a good friend of Maureen Jack's. During rehearsals I saw quite a lot of the Waughs.

Quite coincidentally, Maureen was also in *The Burning* – playing a witch! But tragically for me, in those few short weeks since filming, she had sold her car! Life in Edinburgh thereafter was never the same.

At the end of the run, I was due to go to Glasgow for the Clyde Fair. Instead I went back into the Western General. Not that I was seriously ill or anything. It wasn't at all like the previous year. It was just that Dr Sircus and his team wanted to make more tests and asked me to give them at least a month. This wasn't easy, but it was arranged, and in no time I was back in my old place in Ward D1 and Jenny the tea-lady was telling me how delighted she was to see me! I think the doctors were worried that my intestinal troubles would prove more serious and they wanted to keep a closer eye on me for a time. Anyway, Dr Sircus wanted me back and that was that.

So here I was, back in bed, with the sun streaming in on me. *The Scotsman* crossword still undone and the lady with the book trolley advancing on me beaming. "Back again, Mr Cairney," she said in her best Morningside.

"I'm afraid so," I mumbled.

"Ah well, it's always nice to see you anyway. It's always good to have interesting people in the ward."

"Oh, yes," I said.

I never ceased to marvel at these volunteer ladies and their mastery of small talk. Whatever the situation, they could always turn it round to a social smile. But I always had the impression that it never touched them. Yet here they were out of the goodness of their hearts and a plentitude of leisure time doing their good works among sick people, and pushing their trolleys down an alleyway which had death on one side and pain on the other.

My ward-mate this time was an Edinburgh Italian called Gimi Sciapatticci. He was a well-known city restaurateur, who insisted on wearing his dark glasses, even with his pyjamas and dressing-gown, and was also prone to a small cigar whenever the sister was not in the ward. We became quite a pair. On one occasion there was a sudden panic call from my agent in London that the *Today* programme in America had been on to them requesting my urgent appearance on the ramparts of Edinburgh Castle the next day to quote something from Robert Burns live to New York. They didn't know whether to say yes or no in view of my hospitalisation. But if I felt fit enough, I was to report to Edinburgh Castle the next morning at 10.30 to meet the Production Manager, with whom I would discuss my programme contribution and the requisite fee.

I thought it was unlikely that I could do it, but I reckoned without Gimi.

"Course you gotta do it," he said in his Lothian Italian. "This is America, this is TV, coast to coast — this is big time."

And nothing suited little Gimi more than the big time. He talked just like Barry.

"But I've no costume, and I don't think I could get anything by tomorrow morning. And anyway how do I get there? My car is —"

"Leave it to me," said Gimi, now frantically chewing the end of his cigar.

He bellowed to the nurse to bring the telephone back to his bedside. He was perfectly capable of going out to the hall and using the public call box, but that wasn't Gimi. Despite this "Little Caesar" tendency, he was popular with everyone and had no shame in using that popularity to the hilt. Now he was talking in Italian into the receiver. I wasn't all that worried if I never did the job, I had my crosswords to keep me going. It all seemed too much of a hassle for just a couple of minutes' television. How could I change from a patient in pyjamas to an actor in costume overnight? I mean, this wasn't exactly a dinner-jacket job like all the others. But Gimi did fix it!

Next morning, after breakfast, Monica arrived from Magdala Mews with my Burns costume, which I kept there along with a dinner jacket, and a pair of pyjamas. And, shortly after, Gimi's driver, or someone from one of Gimi's "shops" as he called them, arrived in his Rolls-Royce, and by the time I had got into my costume again in the bathroom, I came out to find Gimi dressed in his best camel-hair coat waiting for me. We then drove off from the ward doors to the cheers of all the patients and young nurses and only the slight disapproval of the sister, who had reluctantly given her permission for the brief excursion. We swept down the drive like royalty, which I'm sure in any case Gimi was convinced he was.

As it happened I had been with him when they came to take him away for his operation, and I had happened to be at the end of his bed when he woke up again, so Cairney was forever impinged on Gimi's subconsciousness! from then on, as far as Gimi was concerned we were blood brothers. It's extraordinary how relationships build up in a hospital ward. Like the army, I suppose. Or a ship. Confinement makes for companionship. At any rate, this was the man who was beside me now in the back of the Rolls speeding towards Edinburgh Castle.

Eventually we found a very anxious American production manager who introduced us to Jack Cassidy, the host for the programme. I left them both in an earnest huddle with Gimi while a young director and his even younger female assistant led me to the very top of the castle, where the lone piper plays at the Tattoo. Technicians wired me up for sound, then they left me to it. I was to say some appropriate lines from Burns, then turn away, and walk to the end of the parapet to look over Edinburgh and the Firth of Forth. They would then create a false mist with dry ice and cut to Jack on the Esplanade for the end titles and the end of the excerpt from "Bonnie Scotland".

I then realised that I had forgotten my black cloak. I thought this might add quite significantly to a small figure on the ramparts. A cloak, like a cane, or sweat and stubble, is always a good actor, as any performer will tell you. But there wasn't time to send a car back for it. Instead, Gimi, with the remarkable presence of mind that made him the commercial success he is, bribed a policeman to lend me his cloak, which he did, and I wore it grandly all the way to America. Naturally, I chose "A Man's A Man" . . .

> Then let us pray that come it may,
> As come it will for a' that,
> That sense and worth, o'er all the earth
> Shall bear the gree an' a' that.
> For a' that, an' a' that,
> It's comin' yet for a' that,
> That man to man, the world o'er,
> Shall brothers be – for a' that.

During the final lines I turned away as directed. The dry ice swirled about my feet and rose up all around me. It must have made a striking picture and some instinct told me to hold it as I gazed over the city like Napoleon on Elba. All my training told me to wait for the director's "Cut", but it never came and I stood there for what seemed an eternity, until the sound technician was beside me patting me on the back and unwiring me from under the police cloak.

It seems that the second camera on Jack had broken down and they held on to me for the whole final section of his voice-over and the closing credits. If I had turned round, I would have killed the shot. Years later, I learned from my cousin Virginia in New Jersey that they all saw the programme over there at breakfast-time and thought it was thrilling. Virginia thought I looked and sounded just like James Mason. It must have been that policeman's cloak. I wonder what she would have thought if she'd seen the hospital pyjamas underneath.

On the unit, the Americans were delighted with me and showed it in their likeable, exuberant American way. I had given them a good

102

"out" in what was after all a live programme coming from Britain straight on to American screens – a fact of which Gimi took total advantage, when it came to discussing the fee. They were convinced he was my manager and he made no attempt to dissuade them. I had to hide my face as they drew him aside and counted out some of the larger-denomination notes into his hand. When they finished, I heard the American production assistant say, "OK?"

Gimi said, "Sure, for expenses."

And that wily Edinburgher got an extra fee, which he considered he fully deserved for personal management.

We swept out of the esplanade with even greater ceremony, and straight to his restaurant in Cockburn Street, where he paid for a splendid lunch in his own restaurant " with my fee – or, shall we say, that part of it which he had earned. It was a very good lunch. By four o'clock, we were both back in adjoining beds, sitting up, smiling seraphically and reeking of garlic, waiting for Dr Sircus and his usual afternoon round.

"You can go home, Mr Sciapatticci," he said. "And so can you," he said to me.

When he passed, Gimi and I reached across and shook hands. Then the irrepressible Italian winked and produced two large cigars.

During my second recuperation, I appeared in a lunchtime play, ironically called *The Knife*, at the Lyceum Studio Theatre; opened the Log Cabin complex at Kirkmichael, drove to London to appear in *Special Branch*, had lunch with the Ivor Novello Trust people at Simpson's on the Strand about my idea for a Novello evening, and recorded another *Jackanory* (my fifth!) for the BBC. Then it was back to Glasgow for *An Evening with John Cairney* at the Eastwood Theatre and a *McGonagall Night* at the good old Duke of Touraine for the Matteos. I asked my mother if she wanted to see it, but she disrespectfully declined. She didn't like McGonagall, said I looked too much like how she remembered her father!

"Ye'll hiv nae luck while ye dae that daft McGoonigal!" she said.

Maybe she was right. My mother's hunches were fearsomely accurate. It was the Irish in her. She had the gift of precognition, which I too have to a limited degree. We see future pictures. Neither of us thinks it a blessing. I took her back with me to Kellie Lodging for Christmas and New Year. Father-in-law Willie Cowan made a great fuss of her. I'm not sure Mrs Cowan approved – "I'm sure Mrs Cairney would prefer not to have your arm round her, William." At the Hogmanay toasts, after the bells, when we came to "Absent Friends" I'm sure Sheila looked me right in the eye!

Hogmanay is always more a sad time than a mad time for us. My mother particularly never liked the New Year time. Too many old folk go at the back end of the year for her liking, and it wasn't a good time to look ahead despite the traditional resolutions. It was still dark winter. Easter would be a better time to start again with the spring and new life happening all round us. It had been a terrible year, a lost year, yet we were still here – just. That's all that matters in the end – survival. To make it from one new year to another. I looked around my family circle; Sheila, Jennifer, Alison, Lesley, Jane and Jonathan, my mother, the Cowans, Bonnie, the cat, Clyde, the dog, the hamster in the garage, two ponies out in the field – that was my kingdom of Fife. My crown was shaky but it was still on my head. My subjects were inclined to be restless, but my Queen . . . yes, what about my Queen? As far as I was concerned, she was still enthroned. And always would be. Happy New Year everybody! What would '74 bring?

Who knows? That was part of the excitement of Ne'erday – the not knowing what was to come, and always assuming that it would be better. Why not? Optimism is part of the actor's survival pack. As long as there's hope, there's life.

The first three months of the new year were given over entirely to *Evenings With Robert Burns*. This time it was Robert Burns with a bow tie, ad-libbing freely through *The Robert Burns Story* and quoting from the works as found. It was a happy formula. The material was by now almost second nature to me and I picked it up and laid it down with all the familiarity of a comfortable old cushion. It gave me a rare performance ease and freedom, yet allowed me to tell the story and perform all the mandatory excerpts; "Advice To A Young Friend", "Holy Willie", "Tam o' Shanter", "A Man's A Man" etc. It also kept me busy and on the road, and away from home. I seemed to be running all the time, but I wasn't sure from what or to what.

The dates were there to be played: Glasgow Art Club, the Cowdrey Hall in Aberdeen (what superb acoustics there – nearly as good as the Town Hall, Maybole, which surely must be the best in Scotland), and the Civic Theatre in Ayr, where they opened the curtains too early and discovered me directing the lights. Such incidents just became part and parcel of the performance and nobody seemed to mind. It was at this Ayr performance that I invited an older lady in an Inverness cape up on stage at one point and I couldn't get her off! So I gave her a chair at the side and she stayed with me till the end!

I played the Carrbridge Hotel one night and the next night a huge lorry came over that bridge and crashed right into the glass-fronted dining-room where I'd been performing. Thank goodness my timing was better than his!

At Wick I was accompanied by the Provost on the accordion who, to the detriment of his playing technique, wore his chain. It gave an unexpected resonance to some of Burns' melodies. It was at Wick, standing on the beer crates which made up the stage in the packed club where I was playing, that I saw right up in front of me one huge Northerner with his arms folded over four pints of beer and four small whiskies. I looked down at once and said,

"You must be thirsty!"

"I hear you're gonna talk for an hour," he said.

"You must have been in the Scouts," I retorted.

I always asked that the bar be closed when I played in clubs. It was difficult enough to get attention anyway, but nearly impossible to keep it when half the audience is lining up and shouting orders at the bar. News of this embargo seemed to have got as far as Wick and this fellow was well prepared. However, he made the mistake of sitting right underneath me, so every time he reached forward for a beer, I would reach to him to say, "Consider, sir . . ." and then would direct to him some item in the Burns story which naturally prevented his drinking, or "A moment . . ." or "But, hold . . .", so much so that the poor fellow never got a chance to touch any one of the four beers he had in front of him. And even when my attention was away from him the audience would call out whenever he was about to drink and I would whirl round on him once again. He took it in good part but, of course, it couldn't go on all night. And he solved the problem very neatly himself, when he stood up and said, "Here, for God's sake," and he gave me one of his whiskies. "Hae a dram, man, an' be done wi' it." The audience cheered and, drinking a toast to each other, I left him to his libations.

Next morning, I went up to have my first glimpse of John o' Groats and was waved down outside a farmer's house by a man in trousers and singlet. When I rolled down the window, he leaned in saying,

"Here, yon was a great night last night in Wick."

"I'm glad you enjoyed it."

"Oh, I wisna there. I juist heard it was a grand night." And so saying, he cheerfully waved me on. How he had heard, or how he knew it was my car, is a mystery to me to this day.

My next date up that way was at Brora, where I played in the hotel for the Freemasons. It was a great evening. They knew their Burns and it made me concentrate. So much so, that it was standing ovation time at the end, and a 4 a.m. bedtime. I was awakened, however, for an early breakfast because, it appears, in my excess following our success, I had taken up the chef's challenge to play him a round of golf, and we had to be on the tee at 9 a.m. We didn't have far to go as the first tee was in front of the hotel terrace, and there was the chef minus his whites, dressed like Lee Trevino, all set to meet me for the first tee-off. I was given the use of the hotel owner's clubs and was pondering on how I could carry them, never mind how I could play with them, when I noticed on the terrace above me last night's audience gradually spilling out as word got round that "Robert Burns" was on the tee.

Soon quite a crowd had assembled, and I suddenly felt a whole golf bag of nerves. Oh, I was no Jacklin, I know that, but like every Scots boy, I'd played the game. I thought I could hit it sufficiently, in other words, I thought I could get round. But here I was, holding a driver in my hand, with last night's ecstatic audience now gathered even more critically behind me in the cold light of morning. I took up the driver and addressed the ball. The cook, who was an Irishman, saw that I was uneasy and said, "Sure, go ahead, they're all on your side anyway after last night."

I drew back the driver – and missed. I tried again – and missed again. By this time, the perspiration was running down my face, down the small of my back, down my legs and into my running shoes. At least I think it was perspiration. The chef looked sympathetic.

"Maybe you'd be better giving them "Tam o' Shanter", he suggested kindly.

I had my usual good luck at the Brunton Hall in Musselburgh (they've always been good to me there) and a wonderful evening in Moffat. I was having a good run. It was at Moffat that the janitor explained that the lighting system had two positions – on or off! On that particular night, the windows on one side of the hall were open wide for some reason and the most beautiful birdsong accompanied me almost throughout. But what I remember is the picture of a couple of little boys whose faces appeared above the open window at the beginning of the night, and then in a gorgeous silhouette as twilight fell. One of them left before the interval but his pal remained right to the end of the first part. When I came out for the second half, he was still up there sitting on the window-sill, all ready for the rest of the show. But when I invited him to come into the hall and join us, telling him that it would get colder and darker before I finished, he blushed and jumped down on the outside, leaving the window frame empty and the twilight gradually fading into evening. I had forgotten the sensitivity of boyhood. I should have left him alone.

Moffat was typical of many of these touring nights – a bleak, empty stage, virtually no setting, but good warm audiences and a lovely, lovely intimacy. I ended up in the Five Village Festival at Fenwick, which conveniently brought me up, via Greenock and the Playtex factory to the Duke of Touraine in Glasgow. It was great to see so many familiar faces in this very familiar setting. "Familiar" is exactly the right word, for that's what the "Duke" had become for me – "family-like". I felt so at home there now.

You mustn't imagine that it was all one long succession of triumphs, this kind of touring, but quite honestly it was nearly so. I was on that kind of high, and the only difference was that it took longer in some places to "catch" the audience than it took in others. One such date which comes to mind in this category from that tour was the night I did battle at the Gartcosh Social Club. They firmly refused to close the bar, and I had to cope as best I could. I remember being shown into a cupboard room backstage, which served as a dressing-room, the walls of which were festooned with curling pictures of previous pop stars, show bands and comedians. I felt singularly out of place, but knew I had to go through it. There had been so many cars outside I thought it was a car factory. During his very long introduction, the Chairman of the Social Club wore a bow tie which bobbed intriguingly on his Adam's apple. I felt sure it would complete a full circle as he addressed his workmates. Or, as he called them, "cronies".

"Cronies," he said, "this next act has been a hell of an expense, I kin tell ye that. But the Committee thought it was time for a wee change. So we've brought you tonight, all the way frae Edinburgh, Mr John Cairney, who we've a' seen on the telly dae'in' his Burns. Noo, he's no' a singer, an' he's no' a comic, an' he's no' a speciality act, in fac' I'm no' right sure whit he is, but he needs the best o' order for his – er – speechifyin'."

I was groaning at the side of the stage, listening as he killed me stone dead. But he wasn't finished.

"Noo cronies, I've nae idea whit he's gonnae dae for a hale 'oor, but we'll hiv tae gie him the benefit o' the doubt. I just was told to come here and bring him on. I just want you to know by the way, that I didnae want him here in the first place."

He glanced over in my direction without a blush. I grinned weakly and couldn't keep my eyes off the rotating bow tie as he blundered on.

"As ye know cronies, I wid sooner hae Callum Kennedy, but the Committee thought that it wis time for a cheynge and you never know, the members, that's you, might enjoy it. Well, we'll see. Anywey, here he is."

And with that, his bow tie still jiggling furiously, he walked off the other side leaving me to get on with it. The way his tie was going, I'm surprised he didn't take off like a helicopter, but he disappeared into the Committee Room, never to be seen again!

I took a long time in starting that night, and was even longer warming them up. The "warm-up" for a straight actor happens in the course of the show, not before it. I dispensed almost entirely with the script and ad-libbed a kind of defence case against Bow Tie, which pleased the members and allowed me to gradually interest them in what was left of *The Robert Burns Story*. It was here at Gartcosh, after that show, that one man kept caressing my upper arm, and when I turned round on him, all he said, with a kind of glazed look, was "I hope you don't mind, Mr Cairney, I just wanted to touch you."

I didn't stay long. I was in such a hurry to get out of the place that I forgot to collect my fee. I had to come all the way back from the car park, but there was no sign of Bow Tie. The barman called out, "Is it this ye're after?" And he threw me a tight wad of notes folded in an elastic band. I caught it before it hit the wet floor. "The Committee says ye've tae hiv a drink afore ye go," called out the barman. "No thanks," I called from the door, "keep it for Callum Kennedy!"

While I was in Glasgow, Father William Dempsey died. He was the priest who had married Sheila and me in 1954 at the Jesuit church of St Aloysius in Garnethill. Now he was gone. Another thread broken. Yet another blow was the sale of my beloved Kellie Lodging while I was away. I wasn't at all sorry to leave Pittenweem but I was heartbroken to leave the house. I thought I would be there till the pension. It *was* my pension! But it was in Sheila's name; she was there all the time; she knew better than I did what our real finances were like after the long hospitalisation, so the house had to go. I then had to approve the new house she'd found on a hill overlooking Loch Fitty at Lassodie, outside Dunfermline, and five minutes from her mother at Coaledge. The setting for our new home was superb, with enchanting views all round. The aspects were more like northern Italy but the climate was strictly West Fife. The house itself was of good design but it had been built with materials stolen from building sites and labour straight off the Irish boat. Everything was there; central heating, double glazing, Aga range, several bathrooms, balconies and double garage, but it was all fitted badly, and if, by some mischance, it were well fitted, it would either be upside down or back to front. We made a good profit in moving but spent all of it and more on immediate repairs and a vain search for a constant roof leak. It became a very beautiful house in the end, but I never really liked it. I lived in it in a perpetual "huff". I seem to remember we lived behind scaffolding for the first year. Or rather Sheila and the children did.

While I was on one of my many trips away, the BBC rang Sheila one day to ask her to choose a record for their programme, *Celebrity Wives' Choice* – "Something just for you and John," they said. "Sure," said Sheila, " 'Strangers in the Night'." And put the phone down.

In the first part of my tours, I had used pianists: John Worth in the Highlands and north, Ken Greenaway in the east and Edinburgh and lovely old Jim Burniston in Glasgow and the south. But I gradually felt that a greater versatility was required in the background music and accompaniment, since the performance shape changed so often and I was more and more inclined to speak over the music rather than insert the formal songs. So I now looked for a musician who had this flexibility and yet was able to travel around with me, rather than my having to rely on pianists available in each region. I started to ask around about a guitarist and found a pianist – or rather, a chemist.

Colin Harvey Wright was a grave-looking Glasgow-born, Edinburgh-based chemistry student of private means, who was still in his twenties, but in appearance, in demeanour, gave the distinct impression of being late middle-aged. He was slightly built, bespectacled, with thinning hair, and no dress sense whatsoever. But he had indefinable charm and astounding ability. I warmed to his confession that his heart was in science but that his mind was on music. He seemed slightly suspicious of me. He had never had cause to work before and his public school background gave him few opportunities to mingle with gipsy actors. But he was intrigued by the kind of job I had to offer and we shook hands on it there and then. His handshake was limp, his palm was wet, his eyes refused to meet mine, yet in meeting Colin Harvey Wright, I knew I had met an extraordinary young man, who was innocent, gullible, and inexperienced, but had the mind of an Einstein, the fingers of a Rubinstein and all the easy conversation of a Gertrude Stein! He was not an easy fellow to get to know, but I liked him from the start and in no time he became not only my pianist, but my manager, and then my partner in Shanter Productions, and ultimately landlord of our new office in Colinton Road. He also became, although he would never admit it, a friend. It was Colin who engaged our new secretary, Sue Frame, willowy, dark and beautiful wife of John Frame of Scotland rugby fame. Another triumvirate had been formed.

While they got the office in order, I went off to Newcastle to play Cyrano de Bergerac. While there, I met Bob Adams, managing director of the McIntosh Furniture Company in Kirckaldy, who invited Sheila and me to see the New Year in with his family in Aberdour. We were glad to do so – especially for the excellent onion soup and the most potent of home-made wines made by his delightful wife, Mary. Furniture business had taken Bob to Newcastle the month before, where he had seen my performance as Cyrano de Bergerac and had dropped me a kind note. We met for supper at his Gosforth Hotel a few nights later and got on easily from the start. We were both Glaswegians after all. He asked me if I'd ever heard of Charles Rennie Mackintosh.

"The architect?" I said.

"Yes," replied Bob. "1975 is designated Architectural Heritage Year. I wondered if you could do a show on him – perhaps with some kind of emphasis on his furniture which could link to our new 'Cranston Collection'. It's just an idea."

It was a good idea. And we drank to it.

"To McIntosh!" I said.

"To Mackintosh!" said Bob. A good idea had been seeded, and it eventually flowered not only in a stage show, but as a TV hour. But before all that happened the Burns Roadshow was preparing once more to get under way.

My first engagement that year was at the Adam Smith Centre, Kirkcaldy, to present *The Robert Burns Story* with the Kinghorn Singers. This was a good device which not only added to the overall artistic value of the evening, but helped at the box office. Choir members are always good at selling tickets. We also had a champion fiddler, Angus Cameron, and Ken Greenaway, a colleague from previous Fife engagements, was at the piano. The whole package promised well, and it did not disappoint, for we had great notices and a week of full houses. With Colin, now professionally known as Harvey Wright, well rehearsed, and his accordion, known professionally as "the box of tricks" well run in, we were on our way.

"With pale, etched face, framed in a steel grey mane, John Cairney strolled casually into the Whitehall Theatre and began to rummage through Burnsian bric-à-brac collected over the last decade. Quickly the past tense of There Was A Man *no longer applied. King Cairney was back."* Embarrassing as that effusion may seem now, what Alan Dunsmore wrote in the *People's Friend* at Dundee then was exactly right for the kind of show that *An Evening with Burns* or, as it was sometimes called, *A Nicht Wi' Burns*, was then – time spent on stage with John Cairney, based on scenes from the life of Robert Burns. Audience involvement and participation was the keynote and at the Whitehall Theatre I had the pleasantest of surprises.

Walking through the audience at one point, encouraging them to sing, a pure soprano sailed above the rest from somewhere in the middle stalls. It belonged to fifteen-year-old Elaine Ness, a local girl who was there with her mother. I didn't know her name then, of course. I only knew I must use that voice at some point. And that point came just before the death. When "John Anderson, my Jo John" came up in the script, I indicated to Elaine that she should sing it, and the innocent simplicity of her tone gave the song all the performance it required and the moment was sealed in the dying fall of the scene.

> John Anderson, my jo, John,
> When we were first aquaint,
> Your locks were like the raven
> Your bonie brow was brent,
> But noo, your brow is belt, John,
> Your locks are like the snaw,
> My blessings on your frosty pow
> John Anderson, my jo.

Any evening that can provide such a moment deserves to be called a Burns Night.

Audience participation was also the highlight of my night with the Liberals at Galashiels. Their traditional Burns Supper was in the orthodox manner with speeches and songs, but on this occasion they had decided on my solo professional performance to tell *The Robert Burns Story*. This gave their committee a little bit of a problem as to what to do with their usual singers, not forgetting their usual accompanist. I said they were entirely redundant as I was, to all intents and purposes, a One-Man Burns Supper. Look what I saved

111

them in singers' fees. The script that I worked from made all the sufficient Burnsian comment and saved a lot of boring speeches. The format gave ample opportunity for the normal kind of songs and why I enjoyed doing it was that it pre-empted all the dirty jokes. The traditional format, in my opinion, had become moribund and it is only with first-rate speakers and top-class performers that a Burns Supper is at all bearable. Otherwise it is merely a continued proselytisation of ignorance and irrelevance. But, on my own, I really couldn't go far wrong. After all, for the most part, I was using his actual words.

However, it was tactfully pointed out to me that these same singers had given good service over the years to the club and, by the way, did I do "Tam o' Shanter" in my "recitation"? Yes, I did, I said, hoping to please.

"Oh dearie me," said the secretary. "Rob Webster always does that. He comes frae Selkirk, see."

I didn't see what difference that made, but I was sure a place could be found for Mr Webster somewhere. But I was adamant that I should do Tam. I had sat through too many earnest, verbatim, line-exact, boring, interminable "Tam o' Shanter(s)" to yield to any now. It's not that mine was any better, but at least it was faster. Besides, I also knew its place in the story and could set it in context.

Galashiels persuasion is irrestistible, however, and I said I would work out something to accommodate the singers and Mr Webster, if they could meet me at the Liberal Club, an hour before the evening opened. All I did was to ask the singers what songs they had in their repertoire, then I selected their running order, as it were, from where these songs occurred in my script and gave them numbers. In this way, Bill knew that he was to follow Kenny, Miller knew he followed Bill, and Jim followed Miller. I would indicate the musical intro to Barclay with a nod of my head, as he had the running order in the music before him, and then, with either hand, indicate the singers. I asked them not to come forward from their seats at the tables to stand at the piano, but merely to push back their chairs, catch the keynote and sing from their place. This worked beautifully. The audience was taken with the spontaneity, and I was grateful for the adaptability.

David Steel, then a very young MP (he's still a very young MP), was the guest of honour, and I'm sure when he left to catch his London train, the collective echo of his constituents singing was still sounding happily in his ears. I wonder are they singing yet in Galashiels, and are there sausages still for tea?

> Here are we met, three merry boys,
> Three merry boys I trow are we,
> And many a night we've merry been
> And many more we hope to be.
> Oh, we aren'a fu' – well, no' that fu'
> But just a drappie in oor e'e.

I paid my tenth and final visit to the Brunton Hall, Musselburgh, on the night of the Scotland-Spain football international, which was also televised. As a result, there were less than two hundred in the hall, where before they had been queuing in the foyer for ticket returns. I think I got the message. I took the chance to experiment further with the format. Colin had now bought an electronic accordion which was only one state less than Cape Canaverel, but what a wonderful sound it was to speak verse over, and we had a whole effects studio in it as well. Unfortunately, it took two of us to carry it from the van.

This time, instead of a choir, I added a troupe of young dancers and also put all the songs on tape. The first device was a lovely addition, especially in "Tam o' Shanter" where they mimed the action beautifully, as I narrated. But the taped songs seemed to inhibit the audience and the lovely audience voice was missing. The tapes, by professional singers, were so good the audience wanted to listen to them instead of following the action. We dropped them after the second night, and the audience sang again.

I was constantly experimenting – perhaps too much. Maybe I was getting bored with the part, or becoming jaded in it. But I was never bored for a second in any of the performances. The audience saw to that, and even at the end of the Brunton show, I had to stop and go to an elderly lady who was in floods of tears near the end, and I told her, "It's all right, it's only a play". And she said, "It's no' that. It's just ye mind me o' my son." I could say nothing to that, but held her hand as we led into "Auld Lang Syne"

> For auld lang syne, my dear,
> For auld lang syne,
> We'll tak' a cup o' kindness yet
> For auld lang syne.

In the spring of 1975, the Pitlochry Festival Theatre invited me to do a late-night *Postscript to Burns* in the foyer of their theatre following a performance of Robert Kemp's *The Other Dear Charmer* in the main auditorium. Doctor Kenneth Ireland, in charge at Pitlochry, had always insisted he was my very first employer as he had given me my first paid job as an actor: £4 a week with the old Park Theatre in Glasgow in 1947. He asserted his primal rights by hiring me very cheaply for the Spring Festival. In addition, Bells Whisky of Perth promised a free bottle with each ticket. It actually turned out to be a miniature but, nonetheless, the attractions of Pitlochry were manifest and I was happy to create another Burns show. Colin was again partnered by his mighty Wurlitzer and was joined this time by the Finn MacCuill folk group (Nick Weir and Tony Ireland), as well as award-winning folk-singer, Lesley Hale. Lesley was delightful and we had some lovely times with her. (It is her voice you hear at the opening of the Burns Double Album).

This four-sided presentation was not my first attempt to put Burns on record. Years before, in 1969, I made a long-playing selection for HMV which *The Gramophone* described as "a masterpiece". It was immediately reissued as "educational" and disappeared without trace. But I am still sneakily proud of it, for it was made in Putney with much love.

The second Burns recording was a very different affair and nearly wasn't made at all. Mike Westcott at Edinburgh University, who had helped us ten years before to find a venue for *There Was A Man* at the Edinburgh Festival, rang to ask if I would provide the Oration at the Inauguration of the School of Canadian Studies.

"Has it to be in Latin?"

"Good Lord, no!" said Mike. "A bit of Burns perhaps – perhaps *not* McGonagall this time I feel – some Stevenson – anything you think might have a little Scottish dignity – keep up the tone – not offend the Principal."

Mike was a stickler for protocol, but he trusted me, and left me to it.

"No more than eighteen minutes please, to allow for introduction. And no less – we don't want any longueurs, do we?" He was also very exact.

I did my eighteen minutes, no more, no less, which was a bit of Burns, of course, MacDiarmid, some of the Makars and my own Scotch Catalogue. Alan McEachern, the Canadian Foreign Minister, was the principal guest, and he protested good-humouredly that there had been no Gaelic names in my xenophobic litany. "Only because I couldn't spell them," I replied. The only one I knew was Ossian and he was a phoney. Mr McEachern invited me to his table to join him and his friends, who were all, like him, Nova Scotians and Gaelic-speaking – and Gaelic drinking! It was daylight before I left the Caledonian Hotel.

I was wakened by the telephone downstairs. No one was answering so I had to crawl out of bed and carry my head under my arm into the office. It was Neil Ross wondering where the hell I was? Neil was the owner/director of REL Records and I had been due an hour before at his basement studio in Atholl Place to record *The Robert Burns Story*.

Apparently I had just slept through several hundreds of pounds of studio time, but since it was my money . . . I was down in that studio within minutes.

I remember little of that long morning, except that the earphones weighed like coal-bags either side of my pounding head, and that Neil's comments from the control box were as incomprehensible to me as a loudspeaker announcement on a railway station. Yet somehow we got through it, helped by Neil's pragmatic inspiration in having a dram ready on the table for me as I entered, and keeping a constant supply of black coffee coming from Holly, his ultra-attractive assistant. Not that I had any eyes for Holly that day. I could hardly see the script in front of me. Luckily, most of it was by now well ingrained, the difficulty was in remembering the cuts. At lunchtime Neil took me round the corner and fed me on pasta at the nearest Italians, not forgetting the Bardolino – a couple of bottles of which we brought back. We were joined by young Jim Hutcheson, Holly's artist friend, who was to design the cover. He promised not to give me red eyes! The afternoon session sailed past, and by the time we got to the "death" I was just about coming alive again. It was late when I got back to Colinton, but next morning I was back bright and early with Colin to lay down the music. That night, *John Cairney Tells the Robert Burns Story* was complete, and that is the double album which sells today on cassette. But not till now will people realise that the Richard Burton vocal effects ascribed to me were created entirely by several bottles of Bardolino, and that the so-called "performance ease" was only the result of a hangover!

Yet there is a baker who listens to it every night in his bakehouse. He says he sees different pictures in it every time he listens, and he has set himself to learn it word for word, so he says it aloud with me as he makes the morning rolls. Ah well, chacun à son goût!

The Canadian link with the product was maintained in the story I heard from a friend of Colin's, who teaches at a school for autistic children in Victoria, British Columbia. One particular pupil used to come into the Headmaster's study nearly every morning and break the pencil on his desk. The Headmaster soon learned to leave a plentiful supply available and try not to show a reaction, although as a good Scot, he must have been appalled at the waste. He thought.the boy would soon tire of the obvious provocation. Then on one morning when he came in for his usual "snap" exercise, my voice was booming out from the loudspeaker in the corner. The Headmaster was working his way through the four sides of the album day by day as he did his mail, since he was too busy to sit down and listen for almost two hours. This particular morning he was on Side 4 and I was in the middle of dying. The boy stopped with the pencil in his hand then, still holding it, went over and sat by the speaker. When I finished, he got up, politely replaced the pencil on the desk and went out.

Next morning, he was back again, but went straight to the speaker and not to the desk, and sat cross-legged in front of it. The Headmaster was puzzled, and then remembered the record. The boy sat fidgeting through Side 1 and the Headmaster feared for his pencils, so on an impulse, he put on Side 4 again, and the boy listened solemnly throughout. At the end, he got up and left without a word, and never came back. To this day, the pencils remain unbroken, and the Headmaster ponders on what was in an actor's voice at a particular time that struck a chord in a clever, sensitive but sadly, autistic boy in Western Canada. Scientific friends like Alastair Knight in Edinburgh tell me that there is a neurone response to specific ranges in the human voice. Certain notes excite a certain nervous reaction.

I don't know about that, although I have found that in certain performances I have stimulated a kind of hysteria in the audience when the collective nerve responds to the emotional moment. There was a frightening occasion once in a shipboard performance when I agitated one young American woman to such an extent that she had an epileptic fit. There is something in the voice in action. There must have been something in mine on that recording – and it wasn't all Bardolino.

In South Africa, one expatriate puts it on every Burns Night and has a large dram between every side. He has only a hazy memory of Side 4.

In the United States, a Jewish family have had to suffer it regularly as the father has been converted to Burns quite recently, and insists that they play it throughout dinner; Side 1 for the soup, Side 2 for the fish, Side 3 for the meat, and Side 4 for dessert. He also insisted on silence during the playing. One of the sons told me that Robert Burns is not a great favourite with the younger members of the family – and John Cairney is not so popular either!

So much for one actor's work of an October day in 1975. The autumn leaves have long gone from that year, and swirled away with the many voices, but that voice, as Robert Burns, still goes round and round – and round – and round – and round . . ..

But before those autumn leaves had fallen and while they were still bright and green on the branch, Colin and I tried out that idea of a Summer Burns Festival. The original hope had been that one would mount events following in the chronological order of Burns' own life; boyhood and youth in Ayr, manhood beginning in Irvine and continuing in Ellisland and the final years in Dumfries. Greenock and Edinburgh would be acknowledged in some way but, in a sense, it was to blaze the Burns trail, and only in the Burns places.

In 1975, however, some people were reluctant to lend themselves to such an enterprise, and I was only able to persuade Maybole, Cumnock, Kilmarnock, Dumfries and Dalbeattie to take part, the first and last of these places having only a peripheral involvement with Burns. But I wanted to try out local reaction and test if there was a possible overseas interest. With this in mind, the Scottish Tourist Board had offered publicity help in the meantime, and promised to keep a watching brief. So, in that first instance, the whole of the Burns Festival of 1975 comprised Colin Wright et moi – not forgetting his accordion. We bought a white van to hold us all and off we went to the Burns Country

First stop – Maybole. We played at the Town Hall, which, as I think I mentioned, boasted the most superb acoustics. Apparently Continental orchestras cut their master disc here, and the caretaker told me that the timbers had been from a ship that had foundered off the coast in Napoleonic times. That's something for our supposed acoustic engineers to consider. Good acoustics are nearly always lucky accidents – whatever the scientists say.

At Cumnock, the Town Hall was given free as a courtesy by the local district council. I wish the others had been so obliging. The whole of the front row was taken by a party of Chinese from Chicago. They just thought Robert Burns was wonderful and promised to contact us again from the United States with a view to our appearing there. We never heard from them again, although it must be admitted I do not speak Chinese – either Cantonese or Mandarin. I think they must have been crackers!

At Kilmarnock we were in the Grand Hall of the Palace Theatre and the evening was virtually boulevardier theatre around tables. It assisted the intimacy I always strived for and what was memorable about that Kilmarnock show was the very poignant rendering of "Ye banks and Braes" by the women of the audience without accompaniment or prompting, which created its own lovely moment of silence as it finished. This is all I work for. Oddly enough, this show was given on 31st July, the very day on which Burns' Poems were published by John Wilson, less than a hundred yards from the Grand Hall in Waterloo Street where we were performing. I hadn't planned it that way. It just happened. I suppose the same thing could be said for the Kilmarnock Edition in 1786. Supper was provided at the tables afterwards and I had some discussion with the Scottish Civic Entertainments Association who promised that they too would be interested in helping a Robert Burns Festival get started in Ayrshire. But I'm afraid theirs was a Chinese promise.

In the van going home, Colin, who was driving, suddenly said — "Why are you not a big star?"

"Am I not?" I said.

Before I left Kilmarnock, I dropped in at the Dick Institute to see my face peering from the Benno Schotz bust now on display on the third floor. It was standing anonymously by a window. Neither Burns nor myself nor, more importantly, Benno Schotz, was ascribed. When I mentioned this fact to Jim Hunter of the Institute staff, he said, "We've had two identity plates on this already. People keep stealing them."

At Dalbeattie, we couldn't start, because a party of local farmers was hogging the lounge of the local hotel. They were reluctantly allowed to remain by the manager, as I pointed out they would drink their admission in the course of the evening, but they turned out to be a very happy nucleus and added considerably to the night. Next day, at the invitation of Jim McAffery of Gretna, I joined Provost Robinson of Dumfries, at the Brow Well near Ruthwell, in a commemorative service for Burns. Burns had come here in July, 1796, before returning home to die three days later. Mr McAffery and his Rosamond Burns Club had done much to clear up the site. But it was still a sad place to go to. It was, however, part of the Robert Burns story.

In Dumfries, I was back again at the Theatre Royal, although an extra performance was given at the Coach and Horses Inn on the White Sands. It was very crowded and very hot, and not a few were very sick. At the end of the show, this time introduced by Elliot Williams, with his usual succession of non-sequiturs, he told the audience that I had lost my shirt on the first-ever Burns Festival. For some reason he persuaded me to offer the shirt I had been wearing for a local charity. With some difficulty, I peeled off the purple garment and with two fingers passed it on to Elliot. I regret to say it raised only £11.

We lost quite a bit, but it would have been impossible altogether had we been paying ourselves proper fees or engaging any other artists. It had all been done very quickly and on a minimum budget, but it was sufficient to give encouragement, not only to the Scottish Tourist Board, but also to Kyle and Carrick District Council, who announced that they would be more than happy to sponsor, in conjunction with the Tourist Board and Shanter Productions, the Robert Burns Festival in 1976. The gamble had paid off.

I have lived in a Scottish tenement, an English villa, a Fife castle and between them, every kind of home, but I honestly believe that Pinegrove House was the worst house I ever bought. Just about everything was wrong with it, but its setting was breathtaking, high on its hill, looking down over fields to the Loch. The site, in fact, used to be a whole village. And looking down from the balcony on an autumn evening, one could be in Lugano, not Lassodie. I may as well have been in Italy for all I ever saw of the place. The local paper gave up trying for an interview and talked with Sheila instead. She could, as usual, tell no lie. I quote:

"On the 29th May we celebrated our 21st wedding anniversary in our thirteenth home — unlucky for some," she quipped. When asked about her husband's present career she said she was not so sure of the demands it made on him. "We were eighteen years in the south and, while there, John played chiefly classical theatre, but had many television appearances and several film parts. I would prefer to see him back in Shakespeare for his own sake. But he wanted to come back to Scotland because he feels he owes something to the country. He certainly has something to offer, but I feel his one-man performances are too taxing. He is giving up too much. He is burning himself up, conceiving the ideas, writing, preparing, producing, presenting and directing. He has shown great talent as a director, and perhaps if he would channel his energies into that he might be persuaded to take things a little easier. I don't know what it is but when he faces a live audience, something happens that is magical. With his enthusiasm and dynamic energy he could set up a teaching theatre that would be open to all people, young and old, not only for productions, but for teaching drama, or even simply the art of communication. The people of West Fife have an innate culture, and there is considerable talent here, but it needs direction," she said. "Ideally, John would

love to have his own theatre here at Lassodie and present King Lear *with my three daughters in it. And he says there will be a standing invitation on that night to the whole village of Kelty. The family is already very embarrassed about the fact that John is to present the prize at the Queen Anne High School this year. But, as John says, 'the show must go on'."*

Perhaps the show went on too much. We had stolen a wonderful family holiday that summer at Achmelvich Bay between Ullapool and Lochinver. We swam in the bay and we walked in the hills. We should have done more of that.

One good Lassodie memory, however, is of coming back from a rehearsal at the Carnegie Hall in Dunfermline, only a quarter of an hour away. As a result, I was unexpectedly home in the middle of the afternoon. Sheila was nowhere to be found. Still with my coat on, I wandered through all the rooms, but no sign. I heard the sound of singing and thought it was the radio, and it seemed to be coming from the garage. Going through, I heard it was actually coming from the old railway carriage, recently purchased to house our newest addition to the family – goats. Going to the door of the shed, I saw Sheila milking one of the goats with her head on its side, singing quietly to it and to herself. I didn't interrupt. I just stood there, listening to this very unexpected serenade, inhaling the lovely smell that nanny goats have mixing with the scent of the straw, feeling the heat of the sun on my back, watching the beautiful woman who was my wife, singing to her animals. I felt very content.

It takes all kinds of work to make an actor. At this time as well as all the Burns activity, I was doing research on the Mackintosh project, planning further Novello development while the show was on a Scottish tour, which was rewarding in every way. After the Carnegie Hall performance, a lady well-wisher sent me a hundred pounds in £5 notes as a "thank you" gift and in the hope I would put on more shows like that. I only wish there were more patrons like her! On the same tour I was paid at the Corn Exchange, Biggar, in beef. One of the directors was the local butcher. After the show, a solid half-bull was hoisted with difficulty into the boot of my car. The springs protested vehemently and only half an inch of the rear wheels showed. I had to ask the workman in the house to help me unload into the freezer next morning, until the Kelty butcher could come up to cut it into manageable portions. It was a whole lot of bull. I only hope that wasn't what they thought of the show.

Then my brother Jim phoned. He and his wife Val had opened a restaurant, called "The Highlander", at Nobleton, Ontario, in Canada, and they had the idea to bring me over for a six-week tour that would allow us to see something of each other, and let me pick up a few dollars. Dates were arranged in Nobleteon itself, the Chinguacousy Collegiate Auditorium, the Cedarbrae Collegiate Auditorium, the Brampton Mall, the Hamilton Place Theatre and a very special appearance for the Burns Society of Upper Canada at the Hyatt Regency Hotel in Toronto on Burns Night itself, 25th January.

> Some merry friendly country folk
> Together did convene.

Well, to my eye, they were anything but simple country folk gathered that Burns Night in that posh Toronto hotel. There was nothing of The Archers about them. This was an all male, top two hundred selection from the cream of the Toronto establishment. It was your actual super-post-yuppie brigade; accountants, lawyers, medical men, clergymen, academics and the military.

The other speakers included Donald Sinclair and Graham Leggat, whom I well remembered as a footballer for Aberdeen and Scotland in both our younger days. He warmed himself to me by saying that he knew nothing at all about Robert Burns and was just going to do the "gag-a-line" speech that he gave at all functions. "Your Majesties, Your Excellencies, My Lords, Ladies and Gentlemen," he began, "You can see the company I normally keep!" On my other side was a man in a green uniform, and when I asked him what he did, he said he was a General. "A general what?" I said. "Just a General," he replied amiably. I'd never met a General before, and was amazed to find he knew quite a bit about Robert Burns. As quite a lot of Canadians do. My job was to fill the second part of the programme after the intermission, and the hardest part was sitting through all the speeches until then. Performance nerves allow one merely to pick at wonderful food that one would normally scoff. Perhaps these same nerves made me unduly sensitive to the matter and manner of some of the speeches. I didn't really mind the gags and the medical allusions (there was a large contingent of doctors present), nor the military and political references. These were meaningless to me. But I very much objected to the tone of one speaker who, in the interests of Christian charity, shall be nameless.

He had been flown in the previous night from Winnipeg, I think, and to me he was still very high and I'm not sure his feet had touched earth yet.

> O, Lord, since we hae feasted thus,
> Which we sae little merit:
> Let Meg noo tak awa' the flesh,
> An' Jock bring in the spirit.

Well, Jock was exceedingly busy that night!

As a result, this gentleman's Burnsian peroration was nothing but a long, slack-mouthed succession of scurrilities and obscenities. Colin, seated diagonally opposite me some way down the table, could see my temperature rising, and made frantic efforts (for Colin) to catch my eye, which meant waving a hand discreetly. But I was beginning to come rapidly to the boil. An incident was averted, however, by the entry of a young girl, preceded by a piper and a grinning Filipino waiter, carrying a Saltire Cross (at least he wasn't wearing a kilt), and behind her two kilted gentleman with drawn claymores. "What's happening?" whispered Graham. "They're going to cut her head off," I said drily. And all the poor girl was going to do was sing a very shrill and wavering version of "Ae Fond Kiss" before being slowly led out again like Mary, Queen of Scots, at Fotheringhay. This was becoming a preposterous night.

Donald Sinclair lightened things somewhat with his somewhat conventional tribute to the Lassies, naturally well received by an all-male company. But then, when our Scots-Canadian guru swayed once more to his feet with a joke about Robert Burns in his Masonic regalia being mistaken for the Pope, it was enough for me. I rose to my feet and bellowed, "Why don't you sit down?"

There was a kind of hush, and I could see him trying to focus on me.

"Sit down," I repeated, and he started again to tell yet another dirty story. "SIT DOWN!" King Lear could not have bellowed into the storm with any greater impact.

The pitiable man slumped to his seat and an awful silence fell. I was standing at my place trembling. "Gentlemen," I said, when I could muster a voice, "you must forgive my intrusion, but I feel I must speak, if not for Burns, then for myself. But, first of all, I ask your indulgence. I am by profession an actor and, as such, have been hired by your society this evening at great expense to entertain you in the second half with an excerpt from my current touring production of *The Robert Burns Story*. I take this opportunity to absolve the Committee from any responsibility for my fee, so that I may be free to give my personal opinion on what I have seen here tonight." (I am perhaps reporting this outburst in a neater and tidier version of what I actually said, given the luxury of hindsight, but no report could convey the absolute cascade of words that poured from me in an icily controlled, molten flow. I was angry, ashamed, and proud all at once, but I had to do something for Burns – and for Scotland.)

"For more than ten years now, I have involved myself with the subject of tonight's celebration, and to hear that poor young man's brief life traduced by a litany of smut and innuendo and hear his work held no higher than the doubtful, droppings of *The Merry Muses* is to offend not only my studies and professionalism, but that of generations of Scots, who have revered his performance in the literary arts and honoured his eminence as a product of the Scottish nation. Only he would have the compassion and genial charity to forgive the previous speaker his irrelevant inanities. I find I do not have that forgiveness in me and I beg him for the sake of that Immortal Memory I'm sure we all hold dear, to remain silent for the rest of the night and I ask you, gentlemen, for your permission to leave."

With that I pushed my chair back and I remember it fell. I walked straight out of the first door I could see, and found myself in a kind of foyer. Now that I had made the grand gesture and the big exit, I didn't know quite what to do, and felt just a little bit silly now that the indignation was beginning to wear off. I wasn't at all sorry for my outburst. I just wished I'd waited till after the show. I realised I had just thrown away a thousand dollars. I could hear someone coming out after me, so I made a dart for the gentlemen's lavatory I could see on my left. There is no place less welcoming than a lavatory when one has no need for it, so I turned on a tap and ran the cold water on my hands.

It was Jim who came in after me. "John, John," he said. His face was red, he grabbed my shoulders. "God, you told them. Oh, you told them." His eyes welled with tears.

"Here, Jim," I said, "try some of this." And I turned on the cold tap. I didn't know if my young brother was emotional with excitement or with embarrassment, but there was no doubt he was agitated.

In no time, the place filled up with men in variegated dinner jackets, some of whom looked at me very strangely. Jim and I went out into the foyer again, still not quite sure what to do. One of the Committee approached me to ask if I would please return. The offending speaker was already on his way up to his hotel bedroom in his hotel. "He was very tired," explained the Committee man, euphemistically.

"Was that what it was?" I said.

Eventually, I did go in again, but any entrance is hard to make after one has made a good exit. The men rose to their feet, applauding except one table, who pointedly remained seated. I learned later they were a party of doctors from out of town, one of whom said to me they thought that the incident was in fact my performance and they weren't very sure how to take it. All this time, Colin, having nothing better to do, had gone to his accordion and was playing mollifying musical airs for his own pleasure as much as anyone else's, waiting to see what would happen and what I would do. I made some kind of tentative opening and we did do an excerpt from the show, albeit rather restrained and self-conscious. But we attained a reasonable conclusion and the night ended more or less on key. As I was putting on my coat, the Secretary asked me to sign the waiver to my fee as I had said. I did so with gritted teeth, and went out into the snow.

Next day I received a letter from the Society, acknowledging my presence at the Hyatt and waiving of the fee. But underneath this typed statement, in handwriting, it said, "Thank you for your heart-warming presence and sincere remarks. The unfortunate gentleman was sent to us with the highest recommendations, but he has not gone home with the same. I enclose a check which I hope will convey our appreciation and thanks." And the cheque was for the full fee plus a bonus of one hundred dollars!

The rest of our Canadian capers did not quite have the personal drama of the Hyatt occasion though it was not without its incidents. At the Nobleton venue I had to help some of the men shovel away about fifty yards of snow about four feet high from the car park to the front door of the Italian restaurant where the performance was to be given. It was not quite the warm-up I was used to. The Italian proprietor looked on with typical Latin flair.

At the Cedarbrae Auditorium an unusually boisterous leap on to the table during "Tam o' Shanter" split my breeches along the inside leg revealing bright red underpants. I thought for a minute I'd cut myself! It meant that I had to sit through the remainder of the performance like Ironside in his wheelchair, but it gave an added vulnerability to the end section of the script. However, when I stood up at the curtain call, I had to take my bow with my hand in a very intimate position. I felt like a very ill-mannered chimpanzee in the zoo.

An extra performance was suggested by the municipal authorities at Scarborough, who asked if I would do half an hour of Burns in the open air in return for a small fee and a silver salver. I liked the silver salver, so I agreed, and found myself standing in what I thought was the surface of the moon – an entirely concrete structure going up for miles into the sunlight; little heads still visible over the parapet, watching and hearing my offering on closed circuit television. This could only be North America.

The Hamilton Place complex in Hamilton was a much more conventional venue, and here I was, on St Valentine's Night, joined by the Schiehallion Dancers and the Saltire Singers. What amazed me in the programme is that they spelt Schiehallion correctly, but the Singers were listed as the "Seltire" Singers. It was a great night, although the management was rather worried about the probable incidents of beer cans. It appears that the last Scottish artist to visit had left his mark in the huge number of empty Tennent's lager cans that were lying about the Great Hall. I asked who the performer had been. "Billy Connolly," they said. "That explains it," I replied.

I told them my kind of audience was much more pan-loaf and, besides, they couldn't afford to drink that much beer. Anyway they applied the principle of carry-out more to Chinese and Indian takeaways, rather than liquor stores. I had followed Cleo Laine into the plush Hamilton Place Theatre. She had her usual tremendous success, and I was followed by Hal Holbrook in his one-man show on Mark Twain, but I am glad to say Robert Burns kept his end up.

I had walked in that morning, a complete unknown to the stage staff. The stage manager wore what looked to me like a stetson and never removed a cigar from his mouth. "Where's your cast?" he asked.

"At your service," I said, spreading my hands.

"What about props?"

"He's just coming in now," and I pointed to Colin trundling in his accordion and speakers.

"Ain't you got a set?" he asked.

"Ain't you got a table and chair?" I mimicked playfully.

He gave me a look which obviously read, "Get this dumb Scotch cookie!" He couldn't believe the sparseness of the setting and the complication of the lighting, but I assured him that it generally worked and thank goodness it did. While we were setting up the lights, they let in the safety curtain, or iron, as it's called, for the mandatory practise, and there on the back I saw the names of all the stage greats, like Gielgud, Richardson, Guiness, Emlyn Williams, and I said immediately, "I'll have to sign that." But the stage manager said,

"Well, let's see if I ask you first."

"Well, ask me then."

125

"After the show," he said deliberately.

After the show, he did ask me to sign it and brought me the big felt-tip pen to do so. I made to sign in a space among the theatre names, but the stage manager stopped me. "That's for Mr Holbrook," he said. Instead I was directed over to the right where they had a decidedly Scottish section. I could see Kenneth McKellar, Moira Anderson, Andy Stewart. So I put mine under Andy and just above Helen McArthur, where I belonged. Once a Scot . . .!

The Canadian tour continued to extend itself and soon it was, "Go West, young man," as Colin and I flew first to Winnipeg, where we gave our show to about a hundred people in a hotel reception room. It was not our largest audience, but to our amazement, each one of them bought the double LP, so it made for a very profitable evening. We also stayed with Ed Evans, the Secretary of the Burns Club, and his wife, who fussed over us happily and drove us next day to the plane for Calgary. Our date there was not this time for theatre, but in the television studios. Besides, I had made a pact with Jack Whyte, an advertising executive turned singer, who made his living around Alberta doing, as he said, "What I could remember of your Burns show, which I saw when I was a boy in Paisley." I was so disarmed by his appeal that I should not perform my Burns show, that I readily agreed and instead arranged to make a television excerpt for Bill McLeod, an Aberdeen-born director at the local station, CFAC/TV.

This was arranged on condition that I could come into the studio after the last commercial on the Saturday night, and be out again before the first commercial on the Sunday morning! The studio was not otherwise available, but Bill McLeod was determined to put the Burns on film somehow, and providing I was willing to do the night shift, he didn't see any problem in doing so. I was installed in a suite in the International Hotel and ordered to sleep. Colin, not being required for this project, had flown straight on to Victoria where he was seeing friends. I would later join him there. While I slept, or tried to, despite the heavy central heating, Bill and his leading camera man, Paul Morris (whom I had known at the BBC), worked on the set and on a provisional camera plan. Bill, being a good Scot, and a good director, was adept at making the most of a little, and when I came in on the Saturday evening, I was amazed at the excellent setting he had made out of minimal resources. I hadn't expected to see our discussions so well realised.

The technique of shooting was very simple. We were virtually making a silent film with sound, if you see what I mean, in that Bill more or less outlined the segment of physical action, and I fitted in the words as they applied. For me, there was the extra fillip of the improvisation required and, for him, it was the skill with which he made up the shots as he saw them: "cutting on the wing" as it's called. Bit by bit, through the hours of that long night, we assembled the story for the camera, and somewhere about eight o'clock in the morning, we were approaching the death. I was feeling in just the right mood by then, in that I was very tired indeed. But Bill calmly mentioned, "You've only got three and a half minutes to die. Can you sort out the text to fit?"

"Well, let's see," I said, hoping for the best.

So instead of the long, dying fall of the stage presentation, there was something of a short, sharp descent. In fact, Bill came down on the floor himself, and once Paul, on camera, had found me in close-up, he stood beside me, and counted me down with his fingers – $10 - 9 - 8 - 7 - 6 - 5 - 4 - 3 - 2 - 1 -$, and as he made a savage cut across his throat, I expired suitably into the lens in big close-up.

The resulting Burns film was shown quite soon on the Canadian screens, and many times since then. It has also featured on the Public Service system in the United States, and I do believe it was perhaps the best of the three screen performances of the Burns I have given so far. It may lack the ingenuousness and enthusiasm of the original solo for the BBC in 1965 and the technical polish of the Border/STV version in 1977, but there was something about this "made on the run" Burns hour for Bill McLeod in that little studio that captured the reality of the theatre performance, and perhaps something of the man. Because of it, there is a corner in Western Canada where I shall never grow old.

I took the train through the Rockies to Vancouver where I met up with Colin again and we flew back to Toronto, and then to Nobleton and another week of crowded Burns Nights at the Highlander.

I used to enjoy my young brother's rather idiosyncratic introductions. After he had supervised the meal in the kitchen, he would be brought out to the dining area, still in his apron and tartan tammy, and made to face his patrons, "Well, Ladies and Gentlemen, and those of you from Mississauga (a district in Toronto), now's the moment you've been waiting for – and here I am! (Cheers) I would like to stay and entertain you all for longer (on occasions he would sing very pleasantly, always from his extensive Sinatra repertoire!), but I can't. (Groans) I have to get the liqueurs and brandies ready (Cheers) but, we've managed to get a substitute (he could never forget he was a professional footballer!). He's not quite in my class of course (Laughter) but he's the best we can do in the circumstances. He's been outstanding in London, outstanding in Edinburgh, outstanding in Glasgow, outstanding in Aberdeen, outstanding in Dundee – and now he's out standing in the porch waiting to come in!" And he would lead the applause as Colin struck the first chord and I came in to begin yet again, a cabaret performance of *The Robert Burns Story*.

On my return to Scotland, I was soon back in the heart of Burns Country to get the first Burns Festival off the ground. I couldn't believe that I was seeing my idea put into official practice at last, but, standing in the evening air of the Courtyard Theatre, wrested out of the Roselle Mansion House Stableyard, I delivered the opening prologue and declared the Festival open.

Four towns were involved; Ayr, Dumfries, Irvine and Kilmarnock, all of them closely associated with Burns, and all reflecting their various aspects of his story. I gave my show in each centre, but there were also recitals by soloists and choirs, a performance of *The Jolly Beggars* by the Quatrain Singers, and the music of Burns given in their different ways by the Reel and Strathspey Society and the modern folk groups. There was also a ceremony at the Brow Well and, perhaps most important of all, a Symposium on Robert Burns, given in a marquee tent on the Roselle lawns. In the house itself there was an exhibition of Burns books and various solo recitals. It was not bad for starters.

The Symposium was chaired by Tom Wright, no less, and guest speakers included Tom Crawford, Jock Thomson, Cedric Thorpe-Davies, Lord Elgin (on Burns, the Freemason – he brought with him Bruce's sword, but didn't use it), and inevitably the kindly, and kenspeckled Reverend James Currie, who spoke on Burns and his God. I gave the title "A Man for All Reasons" to the Symposium and it seemed to hold good for the Festival generally, but there was no reason for the lack of support given the project by the local councils, in that not one councillor, apart from Provost Paton, attended any event.

Yet visitors came from as far away as Seattle and Adelaide, and there were even some groups from England present. Anyway, sufficient was accomplished to warrant the promise of a repeat in the next year and plans were accordingly set in motion. I was quite happy. It had been a trial-and-error kind of festival in many respects and relied extensively on local patience and goodwill.

Stage management was more a matter of whose social engagements did not clash that evening. It was a community effort after all and, anyway, there were times in some of the performances when only God could have been "on the book" as it were. On one golden evening, and summer nights can be golden in Ayrshire, I was in full flight in Part One, and had just embarked on that section beginning:

> Ye banks and braes o' bonnie Doon,
> How can ye bloom sae fresh and fair –

when suddenly there was the most ravishing burst of birdsong from what seemed right over my shoulder. I turned, and could actually see the birds on the tree above the perimeter wall of the courtyard. And so could the audience. And they too knew that my next lines were:

> How can ye chant, ye little birds,
> And I sae weary, fu' o' care . . .

The audience applauded, and the birds stopped. But it was a moment of pure magic, and both the audience and I knew it. I wonder if the birds did?

The same kind of lightning, metaphorically and literally speaking, struck again later in the run. The Courtyard Theatre at Rozelle House was in the open air, and provision had been made for weather cover by the erection of a vast marquee on one of the lawns at the rear. It rains quite a lot in Scotland. That's what makes it such a good growing climate. Anyway, this night it really rained and we moved our audience into the tent. Just in time too, for the heavens opened, and God could see us better! This time, He took a hand in the second act. I was in the middle of "Tam o' Shanter" and was improvising the moves around the makeshift stage when I reached the lines –

> The wind blew as 'twad blawn its last –

It was certainly doing that.

> The rattling showers rose on the blast –

We could hear it on the tent roof above us.

> The speedy gleams the darkness swallowed –

And at that the lights, hung on poles, were suddenly affected by a flash of lightning or a power cut or something and all flickered ominously, but worse, or better, was to come. On the very next line:

> Loud, deep and lang, the thunder bellowed!

there came the loudest clap of real thunder that I've ever heard! True! At that I just sat down on the stage, and said, looking up, "All right, God, you get on with it". It was some time before a kind of order was restored.

Thus, the first official Burns Festival was unique on at least two occasions, and neither will be forgotten by those who witnessed them, least of all, me.

Despite the teething troubles, new friends were made, particularly the Braids, Derek and Maureen, a couple who were at the heart of the local Rugby Club. Derek was more interested in golf than Burns, and Maureen, because she and her girlfriends were habituées of the Pickwick Hotel, found herself appointed, by osmosis, as my very reluctant local Secretary and Girl Friday. She proved to be most witty and supportive at a very awkward time. And when I mentioned that I didn't want to lose my shirt on Robert Burns, so this Festival must succeed again, she arrived next morning at the Pickwick Hotel, with a brand new shirt, which she insisted would bring me luck. It did. It brought me Maureen.

Her father, Mr Quintin Currie of Troon, had been an avid Burns man and she showed me several of his books. He had only recently died and she had taken up this Burns work as a way of remembering him. I suppose she looked on her assistance to me as part of that same memory. All I know is that I was very grateful to Maureen for pointing out the many local pitfalls – many of whom she knew personally. But at all times, she gave me heart. I don't know what real good we did but Derek's golf improved considerably!

Mr Walter Maronski, Chairman of the St Andrews Burns Club, asked if I would give a performance of *The Robert Burns Story* on St Andrew's Night, as he said I was always booked up when he tried to get me in January. Oswald Prosser of the Royalty Burns Club in Glasgow had the very same thought, so here we had two Burns offers for the same night. We tossed for it and Mr Maronski won the actual date and I went to the Royalty on 29th November. Both occasions were well received and I was gratified that once again I could slip on Robert Burns with my dinner jacket and give the audience the same kind of experience that formerly required full costume, sets and lighting. Whether I liked it or not, the Burns image still stuck.

The John Cairney Burns Club was formed by some men in

Edinburgh and registered with the Burns Federation as number 947. I was legitimate at last! So much so that when Yelena Igorevna Proklova, the Russian ballet dancer and film star, came to Glasgow to publicise a week of Russian films, I was asked by the Scottish Office to be her escort. I was more than happy to do so. Suddenly I was in a James Bond world of Foreign Office and Scottish Office officials, actors from the Gorky Arts Theatre as well as Yevgeni Leonov, the leading actor from the Lenin Komsomol Theatre in Moscow. Six Russian films were being shown at the Odeon, Eglinton Toll, one of which starred Miss Proklova. She was more than happy to sit through it with me on one side of her and Boris Isarov, the interpreter, on the other.

I saw her to her hotel, but was permitted only the formal bow and kiss of the fingertips in the foyer. One mustn't rush things of course! Next day we had lunch with Lord Provost Peter McCann at the City Chambers and the party went on for an official tour of the BBC. I found it hard to keep a straight face wandering around behind the dignitaries with my hands behind my back, and trying to avoid all the winks I was getting from old mates, indicating Yelena, with only too obvious "nudge-nudge" implications. If they only knew. The poor girl was more heavily defended than Stalingrad! That night, however, I had dinner with her in a completely Soviet group at the hotel and it was much more relaxed. And before she was quietly ordered to retire, I had the pleasure of introducing her to a very Glasgow version of "one two quick quick slow", something I'm sure she never attempted at the Bolshoi. It was nothing to a veteran of the Dennistoun Palais! I was to meet the lovely Yelena again – but in very different circumstances.

I opened the year of '77 with Robbie Burns Whisky in the Albyn Rooms in Edinburgh. What seemed to me a very distinguished company crowded under the chandeliers and such was the heady availability of the company's product that they must have had a very hazy view of *The Robert Burns Story*. But by this time I was becoming a little more adept at after-dinner performance techniques, and I wasn't afraid to go among them if need be. However, I was always careful to get back on stage by the end. There are moments when one needs the separation, especially when someone might be sick over your feet! Not that this night was at all perilous in that respect. Indeed it was very grand and such were the contacts made in so many different areas of influence that Colin and I considered the engagement extremely rewarding. Not to mention the two cases of Robbie Burns Whisky that were delivered next day to the garage in Colinton Road.

The old West Church at Greenock is reputedly the last parish known to Mary Campbell, Burns' Highland Mary. Out of the facts and the material of the legend, I had created "The Lingering Star" which we performed in the actual church with Patti Duncan as Mary, James Burniston at the piano and two excellent singers, Peter Wilkie and Bill Dennison, who sang the other parts. I meandered through the piece as Burns merely giving cues for the many songs. I had to sing in this one but I kept it as quiet as I could. Since the songs were so good and the settings so unhackneyed, it was a pleasure at times just to sit and listen to the others sing. The script also served as a basis for a fuller Burns dramatisation in time to come but, for the moment, it shone a welcome light on a much misunderstood and sometimes overrated Burns heroine. It was also good to link Greenock to its place within the Burns odyssey and to perform in a venue that had genuine ties with the subject. Besides, I also enjoyed Jim Burniston's company over a dram. Dear Jim loved his dram, and his piano was all the better for it.

We carried on down to Carlisle with *The Robert Burns Story*. This was the full costume performance again and it took place in The Tithe Barn, a newly renovated historical edifice in the town and an ideal place for my kind of intimate performance. We chose to place the acting area in the centre and played in the round, I think to some effect. The acoustics were superb and at the end of the evening James Bredin, the Managing Director of Border Television, came to the little dressing-room at the side and said, "This is something we must do on television." I couldn't help but agree, and a date was soon fixed.

It was still not quite Burns Night when we drove north to Aberdeen for a return engagement at His Majesty's Theatre. This was the return demanded by the audience's petition and I was engaged for the week. The reaction this time was even better than before. Perhaps I was improving. I was able only to do the split week in Aberdeen, as I was due on the Thursday to fly out to Russia. I tried to get out of the Russian trip, as it was no longer the extensive Russian tour that was first discussed, but merely a couple of performances for a party of Scottish Burns enthusiasts. This didn't enthrall me enormously and I knew I could arrange a longer Moscow visit through Geneva at a later date. But I had a slight suggestion from the Scottish Office that perhaps I ought to go since there had been a link to my acting as guide for that group of Russian actors the year before. Oh, yes, I suddenly thought. Yelena Igorevna Proklova. Of course, I would go. After all, if it is in the interests of international cultural relations . . .?

Jimmy Donald quickly arranged a fill-in for the rest of the week; a pair who were also making a welcome return to Aberdeen: Hinge and Bracket, alias George Logan from Glasgow and Patrick Fyffe, Jane Fyffe's brother, whom I had met so long ago in Worthing. I understand from James Donald that I held the H.M. Theatre attendance record but this was beaten soon afterwards by my good friend, Andy Stewart – but then he brought all the family! Well done, Andy. I left Aberdeen very reluctantly after the Wednesday show to drive overnight to the Airport hotel in Glasgow.

When I was first asked to go to Russia by London Productions in Geneva it had been intended as a three-city theatrical tour with a week each in Moscow, Leningrad and Rega on the Black Sea. But now on my first visit, in 1977, this was reduced to a five-day stay in Moscow with only what amounted to a very long speech at a banquet on one hand and an excerpt from the Burns show to be given as directed. My fee was being paid by the Scottish Soviet Friendship Society and Nairn Travel, with some assistance from other parties I gather. I was not told very much about this, as I was sort of persona non grata with most of the company, due to the publicity given my reluctance to join them.

Luckily for me Pipe Sergeant Jimmy McCallum from Ayr was kinder, and he and I sat in the back of the plane on the way out, being left somewhat to our own devices by the company of car dealers, hoteliers and publicans, who formed the main part of the travelling party. One man was particularly aggressive about my general attitude to Burns Clubs. As it happened, he didn't return from the trip. Poor Tommy Gannan had a heart attack a few days later and died in the Moscow hotel. It was not so much that the others resented me, but they didn't like what I'd been saying to the press from Aberdeen about drunken sprees to Moscow in the guise of a Burns commemoration. But I did think it was all too much of a great big haggis bash. I wasn't any kind of killjoy or spoilsport, but Burns was surely more meaningful to Russia and the Russians than Scottish vodka or the miscellaneous ingredients of a sheep's stomach?

A further regulation imposed was that we should all be kilted – "for the purposes of group security". This, no doubt, gave the 150-strong assortment a colourful cohesiveness as we set out from Glasgow airport, but it was a different matter when we arrived at the equivalent in Moscow. The temperature was nearly 50° below (the knees!), and security took on a wholly different meaning as we stood there freezing on the tarmac, waiting in a long line that extended to the Immigration and Customs counter. Piper Jimmy came to my rescue again, giving me the benefit of his wide experience. "Just hop frae one fit tae the other, John," he said. "Get the kilt swingin'. You know, the way the lassies dae it at bus stops." And sure enough I got my kilt swinging as directed. Nothing else did though, in that freezing temperature. I just hoped that it was still in good working order! It was so cold that my nostrils kept freezing over. I had to keep sticking my finger up my nose in order to breathe. It hardly made for an elegant sight, a group of shivering kilties with their fingers up their noses, but no doubt the Muscovites have seen worse in their time at their gates – no wonder Napoleon retreated!

The soldier who looked at my passport with an impassive Slavonic stare suddenly looked up with a smile when he saw the word, "actor", and he repeated it in English. "Actor?" And I said, "Yes – er – da." (I had done my pre-trip homework!) But this soldier or immigration official or whatever he was, gave me the first hint of how the average Russian reacts to the arts and any kind of artist. Almost the way that we, in Scotland, react to football players. He saluted me through.

The Rossiya Hotel in Moscow was one of the largest I have ever been in. It was an enormous place, and each floor was presided over by a stern female, the baboushka, whom one daren't address as Ms. She noted every person who passed, and I'm sure if two people came up, and one went one way and one the other, her eyes would follow both. The Russians were the first to put a man in space, but they still haven't completely fathomed the complexities of interior plumbing. I was just as mystified, and it was Gordon Hepburn, our leader, who suggested that the best way was to lift the shower from the bath and apply it as required.

I was wakened at about 6 a.m. the next morning by the telephone beside my bed. It was the BBC in Scotland calling me directly. As I talked, two ladies came in to service the room, and I signalled to them to leave, but they just nodded and smiled and switched on what sounded like aeroplane engines, but turned out to be very old-fashioned vacuum-cleaners. I explained to the BBC that the KGB had just come in in the guise of cleaning-maids!

The food for the most part was terrible. Breakfast was quite unappetising. It looked like cheese and pickles with sour black coffee.

But I was glad to be up early, for I couldn't wait to get out and see Moscow. Anyway I had my own arrangements made. I didn't tell anyone, just in case they said no. I called the number I had been given in Scotland and said, as directed, "Roberta Burnsa". There was a squiggle of Russian at the other end, and then the phone went dead. I put it down not knowing what to do next. I went down to the foyer, and it was a whole confusion of people, but I saw our leader again, Gordon Hepburn, who said we were on our own devices until the drinks reception to be given by Famous Grouse. So I went back up to my room, genuflecting past the baboushka at her desk, to get my British warm coat and fur hat. I was putting them on when the telephone rang and a very precise voice in English said it was speaking from the Pravda newspaper office. I thought for a minute I was going to be interviewed, but it merely told me that in one half-hour, someone would be downstairs to meet me. He would have the Robert Burns red rose on his coat, and he would be holding the newspaper. This was all very James Bond, I thought, but what else could I say but I would be there.

Détente was still in vogue and "glasnost" had not even been invented then, so I had been warned to be careful. In the foyer, I was just praying that there wasn't a glut of roses on the Moscow market. Then I saw him, standing reading his paper, with the red rose in his lapel. My heart was thudding as I went up to this complete stranger. I mean, I could be letting myself in for anything. His eyes looked over the paper at me. I felt myself blushing when I said, as I had been told, "Roberta Burnsa". He gave me such a wonderful smile, folded his paper, and said, "Come" and, taking me by the arm, pulled me through the door and there we were in the brisk crisp air of the Moscow street striding towards a very small car.

I noticed even in that first few minutes how few cars there were. Only the occasional chaika or big black official limousine – strictly for officials or party members – or prisoners? He motioned me to get into his tiny vehicle and we drove off along the clean, neat, dull streets.

The boy in me was absolutely thrilled at this adventure, but the saner part kept thinking – shouldn't I have left a message with someone? But I trusted what I remembered of my only Moscow friend and hoped for the best. From time to time the man beside me gave me a grin and I grinned suitably back, then suddenly he said,

"Tot-ten-ham Hot-spoor."

"Eh?" I said.

"Arse- "

"What?"

"En-al," he went on. Then I got it.

"Chelsea," I said.

"Voolves," he replied.

"Manchester United," I countered.

"Mankestair Chitty," was the swift rejoinder. As we got used to the game, we became quicker and quicker, throwing the names of football teams at each other. I even managed to get in Celtic and Rangers and Hearts, by the time we arrived at our destination. By this time we were laughing like mad as I had thrown in Cowdenbeath, which had him absolutely floored.

He put his fingers to his lips for silence and indicated right.

"Lubienka," he said.

"The prison?" I gulped.

As soon as we passed it he resumed our game. It seems my driver, while he had no English, had a passionate interest in world football, and knew the names of all the leading British football teams. We were still laughing as we went up the stairs of what looked to me like a Moscow tenement, past the same kind of Mother Courage figure I had seen in the hotel who paid no attention to us at first, possibly because we were laughing, although I did see her glance a bit curiously at me, because, with my kilt under my coat it might've looked to her as if I had no trousers on. I should've known that a kilt was hardly the kind of dress one would wear to pass unnoticed, especially in Moscow. But at that stage this fact had not crossed my mind, and I stood puffing happily opposite a very elegant door. No graffiti up this close nor any sign of vandalism – it was almost too clean.

With a rattle of chains and a whirl of locks the door was suddenly opened and there stood Yelena Igorevna Proklova! Her arms were about me in a moment then I was dragged into the flat, the driver following, beaming. He, in fact, was her husband, and waiting to meet me in what seemed a very cluttered dining-room was Yelena's mother and her daughter. In Russian fashion, they applauded me as I bowed to each of them, and I, in turn, applauded them. None of us could speak English, and at that moment, me particularly. I was absolutely overwhelmed. What was I doing here in a Moscow home on my first morning in Russia? But wasn't it great?

The table was laid out as for a feast, and at my place was a semi-circle of eggcups, each one containing every possible kind of drink; whisky, gin, brandy, rum, port, sherry and vodka of course.

Still laughing, we all had our first toast, "Roberta Burnsa", and with the next, I said, "Alexander Pushkin", and then Yelena made an attempt at my name, which came out like "Hon Ciarnev". I naturally replied with "Yelena". After the toasts I was very glad to be asked to sit down. I knew I had to! What was so extraordinary about that meeting is that we all got on so well, and seemed to understand each other by a kind of aesthetic osmosis rather than by any cybernetic skills. This was more than mere semantics. We had our own kind of terminology that day.

The little child detached herself from this adult babble to kneel down in front of the television set which was black and white, but which, in fact, coincidentally, was showing a film of Yelena's. I knew that Yelena had been given this flat as a reward for her services as a Russian artist, and I thought what a good idea. I wished Scotland would do that for us. She had also been given an English sports car for another fine performance.

But for the moment, she was being a very kind hostess indeed, and was showing me all the photos of both of us in Glasgow. She had been sent them all by the Scottish Office. Her mother, meantime, had been staring quietly at me and when the scrapbook was moved away and while my mouth was full of some other mouth-watering confection from the table, she was pointing at me, then at her wedding ring. And I couldn't resist saying, "No, I do not want to marry you, madam," but I got her meaning, and said, "Da," nodding vigorously, pointing to my own wedding-ring finger, which in the Scottish tradition didn't boast a wedding ring, but I nonetheless got it across to her that I was married. Her face lit up and, in Russian, she asked me if I had any children. I somehow knew that's what she was asking me and in response I indicated my step-ladder family. She clapped her hands and said, "Oh!" and then started counting on her fingers for me to tell her how many, and I showed all the fingers on my hand. "Oh!" she said again, and started applauding.

Her son-in-law, meantime, stood against the fireplace, smoking. At one point, drawn in by the increasing joviality, he had tried out his very basic English in offering me a cigarette, at the same time showing his grasp of the colloquial, "You want a fag?" he said. The way he pronounced the last word made me jump. He made it sound very Anglo-Saxon! I was saved by the little daughter who was by now fascinated by this strange man in a skirt.

I had to stand up and whirl round to let her see it fully, and she unashamedly lifted up one side, much to the amusement of the two women. I knew the obvious remarks were going on, but it was all such a happy occasion that nobody seemed to mind and, to tell you the truth, perhaps I was just a little drunk and couldn't have cared less – until the telephone rang. The husband went to answer it. I could feel the atmosphere change at once. The husband cupped his hand over the receiver and spoke tersely to the two women. The mother started to clear away some of the dishes and Yelena took the little one into another room. The husband put down the telephone and made signs to me. I gathered it was time for me to go. Yelena returned looking serious and I took a rather sombre farewell of that very beautiful Russian dancer, actress, wife and mother while her husband got my coat and fur hat.

We didn't play football teams on our way back to the hotel. In fact we didn't speak at all. He dropped me at the corner of a street some distance from it and let me off at the Underground. The Moscow Tube is like an Art Gallery, with paintings and murals and tiles. It was beautiful but perplexing and I hurried out again. Trams and buses were frequent enough going towards the Centre but I decided to walk. I was glad to. The late afternoon air did much to clear my head. I got used to the giggles and stares from passers-by, but I got a fright when a policeman yelled at me for crossing the road at the wrong place. I was relieved to find the hotel again.

As soon as I put my nose into the hotel foyer, I was jumped on. Oh, not by the KGB or anything, but by our own people, the Embassy Secretariat and the Sov-Scot officials. It seems that somebody had sent up to my room for me for some reason or other and, when I wasn't there, they searched the hotel. They found out that I wasn't with any of the groups and I think a kind of panic signal went out as everyone else had returned for lunch. The news had got to the newspaper office and one of Yelena's husband's colleagues rang him to tell him to get me back to the hotel right away. Hence the panic. That was why he didn't come back to the hotel. I thought it was something I'd said.

Everyone was very annoyed that I hadn't told them that I had had this meeting long arranged from Edinburgh as soon as I knew I was coming to Moscow, and it was a reciprocal act in view of Yelena's visit to Glasgow the year before. Eventually they were mollified and feathers were unruffled, and I was allowed to go back to my room where I was glad to use the shower for its proper purpose.

The next morning, Hugh Thompson, the company photographer, had Jimmy McMullen and me out on Red Square in what seemed to us to be first light, but Hugh was determined to catch the Scottish Sunday papers with his picture story, so he insisted that Jimmy be kilted and I be costumed in all my Burns gear for stills against the Kremlin wall and in front of St Basil's Cathedral. So, while Jimmy played his pipes, I posed, and just as Hugh had guessed, a crowd gathered, all in fur hats. But so did the army and before long a platoon of Red Army soldiers were goose-stepping their way towards us. The officer had a very brusque exchange with Hugh, which Jimmy tried to drown out on the drones, but when I indicated my costume and mentioned the magic name of "Roberta Burnsa", we got a salute and he marched his men away and we got on with it. Somehow Burns never worked like this in Huddersfield!

By this time the shops had opened and the crowd was added to by young girls from the GUM department store. "Is that where they sell Wrigley's?" asked Jimmy, between pipe tunes. More girls came streaming across the snows of the vast square. "Crif Rickard! Crif Rickard!" they were shouting. Because of the wig and the gear, they thought I was Cliff Richard! We didn't try to disabuse them. Jimmy tried his best with "Congratulations" and I did likewise with what I could remember of "Summer Holiday", and Hugh got what he wanted, pictures of Burns surrounded by lots of Russian girls. It made all the papers, and we were front page in the *Sunday Post*. Now that's what I call fame!

The main event of the trip was the Anniversary Dinner on the Saturday night held in the hotel itself. I was required to repeat the kind of programme I had planned for the Hyatt in Toronto in that they gave me the conclusion of the evening, in which to present a section of *The Robert Burns Story*. The little surprise that I had prepared, in this case however, thanks to Peter Henry and the Slavonic Department of Glasgow University, was a Pushkin sonnet, "Yelenye Pasveeshayitsa", which I intended to deliver as an end-piece. Before which, though, we had to dispose of Bill Keith's hundredweight of haggis and hear some really excellent speeches. This was a first-rate Burns Supper and I was proud to be part of it.

I was a little discomfited to find as I began my own section that two electricians from Moscow Television suddenly advanced on me like truculent altar boys, each bearing a light, and proceeded to follow every step I made in the dance area that was the stage. This became so irritating that I waved them angrily away. They refused to go, so I turned my back on them, and went upstage. They dutifully followed me. So I turned and, taking one by the waist, sat him on a chair at one side, and then much to the amusement of the guests, sat the other in a chair at the other side, and continued the show. What I didn't know was that the programme was being televised live to London, and all this was going out on air. What it looked like on the screen, I've no idea, but it wasn't a prime concern to me at the time, as I had an audience to deal with. I ended to what can only be called acclamation, but then came my "pièce de résistance".

They fell silent for what they thought was going to be the normal actor's mumble of thanks, instead I said:

> Ya vas Lyubil,
> Lyubof yeshcho byt mozhet,
> Vdushe mayey ugasla
> Mafsyem . . .

The reaction was marvellous and I felt emboldened to continue:

> No-pust ana vas bolshe nee trivozhyt
> Ya nee khachoo pichaleet
> Vas neechem . . .

I've written it as I said it, in a kind of phonetic non-Cyrillic script that Professor Henry had given me at Glasgow. But apparently my accent was quite acceptable and the Russians in the audience were absolutely delighted. They said the rest of the sonnet with me, and when I finished they rushed on to the floor.

It had also gone out on Moscow radio, and suddenly I found myself the toast of the hotel. All my previous sins had been forgiven, and it would seem I could do no wrong. But the most positive reaction was not from any of our own people or the Embassy staff, but from an older lady, who introduced herself as Rita Ruina, and whose English was impeccable. She told me that she had worked with Samuel Marshak on the first translation of Burns into Russian in the 1930s.

"You must come to visit me," she was whispering vehemently. "I have much to show you. I will arrange it."

Arrangements were in fact put into the hands of a Third Secretary from the British Embassy, who was blonde, beautiful and, best of all, came from Burnside in Glasgow. In view of my previous exploits, she was seconded to keep a special eye on me, which gave me no small pleasure as she was quite an eyeful herself. I received a call from Burnside, as we shall term her, asking me to be ready at a certain time, and please *not* to wear the kilt. In view of my Red Square success as Cliff Richard, I was a little disappointed. However, duly suited and wearing my brand new bright red shirt, I was ready to be picked up, and we headed once more into the city.

During the trip, we passed the Lubianka Prison again, and this time saw, what seemed to me, very small and very scruffy guards lounging at one of the doorways, smoking cigarettes. It was a conversation-stopper, merely driving past that grim wall. She left me at a block of flats and, pointing to a doorway, let me out. "You have my number. Ring when you want to come back. Remember now, don't go walkabout. And if anybody speaks to you, just repeat what they say and hurry by. OK?"

On going into the flat entry and climbing the stairs, the first thing I saw was another Mother Courage, but this one had her feet on a small chair and over what looked like a lit brazier. As I passed her, she mumbled something, and I parroted a mumble back and, as instructed, hurried on, looking at all the doors for the number I wanted. At last I found it, and saw on the door both a knocker and a bell. To knock or ring. Decisions! Decisions! I did both, peering all the time into the spyhole, which I could see plainly. Suddenly a woman's voice said something in Russian, and I stepped back a little, trying to make myself presentable in the spyhole, calling out what now amounted to my ubiquitous password, "Roberta Burnsa". There was an immediate rattle of chains, shift of bolts, click of locks, and when the door finally opened, Rita quickly beckoned me in. Her daughter, Margaret, was with her, and also spoke excellent English. I was made very welcome indeed.

What utterly amazed me was the tartan wallpaper and, on the wall facing me, a road sign, obviously genuine, which said, "To Alloway Cottage", pointing to the sitting-room. In that room, there was the same overt display of Scottishness. I didn't feel that this was put on entirely for my benefit, it was a permanent feature. Although I don't think that the LPs on display, one of Kenneth McKellar, and the other being my Burns double album, were normally exhibited on the mantelpiece.

Rita was wonderful company. We didn't have the feast that we had in the much richer Yelena's flat, but the difference was that Rita and her daughter were University people. They were intellectuals and, while just as honoured, they were much less rewarded in the material sense. However, in that little temple of tartanry in the Moscow apartment block, our conversation ranged happily from Burns to Shakespeare to Dickens, and back to Burns again. And Rita certainly knew her Burns.

I was also fascinated to hear about Marshak's visit to Scotland and of the many Scoto-Russian ties. Lermontov, for instance, was once an Edinburgh Learmonth, and Cameron, the architect, had done a lot of work in Moscow. And there was a General Bruce fought once for Peter the Great. I told her that we were the world's best mercenaries. We would fight for anybody if the money was right, and if there was no money in it, we would fight among ourselves. She mentioned that there was a man called Federov, now working on Burns in Archangel. It was a fascinating time, but once again the shrill alarm came from the telephone and this time, when her daughter answered, I could see again that same panic. What was everyone so afraid of?

It seems I had been reported by the concierge downstairs, who had apparently asked me, "Where are you going?" to which I replied, "Where are you going?" thus exciting her interest and curiosity. This was someone from the British Embassy to say that the Civil Police were already on their way. Could I get out quickly? There was an immediate flurry, but Rita found time to press into my hand a letter written in Russian to her son, who was working at an English University, if I would just post it when I got back to Britain? She put it into the inside pocket of my suit herself. Margaret then led me quickly to the rear stairway instead of the elevator, and ran with me all the way out to the back lane. Luckily we didn't see anybody, but by this time my sense of adventure was rather less than my genuine incredulity. This was getting ludicrous.

It was also getting dark. In the lane, Burnside was waiting in her little car. She flashed her lights and I ran to her, not even saying goodbye to Margaret. Just as we made our way out into the main street, a bigger car drew up at the apartment entry. We drove away, fast, in the other direction.

"Whew! Made it!" said Burnside.

"What's the panic?" I said. "I was only talking about Robert Burns."

"They're not to know that," she said. "The police here are not noted for their literary appreciation or sensitivity to national icons."

"Who are 'they'?"

"Never mind," she said sharply, keeping her eye on the road and on her mirror. I glanced behind but could see nothing else on the road. I was trying to play it cool.

"Seems silly to me you can't even pay a private visit to somebody without – "

"Private visits are forbidden to non-nationalists in Russia."

"Why did you take me, then?"

"As a favour to Rita," she said. "I should have known – oh, let's not talk about it." So we didn't.

I suddenly thought of the letter in my pocket, and checked to see if it were still there. I must remember to post it. For Rita's sake. Why did she want me to post it for her? There were so many anomalies surrounding life in this strange city that I decided not to ask any more questions, but just to keep my eyes and ears open and try to say nothing. I didn't succeed.

"What do we do now, then?" I said.

"I've got a surprise for you," she said. And she suddenly smiled. It was a lovely smile.

The surprise was a visit to the Russian space station to see a model of the original Sputnik. What was interesting about the visit that evening was that we went by a six-seater sledge, drawn by a magnificent horse. In my ignorance I insisted on going to the front near the driver. As a result I got a greater-than-welcome view of that animal's posterior in splendid motion (in both senses) and a constant spray of snow and sleet in my face from the road as we slid, 19th-century fashion, towards the 21st.

The space establishment was a future world not altogether to my taste. I couldn't get over the incongruity of the "twenties" feeling that even this brief visit to Russia gave me, and the contrast this was to the high 21st-century technology all around us. It struck me that the Russian social structure was fashioned in much the same manner as one of these rockets. There was a very small but highly intelligent and élitist coterie contained in the cone at the front. As it went further back, it gradually broadened to include the favoured party officers, the military and police, and then perhaps the artists and sportsmen, then, broadening down again, to encompass the enormous and frightening mass of the ordinary population, more than two-thirds of them still peasant, stretching endlessly into a vast distance. But not a little shrewd cunning was shown in the displacement of this centre; the fact of this drive being available in this supposedly romantic style contrasted to the eerie impersonality of the space objects. But what a change in the hospitality room. The first thing we heard was the sound of balalaikas and singing. The first thing we saw was a roaring fire, and the first thing we tasted was a tiny cupful of vodka.

This was the real Russia at last, Eastern Slavonic and larger than life. Then followed what can only be described as a party. This is what the Russians were best at; drinking and singing, making long, involved toasts, then drinking and singing again. Everybody in the place ended up dancing. Not only did they successfully attempt our eightsome reel, but we unsuccessfully attempted their Cossack knees-bend – all great fun. It was a very different journey back to the city. This time I made sure to sit in the back and Burnside suggested that we snuggle together for warmth. I was only too happy to oblige.

Our penultimate day was taken up with a morning visit to School Number Six, an afternoon call on actors at the Gorky Theatre, and a reception given to Russian writers in what they called the English Embassy, followed at night by a visit to the Bolshoi Theatre. At the school, I was to talk about Robert Burns to the older children who were learning English. I was glad to do so and couldn't help thinking as I looked down from the stage on the rows and rows of shining faces looking up at me how much like children Russian children were. They then sang to me their favourite Burns song. It is not one of my favourites, but they made of it something lovely as they sang it lustily in English:

> My heart's in the Highlands, my heart is not here,
> My heart's in the Highlands, a-chasing the deer.
> A-chasing the wild deer, and following the roe,
> My heart's in the Highlands wherever I go.

I recited "Tam o' Shanter" with a greater reliance on its onomatopoeic values than on its linear narrative. Nevertheless they seemed to enjoy it and, of course, totally appreciated "A Man's A Man". Much nonsense is talked about Russian appreciation of Robert Burns as being merely based on his political empathy with them. Burns was anything but a grey communist proletarian. It is more that he sprang from the soil a very uncommon man, ablaze with a particular kind of genius for the written word, especially in song. They perhaps failed to appreciate that sometimes he paid only lip service to the brotherhood ideal, but in his heart he meant it, even if his head told him that it was virtually impossible in the mortal world. Men are not born equal. They're only the same in the sight of God. Man continually jostles with his fellow man for greater favour, better position, higher reward. It's only natural, I suppose. But it seemed to me that these young people shone with idealism, or was it only innocence?

As I was leaving, a boy and a girl came up on stage, and presented me with gifts — "for my children", they said. Each made me a little speech in English and I thanked them and wondered why I had not thought of bringing anything myself for the school. But the interpreter saved the day by coming forward and giving me two boxes of chewing-gum. This was apparently a real luxury in Moscow.

144

The children in the hall positively squealed with delight as I handed a boxful each to the boy and the girl. I was told that it had only recently been made legal to import chewing-gum. Ironically I could only remember Celtic Park and "P.K. penny-a-packet", in my boyhood. Any of those smoky-voiced chewing-gum peddlers could have made a fortune here. Except that it was Wrigley's I gave out.

We got into the bus again to go to the Gorky Theatre, the next point on the itinerary. I was given two books on Pushkin in Russian by someone in the bus whom I still don't know. He got off when we got off and disappeared. Perhaps he was just getting a lift? It was good to be among actors again. In some sort of way we had our own greasepaint freemasonry and were able to develop a theatrical lingua franca that made conversation possible in a variable permutation based on English, French, Italian and Stanislavsky. Time was all too short here, because a view of a sports stadium was suddenly included in the fixture list.

This was the other face of the Russian passion – sport, especially ice hockey and soccer. They had nothing to learn from Glasgow or Liverpool in their fanaticism, but we had much to learn from them in the facilities offered. Olympic-sized stadia and every assistance for the young to learn to be good in everything and anything. Similarly, in the arts; in music, theatre, but especially in the ballet. The ballet for most Russians is more than a school for dainty girls and would-be defectors to the West. It is a way of life for what seemed to me half the population, who, if they can't dance, at least watch it. Scottish ballet would thrive on a tithe of their support. We were going to the Bolshoi that night but it was to hear an opera, not to see a ballet. However, first of all we had to meet some Russian writer at the "English" Embassy.

I was slightly taken to task by Mr Tough, the Second Secretary, for my errant wanderings around the city, but having been similarly lectured by the matron of the Western General, I was less intimidated than I might have been. He told me he was looking forward to retiring soon to his hotel in Muir of Ord. It was good to see Burnside with her hair down as it were and what a lovely sight she made. I suddenly realised how young she was to be doing such a responsible job in such a delicate area. There were several Scots working in the Foreign Service in Moscow and they met regularly in the Second Secretary's apartment to talk freely and easily and listen to the football results. They don't have an easy life and I didn't envy them. But they do a very good job under very trying circumstances. There are Embassy perks of course, and one of them was theatre tickets.

Our seats were so far back and so high up that I thought we'd need some of the equipment from the space station to see the stage. But such was the sightline ease and the most fabulous sound relay that we could see and hear with absolute ease. The figures on stage were no more than a quarter of an inch high, but I found no difficulty in enjoying their Lilliputian antics even at such a remove.

Although I didn't enjoy the scramble in the foyer beforehand. We had come, remember, from the reception, and nowhere, repeat, nowhere, could I find a lavatory in that public building. Perhaps the innate discipline of the great Russian peoples allows them to regulate their physical apparatus so that such natural needs can be confined to the privacy of their homes. At any rate, I had to explain to Burnside why I was hopping about from one foot to the other. "Too bad," she said, "you'll have to hold it in."

"It's all right for you," I said, "with your trained female camel capacity, but I need to go."

"Try down there," she said, pointing to a corridor.

I did eventually find the appropriate office after a long search. I think it ought to have been marked "For Emergencies Only". You see, there wasn't the normal repair to the cloakroom when one entered a theatre to wash one's hands, or comb one's hair, or whatever. Here, the Russian theatre-goer pulls off his galoshes and snow boots as soon as he comes into the foyer and leaves them lying there, throws his fur hat on to a heap of same lying nearby, and combs his hair, if he has any, in the large communal mirror available to all in the foyer. I remember standing there looking over a group of Russians at my own reflection in the mirror. I am not unduly tall, but I felt a Gulliver among them. Then I found I didn't have a comb.

The performance itself was wonderful. *Rigoletto* it was, and I came out in a kind of glow. I was amazed to find my fur hat and snow boots exactly where I had left them. The fact was everybody needed a hat and boots in Moscow, but it was astonishing that they all knew their own in the heap. I wouldn't really like to try the same thing at the Glasgow Citizens or Theatre Royal. I fear there would be a smart exchange of a pair of old wellies for a pair of fancy fleece-lined flying-boots! I had a meal afterwards with my female minder which wasn't at the hotel, or at the "English" Embassy, but it was very enjoyable.

It was hard to leave Moscow the next day. Our Russian hosts gave us a farewell concert at the hotel, and I had firm invitations to return next year to give my full Burns performance at the Palace of

Congress. But, more importantly, I had made real friends; Yelena, Rita, our interpreter, Mr Tough and, of course, Burnside. She came with us to the airport, and we had a very fond farewell, several times. The plane was perhaps expectedly delayed for one hour, then two hours. This didn't seem to worry the rest of the party unduly, but it affected me, in that I was due back in Glasgow to give not one, but two Burns performances in Glasgow that night – one at ten o'clock at the Charing Cross Hotel and one at midnight at the Duke of Touraine. Both had been sold out before I even left, but now it looked like I wouldn't even get there for the midnight show.

I reckoned without Second Secretary, S. W. Tough, MBE. He had cables flying in all directions and alternative planes made available in London. I'm sure the Duke of Touraine had never had cables coming direct to Parkhead Cross all the way from Moscow. It probably hardly made a stir to them, but the continuing delay was certainly upsetting me, and I was only mollified by the close comfort of Burnside. We were sitting together on one of the airport benches when I said,

"Who's that woman who keeps looking over at us?"

She wasn't one of the Burns party, nor had I seen her around on the official periphery, but from time to time she looked up from the book she was reading and stared quite openly at us.

"Oh, her?" said Burnside, with hardly a glance. "That's my mother." I shot away from the rather overproximate position I had to the girl, exclaiming,

"What!" in a rather strangled voice. I looked back to the lady and she was reading again.

"She's been on holiday with me for two weeks," went on Burnside.

"But I never saw – "

"She's very quiet," said her daughter as if that explained everything. I looked round again and the woman was smiling at me.

"She's going back on your plane," added Burnside.

"Did you tell her – " I began.

"I tell my mother everything."

She was a mystery this girl, but there was no doubt she was an attractive puzzle. She seemed to be good at her job and know all about life and yet she had a little girl vulnerability which her natural Glasgow metal screened for the most part. But I had seen behind the "wall" when the balalaikas were playing, and at moments in the Bolshoi. There was a beautiful girl there for someone, but I regret not for me, as I was due back in Glasgow that very night on a double booking. We took a long farewell, and then I was in the departure lounge with the Burns party. Jimmy the Piper greeted me warmly.

"Where the hell hiv you been?" he said cheerily.

I couldn't begin to tell him. I was swept through Customs like a VIP. This is how Russia treats her artists. I looked for the mother on the flight, but couldn't see her. Come to think of it, I've never seen Burnside since, but I certainly have my own interpretation of that now too-familiar phrase "From Russia With Love".

At Glasgow airport, a fast car was waiting and I was whisked to the Charing Cross Hotel, where I asked to be pardoned for the delay and excused from a performance. Instead I told them about my Russian visit and they seemed delighted with the difference. Roberto Matteo was impatient with all this as he was waiting to take me on to the Duke of Touraine, where I think I arrived by a miracle, only about an hour late. Jack Weir, who had been hired to do "Holy Willie", had boldly held the fort and had given the packed restaurant, "Tam o' Shanter" while waiting for me to make my appearance, which was well above and beyond the call of duty.

When I did arrive, it was to ribald catcalls and jocular enquiries like "Hiv they nae clocks in Russia?" It was not so much that they were unfriendly, but they had been sitting drinking and eating for about four hours. I didn't think a performance was called for at that time of night, so I tried to repeat the anecdotal chat that had gone down so well at Charing Cross. But a party at the back of the room, led by two otherwise well-dressed and attractive women, didn't think that this was what they'd paid for and started heckling me more than vociferously. They had a point but I thought I could win them round. I was wrong. It was the younger of the two women who called out first, "Whit the fuck's a' this tae dae wi' Rabbie Burns?"

It chilled me hearing such a sound from such an appearance. I know she was drunk, but it shattered me nonetheless. I was also very tired. The rest of the company tried to shout her down as her friend laughed and joined in what was wholly a distaff disturbance.

"Ladies," I said, "it's after midnight. Shouldn't you have turned into pumpkins by now?"

Laughter from some, shrill abuse from the "ladies". I had had enough.

"Ladies and Gentlemen – and our two friends from the Women's Guild – I am obviously not suited to your mood at this hour. Perhaps you're in a better position to entertain yourselves than I am to entertain you."

And with that I just pulled back my chair and walked out of the door which was just at hand, right into the cold air of Duke Street. Of course I had no car, but I was in my own territory and turned north towards Dennistoun like a homing pigeon. I was quickly caught up by the Matteo brothers, who, despite my strong protests, frog-marched me back to the restaurant.

"The show must go on, as they say," said Tony.

"And no show without Punch," added Robert, "and that's what ye'll get if we don't have a bit o' Burns."

"For if ye don't," continued Tony, "we'll have a riot on our hands, and Linda's just had the place a' done up."

"All right," I said, "I'll do it for Linda."

We were just going in as the "Kray Sisters" were coming out supported by a couple of shamefaced, dapper husbands. Despite the latters' efforts and the attempts of the Matteos to drag me in, another exchange followed in the street, in which I got decidedly the worse of a vivid, verbal exchange. In the end I was glad to escape into the restaurant. Yes, it was good to be home in Glasgow again! Needless to say, it became another great night in the Duke, thanks to that volatile start. It must have inspired me because that night went on till dawn.

I walked home in the daylight. I had to walk. My mind was tight with a mosaic of memories, and all in only a week; Moscow street and the sleigh-ride, Yelena's daughter, Rita's coruscating conversation (I must remember to post her son's letter), the schoolchildren and their chewing-gum, Burnside – most of all all Burnside, my fair enigma. I remembered an Ivor Novello song:

> My car will meet her
> And her mother came too,
> It's a two-seater,
> Still her mother came too!

I must take a run up to Burnside sometime, to pay my respects to her mother. I was just turning into my mother's close at Onslow Drive when I realised I'd left my luggage in Robert's car, and the fur hat I'd bought for her, and my keys for her flat were in my briefcase. By this time, I was at the door on the second floor. I had no option but to get her out of bed. She'll kill me, I thought. Ah well, and I rang the bell.

"Who is it?" Her voice was sharp and, unlike her, and something made me reply:

"Roberta Burnsa!"

And standing on that cold landing I started to laugh and I was still chortling as I heard the chain rattling.

Jim's Canadian Highlander Nights were really becoming quite famous. Even more people were crowded in, so that in the acting area now available, there was hardly room for Colin's accordion, never mind the two of us. But if we allowed the wood-burning stove to go out and Colin sat in the fireplace, I had just enough room to sit on a stool, and from there we gave our second season of Highlander Burns Nights. They were lovely occasions in that charming little dining-room. It was a family night in every sense. I can remember the figure of Ken Preston looming large with his party at the back wall. His wife Norma always insisted Colin stay with them. George and Margaret Curry drove up from Toronto. People thought nothing of making long journeys from all parts of Ontario to come to what came to be called Highlander Nights. Some came several times. I thoroughly enjoyed myself, especially as, when we'd finished, I'd merely to walk upstairs and I was home.

The only drawback was the dog. Leroy was a stark raving mad cross between an Alsatian, a wolf and a coyote. I am no Crufts habitué, and I've owned several dogs in my time, but none was as vicious, bad-tempered and mean-minded as this mongrel cur who made everybody's life, except Jim's, quite miserable around the Highlander. I suppose, because I shared Jim's voice, he was relatively meek with me, but I just wondered what would have happened had he got loose among the diners packed into that restaurant on those Burns Nights. There was no doubt he was a wonderful guard dog. Not only did he keep intruders out, he sometimes kept the patrons in as well! He had to be locked up till the car park was clear. Yes, it was a dog's life with Leroy.

With the developed Scots-Canadian instinct to make a buck, Jim took advantage of the Highlander éclat to present more ambitious Burns evenings at various venues in the surrounding area, most of them owned by Italians. The crowds just flocked to these and we sold a lot of records. I was also "sublet" to a butcher called Bill McVicars for a series of dates, and Bill certainly wasn't Italian. He had deliveries to make and he wanted me to travel with him. Colin elected to opt out of this segment and flew instead to New York before going back to the office in Edinburgh. Meanwhile I followed the freezer trail.

The delivery dates took us first to Montreal and Ottawa, and then to St Catherine's and Hamilton. These venues were determined less by audience demand or our desire to visit, but more because they were regular halts for Bill McVicars' huge freezer lorries. He supplied butcher meat and incidentally haggis, Scotch pies and copies of the *Sunday Mail* and *Sunday Post* to all these centres, and he thought I should follow him around and give a Burns performance at each.

"If you do a show," Bill said, "I could sell a lot of pies."

Which he did. I was happy to follow along. What I didn't bargain for was that I had also to give a hand at loading and unloading and setting out the wares at each of the halls taken by Bill and his staff en route.

The idea was to take a large community hall in a particular area. Trestle tables would then be set out in long aisles, and these would be loaded up with various Scottish provisions bought to appeal directly to the expatriate. It would be everything that you could only buy in Scotland, now suddenly available on the Western Canadian seaboard, by virtue of Bill McVicars and Company. In addition to the meat dishes, there were tins of shortbread, black bun, black puddings, Edinburgh rock, Lee's macaroon bars and tablet, not to mention calendars, picture postcards and every single thing that Bill thought could turn a dollar. These were all set up by lunchtime, lunch naturally consisting of a meat pie and a macaroon bar. In the afternoon people would come from all over, their Scottish voices ringing round the hall as they greeted friends and selected items. I was put in charge of the stationery and newspaper stall, and did a brisk trade. By teatime, the tables were cleared away, a stage was rigged and the supermarket by day became a concert hall by night.

The place was festooned with every possible kind of tartan and decorated with execrable "portraits" of Robert Burns. In the space left by the tables, chairs were brought in and in no time we had an auditorium. Bill then changed from his whites to a kilt to preside at the door. Chris, his wife, took off her apron to put on her long tartan skirt to take the money at the one table left as a box office. I changed into the Burns costume or dinner jacket as required. Somebody would play a piano or fiddle or accordion, and we had a show. Next morning it was up to get the show on the road again for the next destination, which, for me, was by plane to Calgary.

Ostensibly I was to make a film on RW Service for CFAC but really it was just an excuse to talk with Steph and Paul Morris on more personal matters. The film got made and we must have talked – and talked – for I lost my voice! But during a three-day stopover in Háwaii I found it again – just in time for New Zealand.

I arrived in Auckland bearing a Hawaiian pineapple, which the customs authorities (all dressed in shorts) were unwilling to let me keep, but were persuaded by the assurances of the President of the Auckland Burns Club, Mr Wallace Overton, and I was allowed to come on to New Zealand soil bearing fruit. I was also wearing a red Hawaiian T-shirt, boasting the legend "Hawaii '77", khaki trousers and sandals. Wallace was appalled.

"You can't bloody well come out dressed like that," he said. I was to find out that New Zealanders were nothing if not direct.

"Why not?" I asked.

"Because I've got a bloody pipe band out there," he said, "and a Maori girl to give you a real welcome – 'Kia-ora' and all that. And half the Burns Club, who've all heard you're coming. So let's see about making you presentable at least. Come on, follow me."

Wallace Overton's kindness always had a peremptory edge to it. I had no option but to follow him as he was carrying both my large suitcases.

He took me into an immigration office, and without any more ado started to undo the cases.

"What are you doing?" I said.

"I'm looking for a suit, and a shirt and a tie and a pair of bloody shoes," he replied.

Very properly dressed in my dark, striped London suit and with the Foreign Office tie I had been given in Moscow, I eventually walked out into the New Zealand sunlight to find myself facing a reception party. A young Maori girl wearing a grass skirt, and twirling pois was doing a kind of dance and singing. When she had finished she came up to me and I bent forward to kiss her cheek, as I thought that's what she wanted me to do, but she neatly avoided this and suddenly we were rubbing noses. Hers was pronouncedly flat, perhaps with all the nose-rubbing. "Kia-ora," she whispered and then gave me a little ornament called a tiki and danced away as the pipe band struck up. I looked round for Wallace to find that he was playing in the pipe band!

One of the ladies came forward and introduced herself. This was Margaret, Wallace's wife, who introduced me to the others in the party, mostly middle-aged women, then led me towards the cars. My luggage had been dealt with. There was no sign of Colin. It had been

The Burns face made in New Zealand.

arranged that I would meet him in Auckland, but perhaps he didn't like pipe bands, or having his nose rubbed. This then was my first welcome to New Zealand. I was most touched. Even then I had the strangest feeling that I had come home.

Everything was so unfamiliar, yet familiar. Grown men were running around in little boys' shorts and yet it seemed absolutely right for that climate and way of life. People spoke in an accent that to me was hardly different to the English I had heard in Berkshire, but then, of course, English was a foreign tongue to me too. The houses I saw as the cars sped towards Auckland were small and wooden and gaudily painted on first impression, but they were very much the bungalow type that I knew from home in the better parts of Giffnock and Newton Mearns. And if the vegetation was luscious and stupendously colourful, didn't we have the same thing at the Botanic Gardens and at the People's Palace? In short, it was all much more reassuring to me than Canada had been. Canada, whether it liked it or not, was the United States' offshore island. It hadn't found a cohesive identity that could easily be called Canadian. There were at least three Canadas to me – English, French and Middle Western. But there was no such hesitation in taking to New Zealand. First of all, they drove on the right side of the road – that is, the left. The cars were familiar to me from my boyhood. I was amazed that so many old makes like Rileys and Wolseleys and Singer Gazelles were still on the road, and still going strong by the look of it. In the motel, the first thing I heard when I switched on the radio was the opening music from "Take if from here", which was not being broadcast as a nostalgic echo, but as a current part of national radio's output. The same station had apparently used my Burns double album as its Robert Burns programme for the year, so I was already being prepared for the national tour that was to follow.

Colin was at the motel when I got there. He had been organising things at the theatre.

"Ah, there you are," he mumbled. As far as Colin was concerned, this was an extremely effusive welcome. It was time now to get back to work.

Peter Fleming was an earnest and likeable Scot who lived in Dunedin, that other Scotland in New Zealand, and he had very laudable ideas of theatre grandeur, to which end he formed a company called Theatre International (NZ) in order to bring well-known names in the legitimate theatre world to New Zealand. He very properly thought that living at such a remove from the rest of the world should not deny New Zealand the best of theatrical talent

154

available. These, at least as he told me, were his intentions, and his partner in the enterprise was a very successful sheep shearer, Craig L. Sim, who had still managed to lose two fingers of one hand. Craig had met Peter in a club at Invercargill when he had overheard the latter say, following my Burns broadcast in the previous year, "Whoever brings that fellow out to New Zealand could get himself a Jaguar".

Craig had apparently said, "You don't say. Tell us more."

"You like Burns, then?"

"Naw," drawled Craig, "but I like Jaguars."

At any rate, this unlikely couple became theatre partners for the purpose of bringing me to New Zealand as a pilot run for their later, more ambitious schemes. I must say Peter had done his work thoroughly and the tour was extremely well prepared and detailed. I'm not really aware that Craig did anything other than put up the front money. If he had made as much as he had with eight fingers, what would he have done if he had ten! Anyway, it was thanks to these two that I eventually arrived in Auckland, as described and walked on stage at the Maidment on 4th April 1977 to make my New Zealand début.

One-man shows were not new to New Zealand. Jonathan Hardy's *Diary of a Madman* had only recently been at the Mercury upstairs, and at the New Independent Dorothy Parker was being played by a young actress called Alannah O'Sullivan. Monodrama appeared to be coming into its own. The advertising for the Burns show made much play of the fact that I was on stage for the entire show. Where else do they think I should have been? On the first night the theatre was not quite half full, and half of those were obvious Burns devotees. They are another kind of audience. My kind of Burns show was intended for theatre-goers, not Burnsians, although I see no reason why they couldn't be both. However, the reaction at the end was sufficient to make me think that we were in for a successful New Zealand tour. This was further emphasised by the numbers in my dressing-room afterwards.

It was something of an overall two-tone effect, flushed female faces under various degrees of blue-grey rinses. I thought I was at a meeting of the Daughters of the New Zealand Revolution. Suddenly cutting through this grey sea came a figure, slight, dark, intense and very New Zealand earnest. Audrey Hepburn, I thought. No, but stronger. Katharine Hepburn, then. No, softer. Who was this? She came straight up to me where I was holding court, stripped to the waist at the end of the room.

"That was very good," she said simply.

"Who are you?" I asked.

"Alannah O'Sullivan."

"Even the name was lovely. I couldn't help but repeat it. "Alannah O'Sullivan. You're the girl – playing – uh –"

"Dorothy Parker" she said.

"Yes, that's it. So you'll know what it's like, eh?"

She was indeed a very striking and attractive girl.

"Well – " she said, modestly, then changed the subject. "I was wondering if you would like to come to the Mercury Theatre some time and meet our New Zealand actors."

"Certainly," I said, thinking I am always happy to meet my fellows anywhere, but I was thinking of how much more I would like to meet New Zealand actresses – especially this one standing in front of me. Suddenly I had an idea.

"Look," I said, "I've got to go to a reception now in the University here given by the local Burns Club. Would you like to join me there and perhaps we can talk about your theatre and arrange a time?" I could see she was uncertain, but I pressed her hard. "It's much easier to go to these sort of things with a partner." She wavered. "Otherwise I'll be pinned in a corner and never get away." She agreed to stay on.

"I'll wait at the stage door," she said, and left me again to bask in my sea of matrons. Afterwards it was merely a matter of going along a few corridors and Alannah, as I soon learned to call her, accompanied me to another part of the University complex and into the Burnsian den.

These were the same kind, well-intentioned people who had arranged the reception at the airport, and I could not but be polite and speak not only generally, but severally, to them, but I also knew that I wanted to get away, and as soon as possible, with this charming, independent girl. Craig Sim was our company manager for that evening, and was handling it with all the finesse and delicacy of a sheep shearer. Goodness knows how many backs he put up, and fronts he affronted! But he was absolutely honest in his New Zealand way and it wasn't his fault he wasn't totally au fait with the intricacies of theatre practice. He was very much a man's man and perhaps a very good antidote against the preciousness of some theatre personnel. As soon as he saw me safely in the hands of the Burns Club, or more pointedly on the arm of the lovely Alannah, he was off to the nearest bar.

Alannah told me that he had resisted her coming backstage at all,

Alannah O'Sullivan – the second Mrs Cairney, definitely _not_ Mrs Burns.

and she had to insist that she was there as a fellow actress, and not as any kind of Burns groupie. She might easily have been turned away. What would I have done then? Yet I feel sure we would have met in Auckland – or somewhere. I think we had to meet somehow. Colin, too, had quickly ducked the Burns reception. He couldn't stand haggis, nor were the little curled-up sandwiches particularly appetising after the two and a half hours he'd been on stage with only me and a synthesizer. For myself, I was longing for the check table-cover of the nearest Italian restaurant and a bottle of wine and this girl here beside me. We must go as soon as it is politely possible, but the problem, with Craig and Colin now gone, was how I was to get back to the motel. First of all, I'd no idea where it was, and only a hazy recollection of what it was called. "I'll take you there," said Alannah. "I'll wait at the main door." And she disappeared.

The Overtons invited me back with them but I made some kind of weak excuse and backed slowly to the door making polite noises as I went. I ran along the corridors realising I had the excesses of a first night to get rid of. When I got down to the main door, she was indeed standing waiting, dressed in what I thought were overalls and holding out a crash helmet to me.

"What's this?" I said.

"A helmet. You've got to wear one."

"Why?" I said.

"It's the law."

She was indeed going to take me back, but on a motorbike. A vast machine, it seemed to me, and I wondered how this slender girl could drive it. However, it gave me a splendid opportunity to put my arms round her waist, so I sat on the back and off we went with me clinging tight.

In no time we were at the motel. Craig was there with his box of beers and a party was in progress. There were girls from the theatre and some from the university, and others whom I didn't know. Not that it mattered. I only had eyes for Alannah. But the attraction was entirely unilateral despite the show, the supper, the wine. The girl's interest was waning. So much so, that after quite a short time she decided to go. "But wait a minute," I began. But she was already gone. She was expert at disappearances. I ran on to the balcony and saw her running down the outside stairs. "Hey wait!" I shouted. I caught up with her in the car park. She already had on her wet-suit overalls and had her helmet in her hands. I grabbed her roughly by the shoulders and turned her round. Her face was very red and properly indignant, and then I saw it – a picture of the two of us, standing, as if being married, at least in a bride and groom posture, before a solid bank of rhododendron bushes. It stopped me in full flood.

I was sometimes given to these prognostications. Future pictures that were totally irrational and inexplicable, but they did happen. My dear old mother had something of the same problem, and she was often confused by vivid scenes she saw – she called them pictures – of vivid events that did indeed come to pass. And now I saw this. At this time too. It all happens in a flash, as the cliché says. The brain computer goes into some kind of overdrive, and there it is – a glimpse, a snapshot, a momentary glance, like a still film frame. I found I was still holding her shoulders.

She threw off my hands and mounted her bike. I tried to explain what I saw but she drowned me out with her engine start and roared off into the night. As she faded into the distance, heading towards the centre of Auckland, I bellowed after her, "You haven't got your lights on." Then I climbed up the stairs again and despite Colin's protests, got very drunk with Craig and the students.

In the course of that first week, I had many backstage visitors, although none made quite the impact of the first. Beryl te Wiata came with her daughter, Rima, and we had a lovely supper together. Beryl was the widow of Inia te Wiata, a very famous Maori singer. She herself had hopes of taking up acting in a one-woman capacity. "Why don't you?" I said.

"Would you help me?" she asked.

"I'll help in any way I can."

She was an attractive woman and she obviously had drive. There was no reason why she couldn't create her own programme. What was more important was that she knew she had to find something to do. She was too young to be a widow. I was beginning to enjoy New Zealand.

The next assignment was to be a television event where I was to be questioned by a team of New Zealand writers, actors and directors. To me it was just another way of advertising the show. To television, it was just another programme. But to the New Zealand theatre people, it was a very valuable opportunity to exchange ideas, using me as a catalyst to further discussion of contemporary New Zealand theatre. I was looking forward to meeting them and it was suggested I go along to the Mercury Theatre after my own show one night to have a drink with them. I was glad to. Or was I really only looking for Alannah O'Sullivan? She was there all right but pointedly distant and struck up what to me was a rather obvious friendship with Colin.

Even when we went to Beryl's one night in a group for dinner, she was aloof to say the least. So I was quite surprised one day to get a call from her.

"I've got half a leg of lamb," she said.

"Poor thing," I replied, "perhaps you should see a doctor."

She didn't even acknowledge this, but wondered if Colin and I would join her and friend, Julanne Greville, for dinner on Good Friday, as I wouldn't be working that night. New Zealand was still civilised sufficiently to close theatres on Good Friday and Christmas Day, much as British theatres used to do in more Christian times. But television, being more pagan, insisted that I attend a camera rehearsal during that day. We decided to take the meal break at Alannah's flat and I got there about five o'clock, already tired out, with the show to go on the air live at 10 p.m. that night. I asked if I could lie down for a bit. She raised her eyebrows somewhat, but showed me her bedroom.

I slept through the prepared dinner party, and when I was wakened around 9 p.m. I insisted on having the share of lamb I missed. I was allowed to eat in the kitchen in solitary splendour, then Colin, Alannah and I drove to the television studios.

In the first part of the show, I had to do a section of the Burns and after the break leave myself open to questions – "Open to Question" is nearer the mark. I enjoyed meeting Bruce Mason, already a celebrated New Zealand actor, writer, musician, critic. He was in the chair for the Forum discussion and did his best to keep me in control, but the TV director's instruction to one of the cameramen was "Just follow him". So they did. And during one section, while I was reciting "My Love is Like a Red, Red Rose", I couldn't resist walking among the audience of actors and actresses to come face to face with Alannah (I had made sure she was in an end seat), and together I think we made a very interesting two-shot for the lines, "And I will come again, my love, though it were ten thousand miles." (I almost substituted twelve, as that is the distance from Edinburgh to Auckland).

I know it made a good television moment. There was a lovely supper afterwards in a Spanish-style restaurant and more to get over the effects of it and of a very long day, Alannah reluctantly agreed to let me walk her home. It was a long, long walk in the pleasant, warm night air, past a householder painting his house at two o'clock in the morning – you couldn't do that in Scotland, because of the midges – being passed by nocturnal nomads I later came to recognise as joggers. New Zealand, remember, is a nation of athletes. I didn't

160

realise so many of them worked at night. Julanne was waiting up for us, or rather Alannah, to tell her how lovely she looked on the screen. She even said we looked good together. I liked Julanne. Her attitude to me was quite different from the previous evening, and I had just the faintest feeling that so was Alannah's. We sat on the back porch of her flat – the three of us – and talked for hours it seemed. Then Julanne went in. Alannah and I watched and listened as dawn happened. Something was changing, and it wasn't only the soft, balmy night into the violet promise of a beautiful spring day.

From Auckland, the Burns show gradually moved down-country in what amounted to a series of one- and two-night stands until we came to the next large centre, Wellington. In the capital I was in the concert chamber of the Town Hall on the same night as wrestling was on downstairs in the main hall – "Gin a body meet a body . . .". But I merely used the cheers and the screams coming from below as if it were a kind of Dante-like inferno, and incorporated the noises "off" as best I could. They were especially valuable in the drunk scenes, so I was able to make something of what would otherwise have been an unendurable distraction.

After the first night I met Coleen, Alannah's second-oldest sister and, to me, the double of Sophia Loren. But she was married to a farmer called Paddy Cleary who wasn't unlike Tyrone Power. Also at Wellington I met Aileen O'Sullivan, Alannah's third-oldest sister, then Mrs Hobbs, who worked in radio and she looked like Gene Tierney! She took Colin and me back for dinner one night to the house where she and Emmet and their children lived on what seemed to me the side of a steep cliff. All the houses seemed to be built on stilts, and homes were crammed into every conceivable corner. I liked quirky Wellington and even thought I could live there. Donald Macdonald gave me a wonderful notice in the *Dominion* and we both remembered the irony of his giving me the first-ever mention of my Burns solo intentions in the Glasgow *Evening Times* fifteen years before. Two nights in Lower Hutt at the Little Theatre found me absolutely next door to the Prime Minister's residence, but Mr Muldoon failed to appear on either night.

We crossed over to the South Island via Cook Strait. I may make this sound like a quick trip across the Clyde at Renfrew, but the crossing of the Cook Strait is something of an ocean voyage. Just as people have a misconception about the distance between New Zealand and Australia, so also do they fail to realise the distance between the North and South Islands. There are more than a thousand miles between the two former dominions and there are very rough seas indeed between the two New Zealand islands. Luckily, I have always been a good sailor and I made it easily to sunny Nelson, which even the locals refer to as a haven for "creaks and freaks". Nelson is famous as a resort for the retired and the highly individualistic, but it is also the home of the charming and urbane John Wheeler and his wife Pat who made me so at home after only a five-minute acquaintanceship. New Zealand is good at that.

From Nelson we moved down to Christchurch and its superb Town Hall complex. Christchurch is the most English of New Zealand towns and I wondered if Burns would be justly received. I needn't have worried, for this was where Wallace Vinnell lived, a New Zealander born-and-bred and vastly proud of it, but a surprising Burns addict and founder-president of the local Burns Club. He had been introduced to the bard while clearing out his late father's books in the garage. He came across a volume of Burns and there and then started reading and from that moment was hooked.

When he heard I was coming to the James Hay Theatre as Robert Burns he booked a whole section of the stalls for his club. On the first night, when I entered from the rear-stage as usual in the gradual light-build and came to the front, both the audience and I were startled to hear a loud and immediate "Jesus Christ" echo round the auditorium. "No sir, I am not," I responded. "My name is Burns, Robert Burns." And I bowed in the general direction of the voice. The audience applauded, and I was off to a lovely start. At the end, I was hardly in the dressing-room before the door flew open and there was Wallace, red-faced and choleric and tears sparkling.

"Bloody marvellous! Bloody marvellous!" he kept repeating. It had been he who had opened proceedings. "I couldn't help it," he said. "As soon as I saw you I couldn't believe anybody could be so like what I imagined Burns to look like."

"Lots of people have said that," I said.

"I don't bloody care. I'm saying it now. Christ – there I've said it again – it's a bloody miracle that's what it is."

I stayed on at the Clarendon during my Christchurch season, in the suite used by the Queen no less. I was suitably impressed and every morning I was able to have breakfast looking out on to the River Avon and the willows by the bridge, where the statue of Ernest Shackleton, the explorer, seems quite unmoved as he peers south to that unreachable Pole. I had many pleasant and interesting visitors to my rooms during that stay, but perhaps the most surprising was Miss Alannah O'Sullivan!

She had a play out at the Mercury Theatre and was home in Christchurch for a few days. This was her native city, but her family now lived about an hour to the north along the old Tram Road at Oxford. She and Aileen (from Wellington) were going out there to spend the weekend – would I like to join them after the show on Saturday and return in time for the show Monday night? Certainly I would, so I hired a car to drive them out myself. I think Alannah was amazed that I could drive at all, she was so used to seeing everything done for me. Colin had his own weekend plans. I wonder what they were?

Mrs Christina O'Sullivan lived with her sister, Mrs Janey Dawson, in a farmhouse called Garden Lodge, but which was known ordinarily to everyone in the family as The Terrace. The sisters were tall, striking, attractive widows in their 60s and 70s respectively, and equally remarkable in character and personality; but what asonished me was that that their even more remarkable mother was still alive and alert at 99! I was introduced with ease and frankness and felt immediately at home, even though Josie, the youngest O'Sullivan sister and the saintliest, eyed me a little uncertainly over the kitchen supper table. Mickey, her twin, and elder by five minutes, was much more certain – she couldn't care less! Janey led me into one of the many guest rooms and sat without ceremony on my bed (almost crushing my left leg). "I don't care what they say – I like you." And patting my numb left leg, she left. A very special relationship with Janey was started from that moment. I lay back on the little single bed thinking to myself, "Now see what a fine mess you've got me into!" However, I slept the sleep of the innocent, even though my night prayers always began: "Bless me Father, for I have sinned . . ." I was always a little uncertain about being blessed for sinning!

Next morning I was wakened by one of Josie's tasteful breakfast trays (she was a trained dietician), always with a flower and a happy awareness of colour in the presentation. Afterwards, failing to finish the crossword in the Christchurch Press, I came out to the others already basking in the morning sun on the verandah discussing a big truck tyre that was lying on the lawn. It was a scene out of Chekhov. I found a seat and was just settling into it when I sprang up again. I couldn't believe it! There, along the whole length of the drive, was a massive bank of rhododendron bushes screening the side of the house. I looked at once at Alannah, but she was engrossed in conversation with her mother. Janey came out from the kitchen and joined me. "Gidday," she said.

163

"Er – good morning," I managed to reply.

"Sit down and take the weight off your brains," went on this formidable lady. I was glad to. My legs were shaking.

Tony Vercoe of Reed Pacific Records arranged a signing session at the Record Room in Colombo Street to help promote the Burns double album and the show at the James Hay. Maureen, Alannah's oldest sister, and the frankest, agreed to take me there from the hotel. She also managed to find me some Hamlet cigars. The shop was crowded. Indeed, there was as big an attendance as we got at some of the smaller venues. As the last customer left, and I put away my pen – it was probably the manager's – Maureen said to me quietly, "You won't hurt my kid sister will you?"

I was a little startled.

"You've never thought Maureen, that your kid sister might hurt me?"

"She wouldn't," was the immediate reply. And she didn't even buy a record.

"I'll hear Mum's," she said, and left me with my customers.

Patsy, the middle and remaining sister, and also clever, beautiful and talented, came to the show with her small son, Sean. Young Sean was much taken with Robert Burns and wanted to meet me. But when he came backstage, and saw me out of the wig and costume, he could only say to his mother, "But he's old!" At ten, I suppose he lived in an enviable young world. Sean is now more than six feet tall and has brilliant promise as a lawyer and he still thinks I'm old.

My voice gave out again at the end of the Christchurch run, but I croaked my way south via Timaru, Oamaru, Gore, and then I was in that other Edinburgh – Dunedin. A statue of Robert Burns has looked down for 90 years from a height above the Octagon with his back to the kirk and facing the pub. The Dunedin Burns Club is one of the oldest in the world and in the town they have a Burns Hall and a district called Mosgiel. The Rev. Thomas Burns, a nephew of the poet's, came here with the first settlers, and a record of the Burns connection is part of the history of Otago. We expected good audiences here and we got them. Audiences and audience reaction was getting better all the time, and we had a crowded press conference at the City Hotel.

I met Peter Fleming for the first time. He was obviously pleased about how the tour had grown since its modest start in Auckland, but he always seemed to be thinking of something else even when giving one his undivided attention. I liked Peter at once, but I didn't think he looked at all well. Or was he just a natural worrier? We were now over the halfway stage – funnily enough, the Flemings stayed at Halfway Bush in Dunedin – it should all be easier from now on in. I also had tea (and a little more) with Lady and Sir James Barnes whom I had met the year before in the original Edinburgh.

The Otago University students were also extremely welcoming and one night some of them gave me a wonderful after-show supper in one of their flats. It was lit entirely by candles set in eggcups. More to hide the dingy walls, they said, than for any decorative effect. As the convivial hours rolled by, the eggcups cracked and exploded one by one to great cheers all round. I heard good talk at these gatherings. These, after all, were the future leaders of this still-young country. There was also good singing, and I remembered that most of them came from very old Scottish-Irish stock, much like my own. When I came to leave Dunedin the students came for me in a two-seater sports car, and I'm sure about fourteen of them piled in beside me in the short trip to the railway station. They sang me off on the train.

Colin had gone on ahead in Craig's car. I was glad to go south on my own. I had some serious thinking to do. I couldn't get those rhododendrons out of my mind.

If Dunedin is the Edinburgh of the South Island and Christchurch its Bath, then Invercargill is its Glasgow. There's an energy here and a vitality, even if it's cloaked in diffidence and Southland reserve. Craig met me and took me to his home. The Sims lived in Hibbert Street and had an interest in a scrapyard nearby. Is there nothing this man won't dip his remaining fingers into? He could not, however, have been more hospitable: day-trips to tourist Queenstown, flights in a small plane over the magnificent Milford Sound, drives to Bluff, at the very end of New Zealand, looking over to Stewart Island where the next stop is the South Pole. I was the furthest away I could ever be in the world from Scotland. Well they did say I would go far in my career!

On returning to Wellington I was booked to do some TV and radio interviews and a radio play. This was *The Other Dear Charmer* by Robert Kemp and I had to play Burns. It was directed by the Head of Drama in NZ Radio, Anthony Groser, whom I remembered as a good actor with Perth Rep years before. The female lead in the play (Nancy McLehose) was taken by Mrs Groser, and how good she was, even though she acted with the script in one hand and her knitting in the other. Craig came to say goodbye at Wellington. What he actually said was, "Well, cheerio you old bastard." I was sure he meant it as the compliment it sounded.

Hastings, Napier, Gisborne, Hamilton, and it was Auckland again. I stayed with the Overtons this time, and went with Wallace to see his printing works and his Kiwi fruit farm – this is what I would call a balanced work output. He also took me up in his private plane. And this is the man who would rather play in a pipe band! The Overtons gave me a wonderful farewell dinner at their home. I remember I spilled red wine on the tablecloth. Wallace raised the roof but Margaret didn't seem to mind and took it out almost at once by spilling white wine all over the red.

Alannah joined us at the airport, driving out on her motorbike. Just to make sure I left, I think. She was playing in *Blithe Spirit* at the theatre. She helped me buy paua necklaces for Sheila and the children. It's a kind of shell and there's a lot of it in New Zealand so they make ashtrays and jewellery from it. At least you can't buy it in Rothesay! On impulse, I bought one for Alannah. She wasn't sure whether to take it, but I forced it on her. She was too polite to refuse. Why did I do things like that? Why did I breathe? As she waved goodbye, standing with Wallace and Margaret, I saw it dangling from her clenched fist.

So we say farewell to little old New Zealand. Now is the hour when we must say – or sing . . .

> Haere ra
> Te mana tangi pai
> E haere ana
> Koe ki pamamao . . .

> Haere mai beautiful Kiwi-land.
> Au revoir to the Land of the Long White Cloud.
> I'm sure we'll meet again.
> Goodbye Alannah . . .

I was so high at the end of my first New Zealand tour I could have flown home without the help of the Boeing 747. The euphoric flight was a haze of poor films, Mozart on the headphones, plastic food on plastic trays and an unending supply of cold red wine. I hardly noticed the stopover at Los Angeles and was still feeling no pain when I arrived at London airport to catch the shuttle to Glasgow and from there the bus to Fort William, then the launch to the S.S. *Calypso* for a National Trust cruise round the coastline of Scotland. It would be a very tight connection in view of the fact that we had forgotten that between New Zealand and Scotland there's always a day lost somewhere – or gained, whichever way you look at it. These and suchlike matters were preoccupying Colin and myself as we came though the customs. As always, I stopped to look on the message board for any messages.

Now, in all my years of travelling, I had always done this. I had never yet seen my name on any message board anywhere, but I always stopped. This time, however, there was a letter. Yes, C-a-i-r-n-e-y, Cairney. Yes, John. Typed plainly – John Cairney. I couldn't believe it. Ah, I thought, as I took it down, this is Alannah's work. Some playful mischief here, a conspiracy with the New Zealand steward perhaps, or even Wallace Overton. Or a derisive note from Craig Sim. I was still smiling as I took down the envelope and tore it open. It wasn't from Alannah. It was from Sheila. My smile vanished. I couldn't believe my eyes. It was a single typed page, headed To Await Arrival, and it began "Dear John . . ."

I had to sit down. I went absolutely numb. My hands were shaking, my heart racing. The last time I felt like this was when my father died. But I couldn't cry this time. Perhaps I should laugh? Colin came looking for me. "We haven't a lot of time." Which is Colin's way of saying "We're late."

I showed him the letter. "Read that," I said.

He looked at it then handed it back to me. "I'd rather not."

"Read it," I shouted. "I've got to find a phone."

I don't remember much about the cruise. I went through the motions. Ordinarily it might have been a perfect job, a dream job, but for me it was dead. Colin kept close. Rhona Cowan, Sheila's cousin, was on board. She wondered why I didn't talk to her. Jean Redpath guessed, I think. At Greenock, to my surprise, a lifeline was thrown by no less than Her Majesty, the Queen, or rather her Secretary of State for Scotland.

Bruce Millan had invited Iain Cuthbertson and me to represent theatre in a Jubilee Banquet to be given to honour the artists of Scotland. Like the Ark, artists of every kind, with every kind of escort and companion, had gone in two by two across the Esplanade and into the Banqueting Hall of Edinburgh Castle to dine with Her Majesty, the Queen, the Queen Mother, the Duke of Edinburgh, the Prince of Wales, the Moderator, the Lord Lieutenant, the Lord Provost, and just about every Lord and Lady within a Rolls-Royce reach of Edinburgh. In view of our changed circumstances, Sheila was naturally unwilling to go, but I understand the children nagged her into it – "But Mummy you'll get to meet the Queen!" "I've met the Queen." "Oh – then you'll get to meet her again! And daddy will buy you a new dress 'specially."

She sat on the edge of the bath. The girls were in the bathroom with us. All four seemed to be talking at once, excited about all the presents I had brought them back, the banquet, and daddy being home again – and in that order. I lay back in the bath looking up at my wife. I should have felt like a sultan – home again, dollars in the bank, all my "harem" round me. Instead, I felt empty, drained, grey – all my lightness and silliness gone. I was frankly devastated. Sheila looked so cool – cold even. Cold as the bath water.

Later that night we lay, stiff as statues, on either side of our king-size bed, an ocean of bed sheet between us, wide awake and staring up into the dark. She wanted to talk about divorce. I wouldn't. I couldn't. A separation then, after all we did lead pretty separate lives these days.

"But I love you." I found it was the only thing I could say.

"What does that matter?" I was shattered by her repose. The whole thing bewildered, dumbfounded me. I still couldn't believe it. In a few days we'd be 23 years married.

"That's the trouble," she sighed, "there's no thrill in it any more."

"For God's sake, woman, what d'you expect? We're man and wife, not Romeo and Juliet!"

She sat up angrily. "Why can't we be Romeo and Juliet?"

I turned to her. "Because we live in the world, not between the pages of *Cosmopolitan* magazine."

"We live in two worlds you mean. You've got yours and I've got mine," she retorted. A hit, a palpable hit. I tried again.

"Sheila – "

"Oh shut up!" She slumped back and I could hear her start to cry. I lay back, and for a long time there was silence.

"I love you," I whispered. There was no reply.

The darkness got darker. How could I have been so stupid? I should have been more attentive. But how could I be, I was miles away. I should have been at home more – where I belonged. I had been such a fool. I was in danger of losing the most wonderful woman and I seemed to be able to do nothing about it. I had no idea she was so unhappy. If I had known I never would have – "Oh Sheila!" I cried out. Silence. I could feel myself starting to cry. "Damn and blast!" I bellowed.

On the night of the Edinburgh Castle Jubilee Dinner we had to leave our car on the Esplanade and travel the 50 yards to the main gate in an army car. Security, I suppose. Big Iain was with us, but for some reason Anne Kirsten, Mrs Cuthbertson, was unable to be with him that evening. At our table, immediately at right angles to the Royal table, I found myself seated beside Mrs Magnus Magnusson, whom I had known as Mamie Baird, the columnist. Mamie is very Glasgow and very witty and, as always, it was a pleasure to be beside her. The trouble was that I was opposite Magnus, her husband, who as the public may not know is a great giggler. Sheila was beside him and was giving a great performance as a professional wife.

Before the royal party entered, various ushers and footmen made appropriate noises and then someone said quite quietly, "Ladies and Gentlemen, Her Majesty is on her way. Will you please rise?" So we all rose in a most dignified manner, but unhappily I found myself staring into Magnus Magnusson's face. To avert my eyes would have been dangerous, so I tried to look at his nose as the Royal Party slipped in, swaying graciously and nodding right and left with smiles. The absolute silence was almost unbearable, and I was staring hard at Magnus's bow tie. Then, someone I couldn't see fiddled with a microphone and yelled into it, "PRAY, SILENCE FOR HER MAJESTY THE QUEEN!" The sheer decibel level made everybody jump and this set Magnus off, which set me off and both wives glared as we resumed our seats for the banquet feast and the first of the wines.

We made a merry corner of our table, and even Sheila, despite herself, revealed something of her old witty manner. She and Mamie made quite a pair. Since neither was drinking that night, it meant that Magnus and I had more than our full share. The food was adequate, though small in portions; salmon mayonnaise, escalope of veal and iced grapes, followed by coffee. But the wines were worthy of a feast; Meurcault Les Chevaliers, Sélection Germaine 1972, Achezeaux, F.B. Mugneret, Côtes de Nuits 1970 and Château Climens, Barsac 1970. All the while, Leonard Friedman waved his bâton over the Scottish Baroque Ensemble and afterwards Jimmy Cairncross introduced a lovely programme, including Jean Redpath and David Ward (whom I was later to meet in New Zealand) singing, accompanied by Mr Alexander Gibson.

Sometimes, in the laughter, I would catch Sheila's eye and for a moment, there was a look – just a glimpse – but then she would quickly look away and I would feel a pang, and gulp down more of the Côtes de Nuits. Deep, deep down I could not have been sadder, but, to all intents, I was what they call "merry" and heading fast to what they call drunk.

When it came time for the Royal Party to leave, the same cathedral silence descended as at the beginning. We all rose again politely, if unsteadily. And waited – and waited as the unnatural silence prevailed. This was a most abnormal after-dinner situation. It could be dangerous. Mamie felt the same and nudged me. "Do something," she said. I looked over at Magnus who beamed at me, then to Sheila who looked suspicious, but my Dutch courage was up and there and then I broke into "Will ye no' come back again?" This was immediately taken up in chorus by that very distinguished company and I think it allowed the Royal Party to make what was undoubtedly a more relaxed exit. At any rate, the Duke of Edinburgh gave me a warm shake of the hand as he passed, and Prince Charles winked. As he in turn passed by the song had reached the line "Bonnie Charlie's noo awa'" which was nicely felicitous. We all then sat down, giving ourselves a warm round of applause. Magnus grinned.

"Well, that's your knighthood settled, Cairney." And turning to Sheila, he said banteringly, "And how would it feel to be Lady Cairney?"

Sheila looked right at me.

"Very odd," she said with the straightest of faces.

Afterwards I had a grand get-together with Jean Redpath and David Ward and Donald Mackenzie, the writer, and many others I knew well, and the party became quite hearty. So much so, that when I spoke to Alex Gibson, I asked why the Queen hadn't knighted him that day, and he gave me a very funny look. Next day it was announced that Alex had indeed been knighted, and that had been his last appearance as Mr Alexander Gibson.

I don't remember much of the journey home. I couldn't have totally disgraced myself, however. A few days later I received a letter from Buckingham Palace and enclosed with it, "By Command of Her Majesty the Queen" – a Jubilee Medal.

We had our wedding anniversary dinner at the Green Man Hotel in Kinross. The only warmth was provided by the claret. Callum Mill and his wife suddenly appeared at the next table and the evening was saved. At the end, Sheila and I drove home in total silence. It was as if there had been a death in the family. There had. Our marriage. An autopsy verdict would have read, "Death by Misadventure". Mine I suppose. Yes, I was to blame. I'd only got what I deserved. I had been away too long. I had gone my way, and Sheila had no option but to go hers. A good marriage had simply dried up for want of watering. But my weekly letters – all those telephone calls – the postcards every day?

"The children liked them."

"What about the children?"

"I've told them."

"What did they say?"

"Nothing."

Inside, I was screaming.

"They won't notice. You're never there anyway."

I couldn't shout at this. I couldn't summon up my big voice when my heart was breaking. I didn't want a divorce, I didn't want to leave. If she wanted it so much, she should leave. This was all unreal. I couldn't believe this was happening – not to us. I couldn't accept it.

"It would seem simpler if you just carried on touring," she said calmly, "then nobody would notice."

I was to play Captain Oates then, and walk out into the snow?

"That would be the decent thing to do."

"But I don't –" I stopped myself from saying any more until we were at our own garage. I found it difficult to say.

"Was there another man?" I croaked.

"God forbid!" she said, getting out of the car, "unless of course you want to consider Robert Burns."

And she slammed the door.

Meantime the rest of the world was still happening, I think. The second Burns Festival in 1977 won an award from the Tourist Board and Colin and I travelled to London to accept it, but really it was just another opportunity of dining at the Café Royal, and let me get out of the house for a while.

While there, I met a Japanese businessman who wanted to import a thousand copies of the *Robert Burns* LP into Japan, but was worried about how his countrymen would understand such terms as "wee sleekit cowerin' houghmagandie". I told him that "houghmagandie" was much the same in any language – and even upside down! I never heard any more from Japan. He probably melted the discs down and made a Honda.

The second Festival featured an exhibition of Burns books in Rozelle House. I had really envisaged this as a Burns Bookfest. It is quite extraordinary how many books and commentaries have been written since his death. Here, I thought, was an opportunity to collect all the available titles from all the available sources and display them as a feast of books, but the logistics of such a project defeated us. Perhaps one day? Various other events were arranged at Dumfries, Irvine and Kilmarnock, and I whirled between all of these places like a man possessed. I knew if I stopped, I would crack. So I kept going – pushed on, I must admit, by Maureen Braid, who with her friends comprised the Mauchline Belles in *The Holy Fair*. Perceptive Maureen had guessed there was something troubling me. As her husband, Derek, wryly remarked: "Here's another lame dog for Mo to pat." All I know is that at that time I could not have been more grateful for the breezy solicitousness of this slim Ayrshire girl who smoked too much, but tried her best to give a harried actor a sense of proportion and at least a laugh or two.

These weren't exactly plentiful as I tried to deal with fussing councillors, temperamental amateur performers, and local drama producers whose noses I had slightly put out. Like all amateur directors, they ruled their tiny little kingdoms like nabobs. Now I had blown in – a gale force from Glasgow – and had the nerve to tell them what to do. I think I had sufficient experience to do so. I thought, too, I had the right as Artistic Director. I knew I had the enthusiasm, but what I was considerably lacking in was tact and diplomacy. There wasn't time to be politely considerate and as patient as I should perhaps have been. I tended to speak first and let my thoughts come running up behind me. "You'll be hung for that tongue," said Maureen.

When I wasn't holding court in the lounge of the Pickwick Hotel, I was on the road between the Courtyard Theatre at Rozelle, the Globe Tavern and the Theatre Royal in Dumfries, the Harbour Arts Centre in Irvine, and Dean Castle in Kilmarnock – where on one wonderful evening I performed the Burns story in the open air under the shadow of the castle wall. At the end when it got cold – it gets chilly in Killie – I led the audience into the Long Gallery like the Pied Piper of Hamelin, following the lovely mezzo voice of Anne Hetherington, who had been engaged for the night to sing the songs, and was later to become engaged to Colin. We repeated "The Lingering Star", added "The Clarinda Correspondence" and gave several further performances of *The Holy Fair*, which now gave me the idea of a full-scale Burns musical. The script was a hurried population of my own solo Burns story, but it gave me a whole new perspective on the piece as a company show, especially in the magical atmosphere of the open-air stage at Rozelle.

On the final night I remember leaving the stage at the end of Part One, exiting off in the archway to find Derek Braid standing there watching the show, as all seats were taken. I joined him and we watched the cast end the first part and slowly go off, led by the lovely local girl who played Jean. It looked exactly like *Cavalleria Rusticana*, except that the man who had written it and directed it felt more like *Pagliacci*. Another Burns Festival was over and we all shook hands on the next. It was getting to be like the Olympics. But who was carrying the torch for whom?

I came back to Glasgow to rehearse "Mackintosh" for Scottish Television and to give Jennifer lunch at the Shandon Buttery. She had just become Jennifer Cairney, MA (Hons) at Glasgow University, and her mother and I proudly attended to see her capped.

As a very unsubtle attempt to involve Sheila again, I had persuaded her to take part in the programme I had written for STV on the life of Charles Rennie Mackintosh. More particularly I persuaded Liam Hood to employ Sheila as an actress. Of course he knew her well, but more as my wife than as the actress she once was. "Has she still got her Equity card?" he asked. She hadn't, but using the excuse that any actress is given a year off to have a child, she thought she was entitled to five years off for having five. She got her card, and agreed to make a comeback. "I've been tied to the Aga cooker for too long," she told Gordon Hislop of the *Sunday Express*. She was asked how I felt about it. "He is very happy," Sheila is reported as saying. "I think that over the years John has felt a degree of guilt for keeping me from working." I felt guilt all right.

Sheila played Kate Cranston in the film, and also played very aloof with me in the rehearsals. She didn't even stay at my mother's flat in Glasgow, but insisted on driving home to Fife each night. I should never have given her that car! "Is everything all right between you and Sheila?" asked my mother. "Of course it is," I said cheerfully.

As soon as the Mackintosh was in the can, I flew off to Canada to make a film about the Scottish Canadian Regiments. I was glad to be in the air again. I didn't want my feet to touch the ground. However, within the month I was back in Cowcaddens for another Scottish Television production of my *McGonagall* show with the *Ivor Novello* to follow immediately as an outside broadcast from the Eastwood Theatre. I came home to Pinegrove every weekend with my washing and to pay the bills and see the children.

I arrived back one Friday afternoon as the *Novello* was being screened. I came in behind Jane, who was sitting in her favourite chair, playing with the television remote control. I entered just as my face filled the screen as Ivor, but all I could hear was Jane's muttered, "Oh, that's daddy again. We don't want that." And I was quickly replaced by a cartoon. I couldn't say that my children were anything less than realistic about my professional efforts.

I returned to Glasgow and STV for the final play in the four-play contract I had with them. This was to film the solo Burns. After Mackintosh, McGonagall and Novello, this would be the last effort of a very long hot summer, and I think I went into the job tired. It was by no means my best Burns effort and, to my mind, was vitiated by the director's need for repeated and, for him, reassuring, runs-through on the day of recording. However, it was finally done and I think I slept at my mother's for two whole days.

The last time the Cairneys appeared en famille was in a box at the Theatre Royal, Glasgow, during the final matinée performance of *The Ivor Novello Story* on Saturday 17th September 1977. Jennifer was about to become full-time at "The Ubiquitous Chip", Alison was at Edinburgh University but had a riding job at the Ayr Stables, so Sheila brought the others through and I took one of the boxes for the lot of them. Rikki and Katie Fulton had the other. We had had a wonderful week in Glasgow with the show, and the children seemed to enjoy it except, however, when I had to sing. As I began the first song I saw three little heads, Lesley, Jonathan and Jane, go down under the parapet of the box, while the three others, Jennifer, Sheila and Alison, retreated back into the recesses, so that I found myself singing huskily to an empty box. Never mind, the rest of the house didn't seem to mind as much, although at the end, when I proudly indicated my family in the box, they weren't there. They had guessed what was coming, so they shot off as soon as the curtain fell. It was ironic, and a rough justice I suppose. I so loved them. I was so proud of them, and when I wanted to tell the world, they weren't there. But then how many times was I "not there" for them?

I began to stay more at my attic-bedroom at the office at Colinton Road in Edinburgh and with my mother in Glasgow. On each visit to either place, I would bring another suit or another shirt or another pair of shoes. Colin raised his eyebrows but said nothing. Neither did my mother – for once. But I wonder what she was thinking. "Ye hivnae been the same since ye got back frae that New Zealand," she said. Then it was my turn to say nothing.

But it was Burns time again. Another foreign tour – this time to Carlisle for its Great Fair. I played in the restored Tithe Barn in the centre of the town under the auspices of Border Television and the *Cumberland News*. It was a good theatre space, although the staging was placed in such a way that it was like playing in a boxing ring, but the English audience was remarkably responsive – for an English audience – and I greatly enjoyed the experience.

Clare Brotherwood was the instigator of this particular appearance, and her efforts on my behalf through her columns in the *Cumberland News* helped greatly to ensure full houses. Len, her husband, took an especial interest in front of house, and was always to be found around the box office. I asked him why he was so zealous for our good in that area. He replied that he was out to make sure that I wasn't done and, besides, if he kept an eye on the box office, he wouldn't have to sit through the performance. I must say he did look the part of a manager with his enormous girth, perpetual cigars, and complete apathy regarding any altruistic aspects. But I must say he looked good in the foyer. Clare said he was too nervous to sit through a performance. I took her word for it. She was just the right kind of girl to be involved with in such projects. Good to look at, good to work with, alert, industrious, in love with show business, infatuated with Robert Burns and quite fond of me. Len and Clare had no children, so from time to time they adopted actors. Roy Hudd, Russell Hunter – I was glad to be part of the family. It was good to discover again the delights of Carlisle as well as Cumbrian hospitality from Trish and John Maxwell, but now it was time to discover America.

In 1872 Captain Pond was engaged to escort Anna Lisa, Brigham Young's 19th wife, around the United States on a lecture tour. It was so well received that it gave Major Pond the idea of repeating the itinerary with another "speaker", and another in the year after with another, and so on. Thus began the lecture circuit and, when Colonel Pond left the army, he founded the Pond Bureau to engage lecturers and hire them out to clubs and organisations all over the country. This was the time of the Lyceum and Chautauqua movements in America which were intended as educational and quasi-religious lecture opportunities, but gradually the public speakers and recitalists infiltrated and by the turn of the century actors were a staple part of their product offering. The Redpath Agency also became prominent in this field. In 1903 the Pond Bureau (now father and son) became incorporated and in 1935 sold out to the Keedick Lecture Bureau, who were to bring many famous literary and academic personalities to the United States and Canada.

By the time Bob Keedick took over from his father at the end of the Second World War, they were even trading in Scotsmen. Although I must mention here that one of the most successful platform speakers in the early days was Dr Robert McLean Cumnock, who specialised in Dickens and Scotch Literature! Well, it could be said that I too specialised in Scotch Literature, and the man I played came from a place not far from Cumnock.

I liked Bob Keedick at once. Tall, urbane, soft-voiced and well travelled, this man had much to do with the continued success of his father's Lecture Bureau. On our first meeting in New York I had toothache and, while driving me to his home in Connecticut, he quietly talked me out of it. He was a great believer in the power of positive thinking, especially in De Silva's theories, and was surprised that as an actor I didn't use it more.

"What is your particular technique?" he said to me.

"The positive power of prayer," I replied. "In the one-man show, it's only you, God and the audience."

"Well, we've got you but only God knows if we'll get an audience," said Bob. He was smiling as he said it.

That Connecticut weekend was my first experience of spontaneous and effulgent American hospitality. Admittedly I was to travel in a very well-heeled lane, but I never failed to be amazed at how Americans opened their homes and hearts to me, a complete stranger, throughout that first eight-week autumn tour or, as they called it, "the fall schedule", and in the seven happy years that were to follow. In 1977, the ticket that had brought me out to take me round was twelve feet long and cost £1,158. I would have this cost returned to me of course as part of the various fees, and all being well I should net around £10,000 for the eight weeks' work. But, in the course of the two months, I would land at 20 airports, and stay in 20 hotels, be introduced by 20 chairwomen and at least 17 of them would stumble over my name, and 19 at least would state that I came from Glas-cow.

It is hard to describe the phenomenon that is the American Lecture Circuit. It's an extraordinary thing. Groups of well educated, much travelled, mostly widowed, very rich, American women gather regularly in the palatial premises they refer to as their clubs to hear speakers address them on every topic under the sun. Every kind of speaker, too, from prominent politicians to penurious poets. Singers and actors also featured in their lists, and it was in the latter category, I suppose, I was invited to perform an hour from *The Robert Burns Story*. Not even an hour – it had to be nearer 50 minutes to allow for a suitably verbose introduction and an equally lengthy vote of thanks.

What I found even worse as I waited to come on was that the introduction usually included full details about the next performance, so I would stand listening to how good Olivia de Havilland was going to be, or John Glen, the astronaut. On one occasion, the introduction took the form of the lady's earnestly reading out every syllable of my advance publicity sent out by Miss Schenck of the Keedick Agency. It must have been at least three pages long. I found a chair in the wings and sat down. But then as the introductee ended, she walked to the other side of the stage – and straight out by the back door! She obviously had better things to do. But, in the main, these wonderful ladies could not do enough to please. That was the extraordinary thing. Most clubs had their own theatres with stage doors, and rear exit and scene docks and full stage lighting. I was coming into an industry that was well established. They had been going now for nearly 100 years providing local entertainment, not to their own communities, but to certain sections of those communities, and they were ladies who had seen Olivier in London and Gielgud at Stratford, Jean-Louis Barrault in Paris, and Henry Fonda in New York. They weren't going to be kidded by an import, even if he had "a cute brogue" as they called it, which he used occasionally to speak impenetrable Scotch verse.

Luckily, it was the man Burns I was selling, and not so much the poet. They found his story fascinating and his many loves intriguing. They weren't entirely apathetic to the man, Cairney, either, as I found in the frequent question and answer sessions which succeeded most performances. Generally I "spoke", as they say, from 11.30 to 12.30 and this was followed by lunch from 12.30 till 1.30, and then this Open Forum for at least an hour after that. I saw now why I was paid so generously.

Work began as soon as I arrived, with the very first meeting at the airport. I learned to look out for the anxious peering woman accompanied by the stolid husband, and I was rarely wrong in spotting my host for the engagement. In the car, the husband would do most of the talking. "You see, John . . ." or "Let me tell you, John, it's like this . . ." or "In our country, we kinda . . .". And so it would go on all the way to the hotel, with the wife (to be so effusive the next morning) nodding primly in the back seat. A meal would be arranged attended only by the Chairwoman of course and certain members of the Committee, all with husbands. And I would be grilled again. But not overdone. They were all so polite, so studiously polite. It was a long time before I learned to "float" in these encounters and try not to get too involved. Certainly I refused at least every second drink. I could see too clearly how Dylan Thomas had succumbed, but Oscar Wilde had survived. I was determined to do likewise.

Next morning, the car would come for me after breakfast any time round 9.30. I would then travel to the venue, giving my first performance from the front seat of the car, dealing with the questions inlaid in the small talk. American matrons are second only to English county ladies in their mastery of small talk, where sound is happily sustained and absolutely nothing is said. I would arrive at the venue by 10 and the first hour would be spent arranging the stage or platform, checking the lights, refusing umpteen offers of coffee and bewildering ladies by my requests for Ribena, of which they had never heard, or blackcurrant juice, of which they had no wish to hear. I explained that this was to simulate claret for the performance. "Why not use claret?" they said, innocently.

By the time I had the set ready, I had to scramble into the costume. There usually was a dressing-room available – very frilly, very flowery, very feminine, and as the time of the show grew nearer, their earnest solicitousness grew worse. I was often tempted to say something outrageous or pretend I had lost my voice or act a temperament for their benefit. They seemed uneasy with someone who just wanted to get on and work. However, once started, once we got used to each other, as Gertrude Stein might say, "an audience is an audience is an audience". Getting started was often the problem.

As I walked on in the costume, or was revealed in it by the lights, there was always a pronounced sighing sound, and definite sounds of "Gee!" They weren't used to an 18th-century farmer poet addressing them on a Friday morning. Once as I was about to start in one venue, I heard a booming Bourbon American voice say, "Where's his cigar?" "Madam, I don't smoke," I replied and tried to begin on the script. "My name is Robert Burns. It is a name that has made a noise – " and the voice interrupted again.

"Gee, I thought it was George Burns!" I might just as easily have been Tommy Burns for all she cared.

When the show was over, it was the same kind of attention in reverse, except that they did allow me time to take off my breeches, although I always needed help with the boots. Usually the janitor obliged but not always. On one date for instance, I was due in Fort Worth to play at the River Crest Country Club. I was lodged at the Hilton and my instructions contained the specific note "The Speaker to wear coat and tie." It was that kind of country club. Every performer was referred to as "The Speaker" acknowledging the

Bureau's history as a speaker's circuit. I was tempted to arrive in my costume, but I thought that might be a bit too much for the earnest expense account executives I might meet in the foyer of the hotel. Breeches and jabot, not to mention the wig, would have been hardly inconspicuous among the uniform business suits and striped ties. Despite the opulence of the Country Club, there was no provision for a dressing-room as such and I changed in the gentleman's lavatory. None of the gentlemen was attending the performance. It was being hosted by the ladies. So I had plenty of room to spread myself about among the handbasins. However, at the end of the show there was a problem, in that while it was easy to get the riding-boots on, it was virtually impossible to get them off, so I asked one of the black attendants to oblige me. But he firmly refused to do so. "Dem boots no business of mine," he growled.

By this time, I was stripped to the waist and wigless and rather irate. I then walked straight into the club room where the gentlemen golfers were gathered, and announced, "Gentlemen, I have a problem. I am a guest of your ladies next door in the person of Robert Burns from Scotland. As you can see, I have dressed for the part, but find it almost impossible to undress, as your staff don't feel it is in their remit to remove my boots. Is there a groom in the house?"

Almost immediately three or four men came forward, and one of them immediately demonstrated how riding-boots should be removed. By asking me to lift my leg, he then got astride it with his back to me, and one of the others pulled. The staff watched with wide-eyed amazement, but in no time I was padding in my socks back to the lavatory and re-dressed in my collar and tie.

Whether the show had gone well or not well, the ladies were just as effusive. I found that if it had gone very well, they were untypically subdued. But in either event I was always led in a procession to the dining-room for the lunch and another kind of performance at the table, followed by the inevitable question and answer session. The first question was always, "Are you married?" The second, "And how many children?" I was a little uncertain about how to answer the first, but I always knew how many children I had. Depending on the intelligence of the Chairwoman and the quality of the particular ladies, these sessions could often be better than the performance. It sometimes led to a lively debate, generally on American taste and its British counterpart. Americans are extremely chauvinistic and very proud indeed of being American. Some relievedly so – those who had left a difficult European background to find their Utopia in this all-embracing continent. I could hear all their stories in their different accents. But they were all women and, like all women, they were all different and all the same.

By the time I was deposited in the car again with my script and Burns bag, it was always the middle of the afternoon and either I was returned to the hotel, or driven straight to the airport for the next date. I never knew which was the more desirable. Certainly the idea of a drink and a bath and a mindless television show was a rest in itself after such a non-stop day. The fallacy was that I worked for an hour. Any performance meant a full eight-hour day from beginning to end with only the prospect of a good meal afterwards or a long relaxing flight to sustain one through the endless chatter.

And I've not even mentioned the radio interviews in stations that had names taken from an optician's chart, with announcers who were surprised that they understood what I was saying. I learned to plug the show with some skill but there was little need to do so. All the performances were private affairs for club members only. I only did one TV interview, and that was in an Arts programme in New York. I was asked at one point what I should like to offer American viewers. "A moment of silence," I replied.

"What?" asked the Chairman.

"Beautiful silence," I went on, "to make up for all the wasted words we hear on TV."

"Yeah, sure," said the host and quickly changed the subject.

And the press interviews as well. The same earnest questions, the worry about what Art is, and "Do you like us?"

"Sometimes," I would naturally answer.

It was a jet-lagging, strength-sapping, mind-bending, tongue-tiring routine. Why did I do it? For the fees of course, for the travel, the places to see, people to meet. And what a people – eager, friendly, adolescent, innocent in so many ways, anxious to please. And for the women. Many of them wonderful women – old and young, beautiful and plain, rich and very rich. And all the accents too, from crisp New England through New York nasal to homespun Oklahoman and drawling Missouri. But it was the south that caught me – from New Orleans to Houston – voices that were either Dolly Parton or Scarlett O'Hara. The trouble was that some of the faces were more like Rhett Butler's. Leathery widows gleaming in diamonds, even in the morning, smiling with all their American teeth under expensive hair and proffering gnarled hands, heavy with rings, for me to shake.

But there were others – lovely, smooth young matrons, already in a sense, widows. Nubile "widows" to their travelling, upwardly mobile young husbands already on the relentless American conveyor belt to soaring success or total failure. There was no middle way, it was all or nothing. That is the American way. And the strain sometimes showed in those lovely unlined faces I saw in the mornings as I was introduced to "Mrs John R. – " "Mrs Wilbur T. – " "Mrs Henry K. – (Junior)". I never knew an American wife who was not introduced in her husband's name, and he always had a middle initial. Yet how they drank down Burns' lyrical words, how they relished his romance, even his soft failings with their own gender. Smooth words are commonplace in America, soft words are rarer. Especially when they come in another tongue from another land.

I had started off the tour in the Four Arts Club at Elkhart, Indiana, as the guest of Mrs Bruce A. McArt. But the outstanding memory of my first American engagement is in going to Mass at Notre Dame University, and seeing the students grouped in a circle round the altar in the centre of a magnificent church and each of them in their different costumes; the football player holding his helmet, the runner in his tracksuit, the academic with his books, the musician with his instrument etc. It was a very touching sight, seeing young, albeit privileged, America healthily involved in their varied pursuits yet, for an hour, joined in a circle with heads bowed round an altar.

I was in the Windy City for the Chicago Drama League, but I always tried to stay as long as I could in that other Glasgow in the middle of America. I liked its energy, its dynamism, and its wonderful bookshop with classical music and free coffee. I bought yet more books to lug around. I also went to the Soldier's Field to see the Browns play football, and away out into the far suburbs to find Frank Lloyd Wright's house. Theatre too was good in Chicago.

On my first free night I saw Van Johnson in a play and the next night I booked to see James Earl Jones play Paul Robeson in a one-man show. Because of my architectural wanderings, I was late arriving at the theatre, and at first they weren't going to let me in, but I pleaded in my best Scottish voice and they relented. I was led in by a torch and placed on an aisle seat on the right. When the lights went up at the interval, I found that the audience was all black! I think I was the only white person in the theatre! No wonder they were reluctant to let me in. Not that I was bothered. I sat back and looked around me, then sat bolt upright as I saw who was beside me – Cassius Clay – I mean, Mohammed Ali. Looking as large as life, no larger, and as beautiful a man as I have ever seen.

He was relaxed and easy but the coloured girls wouldn't leave him alone, so I suggested we change seats to allow him the aisle seat. So we did, and I found myself sitting beside his manager, I think. He was much less amiable. Perhaps he wasn't a theatre fan. He certainly hadn't heard of Robert Burns, but Ali had.

"I'm a poet myself, you know that?"

"I know that," I said. As he signed for the girls he talked with me. He was intrigued by my accent. He had never been to "Glasgow" he told me.

"Louisville, Kentucky, is my home town," he said.

"I'm going there tomorrow morning," I told him.

"You don't say? Well, you have a real good time. Tell them I said so."

"Do you think they remember you?" I joked.

"They sure do," he laughed, "I still owe some bills down there."

The rest of the play, and the sterling performance given by Mr Jones, was rather lost in the charisma of the company I was keeping, and at the end he took time to sign my programme for Jonathan, although he made rather heavy weather of the spelling. I didn't dare add "Cairney". I almost skipped along Michigan Avenue to the Blackstone Hotel. It had been a great day.

I wish I could have done a proper theatrical tour in the United States, but union rules prevented this – Actors Union that is. I am often amazed how anti-theatrical actors unions are. It seems that American Equity was worried about my taking a job away from one of their members, although the number of American actors eager to play Robert Burns, or Robert Louis Stevenson or William McGonagall was not overwhelming. (At the time of writing, two American actors have played Robert Burns in one-man shows!) Bob Keedick had neatly side-stepped the problem of my visa by declaring me to be a "Lecturer in Robert Burns, Poet". This gave me an H1 category and an Emeritus status as a distinguished academic. I quite enjoyed that though I was probably the first "Professor" to lecture in costume and wearing a wig. I remembered all those discussions more than ten years before with Harold Shaw and Sol Hurok about bringing *There Was A Man* to Broadway. No Equity problems then, only the difficulty of being released from *This Man Craig*. I always had a problem with timing. Now here I was in the States at last and loving it.

I found I was a natural tourphile, addicted to travelling, and I had plenty of that. North, south, east and west, I seemed to go in all directions in that first tour, and sometimes all at once. I didn't mind. It was all so strange, and yet so familiar. What Americans seem to forget is that all the rest of us in the world have grown up with the American image via Hollywood. From our seats in the stalls we came to know New York, the Wild West, the Deep South, the Rocky Mountains almost as well as we knew Glasgow, the Clyde Coast, the Burns Country, the Trossachs, but few Americans know Auchtermuchty or Tillicoultry, yet that was the kind of America I was seeing now. Real people in real places doing real things, like coming to hear a Scots actor recite Robert Burns! America is only extreme at the edges – New York or San Francisco. It has a lovely soft centre. Here it is the drugstore, not drug-scene America, just like in the old movies. This was the America I grew to love. Norman Rockwell had it right.

By this time I had deep-frozen my marital miseries. The only time I felt the ache was when I saw a young wife fly into her husband's arms at the airport. I used to steel myself to look away.

The next day I went to Hollywood. I stayed at the Roosevelt Hotel overlooking Grauman's Chinese cinema. For a few days I did all the Hollywood things, went on all the tourist trips, Disneyland and the studios, went to the TV shows at night, and loved it all. The tinsel was a bit tatty, the glamour had worn thin, the paint was peeling all over it, but Hollywood was still Hollywood and it still had a magic for the wee boy from the East End of Glasgow. I had reverted wholly to the avid reader of the *Picturegoer* and the *Film News* and couldn't see enough. At night, I phoned home to Fife. I wanted to share the lovely time with them.

Jennifer, MA (Hons), was at home, and loved hearing all the Hollywood gossip. Alison was only interested in whether I'd seen any horses in the Wild West back lot. Lesley asked when I'd be coming home, and Jane couldn't be wakened. Jonathan wondered if there were any soldiers in Hollywood and asked if I could bring him back some "Confenderate" soldiers for his collection. Sheila didn't have much to say, so I hung up.

My next stop was Washington. There could be no greater contrast to Hollywood than in the sombre concrete neutrality I found in Washington. It had all the inertness of a Government city. I went on the Capital and I'll never forget walking round the pond before the Lincoln Memorial. As I walked up the many steps and was about to enter into the cupola, all the floodlighting suddenly blazed on. There was no need for them to go to this trouble just for me. It felt like a cue, and instinctively I turned round on the steps declaiming the words inscribed in granite in the famous statue before me: "Four score and seven years ago, our fathers brought forth on this continent, a new nation conceived in liberty and dedicated to the proposition that all men are created equal." Luckily there was no one in the place at the time, although I noticed that a jogger, running round the pond perimeter, momentarily stumbled in his stride as this actor's voice boomed out over Washington. It was a wonderful feeling, but then my toothache came back, and I hurried back to the hotel bar and a medicinal Scotch.

At Lakeville, Connecticut, I played at the Hotchkiss School, for what they termed a Special Confidential Fee, and was delighted to find my cousin, Virginia, with husband, Joe, and son, Paul, in the audience. They were my real American cousins, and had made the journey specially from New Jersey. Bob Keedick also attended and I stayed the night with him. It was one of the rare occasions in which he sees one of his clients actually perform. "I mustn't make a habit of this," he muttered.

I don't know what Virginia and Joe made of it all, but Paul was hugely impressed with his mother's cousin in his costume, especially the wig. Why is it all young boys are fascinated with wigs? I had to make sure he hadn't taken it away in the car with him.

Then it was back to Richmond, Virginia, and up again to Akron, Ohio, Then down to Pittsburg, Pennsylvania. As you can see, it wasn't a wholly rational tour. I was going up and down America like a yo-yo. But there was no better way to see it, or at least American clouds. Minneapolis, Minnesota, Hinsdale, Illinois, and then back to Louisville, Kentucky.

I could not have been more warmly received by Mrs C. R. Smith and her party, Mrs Thomas Hardin and Mrs Charles Mays, and they gave me a wonderful night at the Actors Theatre where I saw an excellent performance of a Vietnam play (which reminded me, I still hadn't found Jonathan's soldiers). I couldn't wait for the performance next morning, or rather at twelve noon, at the Women's Club. A coffee morning had preceded my hour, and the tables were still being cleared as I was being introduced. This time I didn't really mind the long introduction as it would give time for some order to be restored. However, as I began, the noise was now coming from the kitchens immediately through the wall. A door had been left open and through it we could hear a very rhythmic rendition of "Dem bones, dem bones, dem dry bones", to the accompaniment of cups, plates and cutlery.

I persevered as best I could for a time. Then I had to stop. My instinct was to go down into the auditorium and close the door myself. But since one very elegantly dressed Kentuckian was sitting right by it, I suggested politely that she might close the door on the noise. She looked at me with disdain, "It's not mah job to close dooahs. If you wish it closed, ah suggest you call a portah."

I was flabbergasted at this, and could think of nothing brilliant or witty to say. Even if I had I doubt it would have been heard, so I merely turned to the rest of the ladies and shouted, "Then Robert Burns met Jean Armour and they lived happily ever after." And I walked off, straight to the dressing-room.

I had been on stage for about ten minutes. I don't know how long they sat there, but by the time they came round backstage to me, I was already on the way out with my suitcase. I pushed past several bemused ladies and found myself standing with heaving chest on the pavement, or sidewalk, as they called it. Luckily a taxi came and I was in it before the pursuing ladies caught up with me. Back in the hotel, I realised how silly I had been. I should have just gone down and closed the bloody door myself and nothing more would have been thought of the matter, but I'm not a motor mechanic or even a dishwasher. I am an actor, an artist working in words, and given to those failings and excesses that mark our tribe.

I phoned Bob in New York to explain what happened.

"It was a spontaneous reaction, Bob. I couldn't help it."

"Well, that just cost you seven hundred and fifty dollars," replied Bob calmly. "But don't worry, I'll waive commission in this case."

He was always the gentleman was Bob Keedick.

Next day I was in Lexicon, and still within reach of the Louisville ladies. But I heard nothing and escaped to Canton, Ohio, and an audience of college graduates. I spent the day at the Football Hall of Fame and it gave me the idea of something similar for Scottish football in Glasgow. Another idea for the future.

The Cincinnati Women's Club was the final date, and I'm glad to say my first American tour ended on a capacity note, and a good reaction. Once again it was an evening show, but this time it was mixed. The women brought their husbands, and the difference was marked. Robert Burns was in a theatre once again, and responded appropriately. Next day I had to buy a big canvas bag to hold the presents for Sheila and the girls – little painted wooden box-bags, and yes, I did find the "confenderate" toy soldiers for Jonathan.

The Jolly Beggars Burns Club in Bathgate debated the motion: "What effect have John Cairney and James Barke had on modern thinking on Robert Burns?" I can't tell you how thrilled I was by this.

That ordinary working men with an interest in the Bard, should not only link me with a great popular novelist of Burns themes, but spend an evening discussing whether or not in playing Robert Burns for twelve years, I had influenced anyone, moved me enormously. What had started out for me as a holiday job between films had become almost a vocation, and in its exercise for more than a decade, it had become something of a cult, from which it has now dwindled to near-legend. It is a strange process and one that is not the lot of every actor. And not every actor's professional efforts have been so formally discussed in a working men's club. I never ever heard the result of the Bathgate gentlemen's debate. But it didn't matter. It was the best Christmas present I had had in years.

The STV *McGonagall* was shown on the network and the *Sunday Mail* sent Sheila a bouquet of flowers because it was adjudged the best show of the week. I was allowed to name the recipient, and named my wife. She didn't send them back. Things weren't much changed but we kept up a public face and we played "happy families" quite easily. Because most of us were – it was only Sheila. The *Fife Herald News* sent ex-schoolteacher and artist, Ian Craig, to interview all of us for their Christmas issue. He was much tickled by the fact that he and I were in a sense namesakes, since I had played Ian Craig for two years in the TV series. His article was a long, articulate resumé of my career so far, and on his own admission, he left around 1 a.m. exhausted. I was more interested in the picture he took of the family.

Jennifer and Alison were the only ones missing. Jennifer was still managing her Glasgow restaurant, and Alison, no doubt, was mucking out some stables somewhere. But Lesley, at fifteen, was already pleased to see the camera. Jane in roll-top jersey wasn't so sure, and Jonathan just stared ahead, not knowing how to look. Sheila was smiling, but it was an uncertain kind of smile. I had my "actor's face" on, despite being rather tired and a bit tense, but all I can see now is that I had Sheila's hand clasped firmly in mine, and I was reluctant to let go.

I started the New Year of 1978 by flying to Tangiers, then travelling by coach to join the *Uganda* at Ceuta. I was to perform *Robert Burns*, *R.L. Stevenson* and *McGonagall* to the passengers as we sailed, but not all at the same time. Colin and Ann would also join me for *The Ivor Novello Story*, so it was certainly a working holiday – but what a holiday. We cruised first to Malta. I spent a day walking solitarily around the harbour at Valletta imagining all the battleships that once formed a single line along its length. I was still the little boy who once wanted to be a sailor on horseback.

We landed at Itea for Delphi, and I went on the excursion to see the oldest theatre in the world at Epidaurus. It was eerie to be on Greek soil in the very heartland of the ancient classics. It was even more so to stand in the centre of this unique, open-air auditorium, whisper a syllable and hear it reverberate up the stone escarpment in front of me where a little row of heads (other passengers) were able to converse easily with me. It was like whispering from the centre spot at Hampden.

"Say something, John," they said.

"Give us a bit of Shakespeare," said one voice.

"What about Burns?"

So there and then, standing in the sunlight, I recited part of Burns' "Advice to a Young Friend", bearing in mind the *Uganda*'s main role as an educational cruise ship for children, but I was beautifully upstaged by a group of Canadian children who followed me on to the centre spot, and standing there in a little knot, sang simply and most movingly their national anthem, "O, Canada", with its most emotive melody. It made Canadians of everyone.

Next stop was the harbour of Haifa and a tourist bus to Jerusalem and Bethlehem, and the cruise became a Holy Pilgrimage, despite the camels and the bazaars and the pestering Arabs. What a change in a year from the frozen wastes of Moscow to the idyllic shores of the Aegean, and I had Robert Burns to thank for both. And he travelled as well as I did. I could take him everywhere! P & O had of course comedians, musicians and singers on board, as they had on their other luxury cruise ships, but this was the first time they had hired an actor to give them live theatre. I was also to preside at the Burns Supper.

I would have loved Sheila to have been with me, but she proffered the usual reasons: Lesley, Jane and Jonathan. So I made do with the pleasant company I found on board under the Mediterranean sky. A young mother was there with her two children and her parents and they adopted me for the trip. But most of the time I was working. I even did the *Burns* in the open air, on an improvised theatre on one end of the upper decks by moonlight. Charlie Kelman from Peterhead saw it, and he said, "Here, yon was really something," so it must have been. "Ye'll hae tae come tae Peterhead, and dae it for us, man." I promised I would, if he would guarantee the moonlight and the soft, still air. "Nae bother," he said.

But my real memories of that time are of the sten guns poking out of narrow windows in the Holy city of Jerusalem, going up the Via Dolorosa watching out for child pickpockets and crowding into the crypt at Bethlehem, being assured by four different black monks at four different corners, "Psst – Christus born here," pointing to their own spots. A sense of humour is necessary in any religion. We were given tapers and told we could offer them at the little altar for any intention. The *Daily Express* writer was just behind me with his attractive, though volatile, wife, who said she didn't believe in all this. "Never mind," said the husband, "let's shove a couple in for a happy marriage, eh?"

"Our marriage?" replied the wife incredulously.

"Why not? We're here now."

He lit his two tapers and I lit one. But mine went out. It must have been a draught.

James Bredin of Border Television wanted me to play a live performance of the *Burns* in Carlisle to coincide with their network transmission on Burns Night of my television solo which they had made in conjunction with STV the previous year. Arrangements were made with the Cumbria Hotel and we got a full house and a full stomach. It was a wonderful meal. It was also a very odd experience to play the show and then watch the audience immediately adjourn to the dining-room where a large screen had been set up, to see me do most of it again. I didn't join them. I had seen it. Anyway I couldn't bear to watch it, so I adjourned to the bar and waited for them to come out. Besides, I had a lot of drinking to catch up on.

What a situation, alone at a bar hearing my own voice droning away through the closed doors. How long could this Burns thing go on? Or is it going to last all my life? What a life! From an occasional happening it seems to have firmed to a permanent engagement. Not that I minded. It was a stimulating, demanding, interesting, profitable job to do. At least it was never boring – far from it. And look at all it had given me. But I was on a roller-coaster. How long would it be before it became a treadmill? And look too at what it had cost already in other ways. And what was I storing up for myself? I broke off. I was on my fourth drink. I was getting maudlin. But then there was applause, the doors opened, and people were all round me.

> God knows I'm no' the thing I should be,
> Nor am I even the thing I could be,
> But twenty times I rather would be

> An atheist clean,
> Than under gospel colours wid be
> Just for a screen.

STV wanted to talk about a project on the Friday and BBC wanted an interview on *Scotland Today* on the Monday, so it gave me the weekend at my mother's flat in Glasgow. It also gave me a rest and something of a fright. I suddenly thought I had a late vocation for the priesthood. Please don't laugh. This was not so ridiculous as it might sound. As a ten-year-old I was almost away to a seminary, capped and short-trousered and with little brown suitcase, but my mother thought I wouldn't be safe in England, so she kept me behind to face the bombs in Glasgow. As an eighteen-year-old in Germany I was very serious about it. It was either that or complete atheism, but instead I was drafted into entertainments, and the notion passed. It's almost a natural thing for a Catholic boy of any sensibility at all to think of the priesthood at some time. And now here I was at 47 with a growing family and everything career-wise going for me and I had the strongest yearning to go into the Church.

I thought at first it was only a reaction to Sheila's bombshell, but over the time since, it had niggled and persisted, and on this Glasgow weekend I resolved to do something about it. But what? I decided to go round to the nearest Catholic church and talk to a priest. As I walked along Onslow Drive I wondered what I might say. The church was empty when I got there, and it was soothing just to sit in the back seat with only the glow from the altar light and early evening at the windows. Outside, the faintest traffic noises. Then there was a jangle of keys and the parish priest appeared. I stood up as he approached. I think he recognised me.

"Good evening, Father," I said.

"Hell, Mr – er," he began in his dry voice.

"I was wondering, Father –" I began.

"Yes?" he said, looking vaguely about him.

"I wondered if I could – er "

"Was it important?" he interrupted. "I was just going to lock up."

Something in me abruptly switched off. I became quite cold.

"No, it's not really important, Father." The priest blinked vaguely.

"I'm always here in the morning," he said. He was a grey man with grey hair and a grey face and grey voice. I couldn't get out of the church fast enough and the thought of a vocation has never entered my head since.

Oh yes, there is sometimes the escapist desire to be a blissful monk in a beautiful library – or building a wall, or tending a garden – but that's only the ideal rejection of the harsh world. However, at that time I seriously thought I could still do something worthwhile for my Church with my particular training. It was out of the question now. Perhaps I was still suffering from shock, a kind of delayed concussion. When I mentioned it to my mother later, she just laughed.

"A fine priest you'd be," she said. "You'd never be away from the Children o' Mary, or have yer haun oot o' the collection plate."

"Come on, mother – "

"An' as for yer sermons – God – " she said, "wi' your gift o' the gab we'd be there a' day." I gathered she didn't approve.

I then decided to do something I should have done a lot earlier. I put in a call to New Zealand.

"May I speak to Alannah O'Sullivan please?"

"Who's calling?"

"John Cairney from Scotland."

"Is that you, John – gidday – this is Mickey. Hold on, I'll get her. She was waiting to hear from you. Hold on."

I held on.

Hong Kong is a man-made opportunity for East to meet West, so that the two shall profit. But the first person I met in Hong Kong was a Highland girl called Evelyn Macrae. I was standing in the Harbour Road trying to cross the suicidal traffic at Wanchi, when this smart young lady touched me on the arm and said, "I think it's safer at the crossing," and led me up to some lights.

"Thank you," I said.

"Where are you going?" she asked.

"To the Arts Centre."

"That's funny. So am I."

And that's how I met my Hong Kong minder. She was an Economics Student from Edinburgh University, and was working there for American Express, I think, or some such high-powered outfit. At any rate, she always had the *Business News* or other financial papers with her. One of the first things she did was to give me her card. Everybody in Hong Kong had a card, a business card. Of course, I hadn't. The only card I knew at that time was my National

Insurance Card – LR642088B – every actor knows his Insurance number!

I had to meet Colin again at the Arts Centre. He was flying in from London with Anne Hetherington. So we made up an immediate foursome while we discussed the Hong Kong campaign. Evelyn was so self-possessed, she wasn't at all put out by being among theatricals, and was an invaluable help to Colin and me in finding our way through this jam-packed city – if it is a city. It seemed to me like one ever-open shopping complex for tourists.

We were to play *Burns* for the first four nights and then *Novello* for three. Originally we were booked into the Studio Theatre, but I'm glad to say ticket demands were such that we were moved into the huge recital hall, and rehearsals started at once with Carol Chapman, a local singer, who also invited the three of us to stay with her and her husband in their very swish home up on the hill. Anne and Colin accepted but I stayed on in the Harbour Hotel, despite the cockroaches. I preferred my freedom. Anne hadn't liked the cockroaches in her hotel bedroom. I said they were no trouble if you slept with the light on. "How can you sleep with the light on?" she said.

"I have nothing to hide," I replied.

Since the Burns really only involved me, I left Colin to rehearse the singers, and allowed Evelyn to show me the real Hong Kong. She had made many Chinese friends and one of them invited us for a meal in their home. This was a rare invitation and I was glad to take advantage of it. The family's name was Sin. Whether this was intentional on Evelyn's part or a mere coincidence, I'll never know, but the whole Hong Kong experience was bizarre – or do I mean bazaar? It was at that house of Sin that I learned that a dirty tablecloth to the Chinese was a sign of a good meal. All I can say is we made a right mess of that tablecloth. In return, I took her the next evening to the Mandarin Hotel to the Dinner Theatre there. To my pleasant surprise it was showing *No Sex, Please, We're British*, and an even greater shock was to find that its author, my old friend Tony Marriot, was actually staying in the hotel, with his wife, Heulwen. I couldn't believe it, and after lots of hugs and kisses all round we shared a table to watch the show. I caught Heulwen looking at me closely, but she said nothing. Nor did Evelyn.

I felt very much at ease with this quiet Highland girl, who seemed a strange choice to be a rising whizz-kid in Hong Kong's hectic financial world. It might have been that she found in me that a change is as good as a rest, and perhaps the same applied to me? Hers was a world as totally alien to me as mine was to her, but for those two weeks she was an invaluable consort. Colin and I had expected that the *Novello* would sell out and the *Burns* would be carried by it. It was exactly the opposite way around. The expatriate community of Hong Kong surged to the Arts in a body for the *Burns* and there was no doubt that for four nights he ruled.

We were even graced on one occasion by the presence of the Governor of Hong Kong. His name was McLehose, so you can imagine the gift this was to the whole Clarinda episode in the script. He wasn't amused.

After one of the shows, I met Mary O'Hara. She was a girl I'd known at Primary School in Parkhead, now married to a sergeant in the army in Hong Kong. It was good to see how well she had adjusted to this strange life in the heights above the bay, and it was hard to remember the little girl I'd known at school whose mother worked in the BBC canteen in Glasgow. She thought Evelyn was my wife. The husband said, "You mean, his daughter." Perhaps she was both.

I never hid anything from Evelyn. I told her how woman-sour I had become without being entirely misogynistic. I mentioned the very delicate state my marriage was in and assured her that my wife understood me only too well, and there was also this girl in New Zealand. With all her powers of logic and realistic assessment, Evelyn read the situation well and nothing more was said on the matter. I was sorry I had no time to get to know this interesting girl better, but I had only three nights left.

The *Burns* finished on a high note, and it was made for me by the young Chinese stage manager, a girl who spoke no English, coming out on stage at the curtain call and singing "Auld Lang Syne" in Chinese. It was a beautiful moment and a good note on which to end.

Evelyn hadn't come to the Souchong Theatre for the last night. She had her boss to see from American Express. Nor was she on the slow boat we took on a day trip into China. But she came to the Kaitak airport with only one request, that I would call and see her mother and father if I were ever near the Pitlochry area. Of course I would. She then pecked me on the cheek and drove off into the Hong Kong traffic. I wonder if she's Vice-President of the Corporation by know? It was a puzzle to me why such a marvellous all-round girl had never married. A Chinese puzzle?

Memories are made of people and the people I have met on my many

The final years: Burns in a bow-tie.

travels convince me that all of life is a matter of personal relationships, and if one is lucky one can find them everywhere and with the most unexpected people. In that respect at least, I have been lucky, I think.

On my return visit to Scotland, I did visit the Macraes at their farm cottage deep in the Highland countryside and happily gave them news of their remarkable daughter. They had apparently heard all about me, so we spent a very pleasant afternoon together. When I went back into the village later I went into the Post Office to check my directions, and the Post Office lady said, "And did you enjoy your visit to the Macraes?" They don't need bush telegraph in the Highlands.

I played the *Burns* at the Theatre-in-the-Forest in Grizedale. It was my first visit to the Lake District and what a wonderful experience it was. The hotel was fantastic and the French chef particularly good. The man in charge of the theatre was Bill Grant, another Scot, and we enjoyed a bit of a ceilidh after the performance. He asked if I might do a second show and I immediately agreed on condition we could do a deal on my children. That is, that I be allowed to bring Jonathan and Jane down for a week's holiday as soon as they were free from school. He agreed, so I did the show.

The children and I had an idyllic Lake District holiday. I even got them to eat snails. Jonathan loved them as long as they were called escargots, but felt quite ill as soon as I told him they were really snails. I also took them walking, climbing, pony-trekking, and we visited our first game fair. It was a wonderful time, and I was grateful for the fact that Robert Burns paid for it all.

Largs was a new venue added to the third Burns Festival and the main feature was an updated version of *The Holy Fair* with a young Ayr actor, Jay Smith, as Burns, and Alison Hamilton repeating her previous year's success as Jean. Rehearsals for this were a tense affair since I handed over completely to Tom Raffel. I had the uneasy feeling that the Burns Festival was gradually being taken out of my hands. I noticed that I was no longer Artistic Director, but Artistic Adviser. An administrator had been appointed and the whole thing was becoming very much a municipal affair. The artistic input was becoming increasingly restricted, and no new work was encouraged. The whole idea that I had originally for the Burns Festival was that it would be a platform for contemporary writers and composers who would be prompted to create work on the Burns theme. Instead there was a fall back to old ideas again.

In addition, we now had representatives from the Strathclyde

Regional Council and the District Councils of Cunninghame, Kilmarnock and Loudon, and the Dumfries and Galloway Tourist Association, not to mention Moffat Woollen Mills Ltd. Now Largs had been added. It was becoming a very top-heavy operation and the original thrust and drive was being lost in bureaucratic procedures and civic protocol. I was rapidly losing my temper with it all and found that I had few friends in the corridors of power. But then I didn't live in corridors. I operated from a stage.

These councillors got ten pounds for every meeting they attended, and the officers had their salaries but I got not a penny at this stage, even though I was often coming from all parts of the country to attend. My directorial fees would only apply once the production had been mounted, but before that I had to sit through all these interminable meetings where they argued for hours about pennies. I learned later that for some political reason, I was expunged from the Minutes. It was all getting very difficult, and yet the whole idea had been mine in the first place. But by this Third Festival it was almost forgotten. Yet the third was without doubt the best yet. It had taken hold, both locally and nationally. I should be glad of that. I was, but seemed to incite severe personality clashes with the people of influence in the town. As a result a kind of anti-Cairney campaign grew up and some of my best friends were part of it. Maureen advised me to hold my tongue for once and let it all blow past. I tried – unsuccessfully – and found it very trying.

I finished the Festival in Russian company. Three Russian writers, Vardques Petrosian, Anatoly Melinkov and Ovidiy Gorchakov, had come to Scotland to do some research and to see Edinburgh Castle, Burns Cottage and meet me. So they said. A day was arranged at the Land o' Burns centre, and a special performance given of *The Robert Burns Story*. I stayed in the costume to meet them, and Anatoly Melinkov remembered my Moscow visit. So did Mr Gorchakov, although he hadn't seen it. He said the writers had talked about it and he hoped I would come to Moscow and give the full theatre performance there. I said I would prefer to bring a plane-load of ordinary Ayrshire people in *Bard* and perhaps they could send a Russian choir to the Burns Festival next year?

Meantime, the Russians' hosts, members of the Arts Council and the British Tourist Authority, stood by sipping their sherries and smiling. The Russians had seemed genuinely interested in talking with me and I was more than glad to talk with them. But a prominent local official seemed put out. He dragged me angrily to a corner. "You'd think this whole Festival was your idea."

195

"Wasn't it?" I said. His face was apoplectic.

"If you persist in interfering, I'll come down on you from a great height," he hissed from lips that were flecked with saliva. I was very cool.

"Really?" I said. "For you to come on me from any height, I would require to be subterranean!"

I walked away and left him standing. It was the only time I've ever said something I was glad to say at the time instead if wishing later I'd said it. I walked away not only from the Land o' Burns centre, but from Ayr, and from the Burns Festival. When the Festival ended, I submitted my report – and my resignation.

By this time, Monica Barry was in Japan, Sue Frame had had her second child and Colin had defected into matrimony with *Novello* singer Anne Hetherington. All the ships were deserting the sinking rat! But meantime, Alannah O'Sullivan had come to London and was working for the Thames Water Board. I invited her to join me at the 1978 Edinburgh Festival and sent her a rail fare – one way. Afterwards, I had to go the United States on my third Lecture Tour. She agreed – in the emergency – and as a temporary measure – to look after the office while I was gone.

Near the end of the six-week tour I was in a quandary. What to do with a free weekend? Should I go on to Cincinnati and spend the weekend there before the show on Monday, or should I stay on here in the Fort Worth/Dallas segment and fly out on the Monday? Mrs Gordon Smedley had no hesitation. "You don't want to go to Cincinnati," she said. "You just stay along with us and we'll make you real welcome Texas-style. My good friend, Jane Turnbow, will be glad to look after you. Her husband, Jack, makes a real good chilli. I understand you like chilli."

I must admit I'd developed a taste for this Mexican food in my American times. And that is how I came to meet the Turnbows, Jane and Jack who, with their children, Jay and Jill, have now become dear and lifelong friends, and permanent Texas hosts.

Two parties followed, one after the other; one in the Turnbows' three-tiered town house, with what seemed half the population of Fort Worth, and the other in the Smedleys' lakeside retreat, complete with jetty and powered motorboat, where the other half of Texas was. This was really the *Dallas* life of the soaps, although JR hadn't even been born then. What struck me was that, well-to-do and hard-working as they were, they were all essentially real. Most of the friendships stemmed from schooldays, and they formed a very tight community indeed, but a caring and very charitable one. All Methodists, they represented the very best of the American tradition, although they wouldn't call themselves American. They were Texan and they were proud of it.

I soon became as proud of them. At least they were more than kind to this actor at a time when he was much in need of it. The Turnbows suggested I move out of the hotel to their place till I left on the Monday. I was delighted to do so and Jack and I between us sure licked a lot of chilli.

The rest of the tour couldn't help but be something of an anti-climax after Texas. I was relieved as the two months' travelling drew to an end. The one little thing that made it bearable was that at each date Alannah had waiting for me National Portrait Gallery cards of famous women in painting. I had a different woman for every date. It was her way of keeping me up to date, but was she also trying to warn me?

From Sewickley, Pennsylvania, I flew to Toronto to see brother Jim at Nobleton to do a radio programme for Denis Snowden at Oakville. It was good to be among family again, especially my own family, or rather my brother's, despite Leroy, that dog of theirs. I was soon settled in one of the boys' rooms and there on the bed was a bundle of mail waiting for me. Most of it was from Alannah, so I sorted it out in date order and, taking another sip of my drink, lay back on my bed to enjoy a long read, first remembering to turn on the radio at the classical station.

The strains of Grieg's "Solvieg's Song" filled the room, and I opened the first letter from my adorable Girl Friday to read:

"Dear John, As I write this, 'Solvieg's Song' is on the radio. It's always been my favourite . . ." I couldn't believe it. This was eerie. There was definitely something in the air and it wasn't only Solvieg's Song.

The next day was November 22nd – St Cecilia's Day, the patroness of music. It was also Sheila's saint's day. Cecilia is the Latin for Sheila. On an impulse I decided to ring her – Sheila, not St Cecilia. I might have had bother getting through to the latter! Come to think of it, I might have even more difficulty getting through to the former. Sheila answered, and was surprised to hear from me. I was surprised to find how emotional I got. I found myself making one last, desperate plea for our marriage.

I summoned up every ounce of feeling from our time together. It seemed a long time since 1951 now. She had been 17. I was the first man she had known. She had trusted me completely. What a crass idiot I had been, but I had been so unthinking. I never seriously thought that any of my "misadventures" had anything to do with my marriage. It was the chauvinism of my generation, I suppose. Which doesn't lessen the contrition, however. Although at the time it had felt hardly venal.

Anyway, it was the nature of the job – or do I mean the beast? I was thrown into the arms of beautiful women in the course of earning my living. Of course I know I should have resisted more often. What was the miracle was that I resisted at all. In any case, many of these relationships were more extra-mural than extra-marital; more a matter of after-hours activity, a beneficial therapy, than anything more meaningful. It made me play even harder and maybe go further now and then than a happy husband should. It's a factor that should be borne in mind when allocating guilt. Besides, as Burns points out, how many are removed from temptation merely because they have never been in the way of it? Several times other relationships might indeed have developed into something more, these were lovely girls in every sense, but I had always backed away. I hardly felt righteous, however – only foolish.

> I hae a wife o' my ain,
> I'll partake wi' naebody –

We had had 24 wonderful years – and now this. It was all those stupid feminist magazines, I thought. They had unsettled her. Made her vulnerable. "I don't get the same thrill when I touch your hand," she had once said. "For God's sake, Sheila, it's been 20 years!" But I had never guessed for a moment she had been so unhappy. If I had, perhaps I might have done something about it. It was just in this last year or so. Was there someone after all? I couldn't believe it. Not my Sheila – she was Caesar's wife.

> I'll take Cuckold frae nane
> I'll gae Cuckold to naebody.

I knew now I should have abandoned everything and stayed with her, but to be honest I suspected that it was just a phase she was going through. Something she would get over if I left her alone. If I stayed away. Our best time was just coming. We were just getting nicely older. How old was she? If I were 48 she must be. . . 43. Gosh, was she as old as that? To me she was still a 17-year-old girl.

On Hallowe'en, I saw a Queen
Hang out her washing on the green. . .

What a young wife she was at Bristol! Dammit – dammit all! What could I do? I was tied to this damned job, to this constant travelling. "I have to pay the bills," I always said. Now I was paying more dearly in another way. I had overdrawn badly on a patient and long-standing account.

On the transatlantic telephone that day I couldn't even speak clearly for all the unhappiness that was welling up inside me. I wept for my lost wife. What will my lovely children think? "They know all about it." It was like talking to a machine. I knew it was ended. Our marriage had gone cold for want of mutual tending. Like every other stupid Scottish husband, I had forgotten my wife was a person. I thought of her merely as my wife. Of course I loved her. Of course I would take care of her. But I took it for granted that she was there, as my mother and father were there. But my father had died. And now, too, so had my marriage. And in my brother's house in Canada I mourned grievously for it. We were only just over a year away from our silver wedding. I asked her to at least do nothing till then. I couldn't tolerate divorce. But I promised to stay away if that's what she wanted. I put down the phone on a terrible silence. I looked out of the window at the Canadian snow feeling just like Captain Oates. Jim was his usual honest, frank self. "Has it anything to do with this – uh – Eleanor?"

"NO," I shouted angrily, "IT'S GOT DAMN ALL TO DO WITH ALANNAH!"

Alannah met me at Prestwick airport in a hired car. She was very shy. I felt unclean, but perhaps it was only the all-night flight. We drove straight to Edinburgh and to rehearsals for the *Mackintosh Experience* at the Lyceum Studio. I went back to Pinegrove House at the end of that week with my washing. It was turning out to be the most expensive laundrette in Britain! Nothing much was said, but it was great to see the children. What fine people they are growing into. All Sheila's doing, of course. Unless one considers the genetic influence!

I went home to my mother for Christmas. We had Christmas dinner at the Duke of Touraine and I plied her with sherry after sherry. At what I thought was the right point, I told her the real situation. She didn't believe me. And when I told her it was true, she said immediately that it was all my fault. She wouldn't have a word said against Sheila.

"It's that other lassie, isn't it?"

"You mean Alannah," I said.

"Aye, it's her, isn't it?" Just like Jim.

"No, mother, it's not." She wouldn't believe that either. She must have seen how miserable I was, for she suddenly said, "Well, I suppose if you done a murder, I'd still have to love ye. But just promise me one thing."

"What's that?"

"You just give Sheila peace if she wants it. But don't you marry again. You've been married once and that's enough. You can have as many lassies as you like, but just make sure you don't get married to any o' them."

"Mother," I said, "are you telling me to commit mortal sin?"

"Don't be daft," she said. "You know fine what I mean."

I knew well what she meant. But I didn't know what I was going to do about it all.

This bleak year ended appropriately in a snowstorm that virtually cut off Edinburgh and Glasgow, not to mention Fife. Mickey, Alannah's younger sister, had arrived to see her in Edinburgh and they were busily demolishing the Chivas Regal at Colinton Road. My mother was all right, I think, in her snug little Dennistoun apartment with her TV, her cards, her fly wee vodka and lemonade now and again, and her good neighbours up the close. But I was worried about my children.

They were at Pinegrove House under Alison's care, because Sheila had chosen to go and visit her friend, Catherine Anderson, in Dalbeattie (no doubt for a good heart-to-heart on the situation). The problem was that she got cut off down there. The children were then cut off up at Lassodie. Alannah and Mickey were snowed in at Colinton. And I was in Glasgow. On a sudden impulse one morning, and being totally foolhardy, I set out from Glasgow for Fife, despite the broadcast warnings not to travel unless absolutely necessary. This, I thought, was absolutely necessary. I don't know how I managed it but I got the car to the top of Lassodie Hill, saw that the children were really enjoying the adventure of it all, and that they were all sleeping down in the sitting-room round the fire in sleeping-bags. They were making a huge game of it all. But I wasn't enjoying it much.

I was reversed into by a snow plough, and was pulled out of a ditch twice. I then had to return to Glasgow to take my mother to the

Citizens pantomime of all things. And all the time road and weather conditions had never been worse but I was determined to know something of the holiday season. This was Christmas, after all. I got my mother home and, despite her misgivings, I got back into my battered car and drove along the lunar landscape that was the absolutely deserted M8 to Edinburgh. Only the radio announcer and I seemed to be left alive.

I could die here, I thought – hypothermia, exposure, starvation – and do you know I didn't even care. I was frozen even though I had my pyjamas on under everything I could wear on top, but the car heater had been affected by the bump I'd had and I had to keep the car window open for visibility in the swirling snow. Rather than Captain Oates I was Captain Scott! I drove right through Edinburgh ignoring every red light in that city and cars stuck in snowdrifts or slewed across my path, not stopping until I slithered to a halt on the drive on Colinton Road. But what a welcome the two New Zealand girls gave me.

The house was ablaze with warmth, but they had finished the Chivas Regal. From my room I brought out the bottle of vodka I'd been saving since Moscow and we toasted the New Year of '79 in high good spirits indeed. Hysterical it may have been, but I had nothing to lose. I had lost everything already. But with the New Year, new hope, and I took all the comfort I could from the wonderful smile Alannah gave me at the Bells.

My farewell solo performance as Robert Burns in Scotland took place at the Netherbow Arts Centre, Edinburgh. Some commercial interests in Scottish theatre had advised me to make a big thing of this and, like Harry Lauder and Melba, enjoy a few years of farewell performances in cities and countries where the *Burns* had been so well received, but it never happened that way. It just seemed to come to an end at its time and that was that. To me, it seemed somehow appropriate that the costume performance came to an end in Scotland, neither with a bang nor a whimper, but with a full house and an assured resonance that belonged to doing the thing on my own terms much the same way as I had begun it all in Edinburgh fifteen years before. It finished with dignity if not with razzmatazz. This was the final impersonation in Scotland.

From now on, I would play him more and more representationally, that is, talking about him as "he", not as "I" and in my dinner jacket, rather than in costume and wig. There was still mileage to be gained from the costume performance, but that was in the next year and the year after that and in lands very far away from here. But for Scotland at least, on the stage of the tiny Netherbow, I bade Robert Burns farewell. I don't think anybody believed me.

Alannah and I then drove to Carlisle for a dinner theatre series and to record a Burns/Clarinda episode for Border Television. Alannah made a lovely Mrs McLehose in her red wig and I was able to resume my costume for the cameras. But I had the sneakiest suspicion that perhaps I was getting too old for Robert Burns. The cameras could not lie. Let's face it, I was well into extra time already.

Before the final whistle, however, I engaged Russell Hunter to join me in a documentary Burns programme, *As Others Saw Him*, to be presented at the Barrfield Pavilion in Largs, but more particularly to star in something I had written especially for him – "A Drunk Man Looks At Robert Burns". This was a deliberate combination of Burns and McDiarmid, playing very heavily on my association with the former, and showing Russell as the plain man against this image. To me, it was an exciting concept, contrasting these two large poets, and the comic performance it drew from Russell more than justified all our efforts.

It was no more than a dramatic reading but within it there were moments of genuine pathos from Russell and real theatre magic. Quality, too, as the Burns and McDiarmid lines jostled and clanked like war horses in a tournament, and the end was finally realised by Russell – "Oh, I hae a silence left . . .".

We played it at the Gaiety, Ayr, at the Volunteer Rooms in Irvine and at the Village Theatre in East Kilbride, and the last was perhaps the most satisfying of all three. By this time we had got it working rather smoothly and Russell now made a practice of entering through the front of the theatre complex with genuine, newly purchased fish supper. Attired as he was in his old trench coat and flat cap, he was not at all out of place in the fish and chip shop queue. He would enter through the front of house and make his way into the auditorium with as much noise as possible. Ostensibly he would then interrupt the recital I was giving of Burns and by the time he made his way up on stage to join me, I was gone and Russell had the stage to himself.

But on this East Kilbride opening night, the front of house manager only took over in the evenings and no one had told him that Russell was making his entrance through his domain. What I heard from stage was indeed an altercation, but this time it was a real one, with the manager stoutly refusing to let Russell enter at all. Russell thought the fellow was making a good job of his improvisation and played up accordingly until, as he said, he realised he was never going to get in. Quickly he had to resort to his Stratford-on-Avon intonations to tell the manager, "Get out of the way, you silly man, and let me make my entrance."

I well remember my mother's face in the middle of those stalls laughing until the tears were glistening on her face. She later told me it was the funniest thing she had ever seen, but she couldn't understand why I'd given Russell a better part than I had. I told her it was written that way for the drunk man to be the comedian and me to play the straight man to him. She still wasn't sure.

This was my official farewell to the Robert Burns Festival. After seven years of planning, preparing, pestering and promoting it had all happened, and once it was off and running it was quietly taken out of my hands. Ah well, that's ever the Scottish way of it. But at least a few things were discovered – it is still a good idea and could be worked at yet. Especially if Prestwick became Robert Burns Airport and they built that Courtyard Theatre in Rozelle Park. On the plus side, I found the Braids, *The Holy Fair* and that I wasn't a good man to have on a committee. I am an unashamed despot, or at least an oligarch, and work best at doing my own thing. And I've come to the conclusion that everything that ever gets done is always the work of one man, and if it doesn't fulfil its promise then it's the work of a committee.

That's as true in any walk of life as it is in theatre – more is not merrier, it is muckier, and the mud sticks to everybody. So how did it end at my final Festival? With a lovely belly laugh, I can tell you. All I know is we made a wonderful combination, Russell and I, and I would have gladly extended the run with it, but I was due in Canada with Alannah for the Gathering of the Clans.

"A Drunk Man Looks At Robert Burns" can't really be done now because my physical and professional links to Burns are distinctly smaller public profile than they used to be; nevertheless, it had its time, and it was fun. There are times when acting is much better than working!

The Festival Theatre at Niagara was famous in North America as a touring venue and took most of the big shows and the big names working between Broadway and Toronto. Another old pal, Donal

Donnelly, was playing there the week before me in his one-man show on George Bernard Shaw, and now I was to give my last *Burns* performance in Eastern Canada from that same stage. Donal had been the first artist in a series of Sunday specials booked, and I was the second. Others were to follow, and it became in fact a regular feature of Canadian theatre life. Sunday was a good theatre day, and the best time was after church in the morning and before TV football in the late afternoon.

I came straight from the airport to the theatre and spent the morning assembling my few bits and pieces. Once again I had that same scoffing reaction from stage management. They couldn't believe that an actor could survive for two hours with so little, but I was used to this by now and just got on with it. I finished the lighting and sound cues with just time to get myself into costume before curtain-up. When I did make my entrance, I was amazed to see an absolutely full house. I had expected a fair response since, by now, I had made a few friends in Canada, but this was without doubt a very special occasion. It was after all a farewell performance.

This must have stimulated me to extra efforts, because the performance finished in "the great silence" as I walked off. When I re-entered to take my bow, the audience rose up like one person. It was a most astonishing sight and almost intimidating. It stopped me in my tracks and made me flinch. This was a genuine standing ovation, not the kind of mock response created by a claque or by the example of a few being picked up politely by the rest. It was a single, involuntary gesture taken by hundreds of people acting as one, and I was literally taken aback by it. I had to take at least two paces back from where I stood. I could only dumbly bow my thanks.

A further cause for rejoicing was when Jim told me driving back to Toronto, "We sold a heck of a lot of records in the interval". We'd all thought he'd forgotten them. He had, but during the rehearsals he'd nipped home to get them. A mere two hours each way – and just made it back for the interval. Good old Jim.

The Celtic Supporters Club in Kearney, New Jersey, is a unique kind of place. It is much more Glasgow than it is New Jersey. A very definite effort has been made to retain a Clydeside atmosphere in that very American place: Scotch pies, treacle scones, black pudding, the *Sunday Post* and the *Sunday Mail*. They were all available at the Kearney Club. Favours from every Scottish football club, including Rangers, were displayed; but pride of place was given to Celtic and especially the deeds of the Lisbon Lions. Joe Arbadji, my New Jersey landlord, had arranged this show in conjunction with my Uncle James, ex-sailor and part-time drummer in a Shettleston dance band. He was my mother's youngest brother and the nearest to an older brother for Jim and me. By chance my mother was also in America at that time to see relatives in New York and visit Jim in Toronto, so she attended along with most of my Yankee cousins and respective spouses – and Alannah.

My mother had been reconciled to her since the previous St Patrick's Night, and now they couldn't be closer. You will understand that the Cairney connection made at least a good half of the audience. That was really the idea that Joe had in putting on the show in the first place – another family reunion, another party. Americans just love parties. So no one was taking the show very seriously, least of all the Kearney Club. Their idea of theatre preparation was just to turn the jukebox down and the lights up.

However, we got under way eventually and I spent more of my time exchanging cracks with the audience than telling *The Robert Burns Story*, which all the more convinced my Uncle James that I should have been a "comeedjin". "You're a right comeedjin, John. That's what you are." I think he meant it as a compliment. Uncle James was a character. A product of the Depression '30s, he had dabbled in most thing and was without doubt a talented drummer. When Alannah and I had dinner with him in a Long Island hotel, he kept up a marvellous accompaniment to the band with his knife and fork. He always insisted he had given me my "talent" as he called it.

It was due entirely, he said, to the fact that he gave me an electric shock when I was a wee boy by making me hold the live wires from our old wireless "It was the shock did it," he insisted. "Talent's just a matter of energy and what bigger energy can you get than an electric current? Made ye a right 'live wire', John. Get it?"

Whatever his theories about artistic conduction, he was a character was James. Everybody liked him, and he liked everybody. But he liked his wee drink more. And it killed him too early. On that night, though, he was in great form. It was the first time he had ever seen me since I was a boy.

At the end, the Kearney Club presented my mother with a huge bouquet of flowers on stage. It was the kind of gesture that takes one by surprise and brings a lump to the throat. That they should have thought of my mother. How did they know? I never realised she was so beautiful.

But the tour must go on . . ..

Our first morning in a Vancouver Hotel was interrupted by a very
Glasgow voice. It belonged to Jack Webster, brother of Sandy,
formerly of the *Sunday Mail*, who breezed in to where Alannah and I
were breakfasting with a television crew in order to film an interview
with me. After about ten minutes he suddenly stood up and growled
in his half-Scottish, half-Canadian voice, "This isna good enough.
Let's fix it for the studio tomorrow morning." So what was to have
been a two-minute insert on the news programme became virtually a
programme in itself as the formidable Jack Webster collided with this
actor across the table. The programme went out live, but there was
no holding either of us. First of all, it was my voice. Or rather my
accent.

"You don't sound very Glasgow to me."

"Well, I'm sorry, but I've got School Board reports that can prove
it."

"It's kind of Anglified," he said.

"What's so terrible about that?" I said. "After all, we're in British
Columbia."

But Jack was like a terrier and would not be put off.

"But you can't say your accent's from Parkhead. Sounds more like
Polish to me."

"Aye," I retorted, "Mansion Polish!" He gaped. "Or French Polish,
if you like, since we're in Canada!" and even Jack laughed.

His method was to goad his guests into absolute indignation so as
to relax them. I don't think he'd got back as good as he gave for a
long time – at least since he last invited a fellow Glaswegian on to his
show. Before long the tables were turned and I was almost
interviewing him. The other guests appeared to have been forgotten
and Jack and I had a great chinwag about old Glasgow times and new
Canadian days. To tell you the truth, I think we forgot we were on
television, and that makes the best television there is.

As a result, we had standing-room only at the McPherson
Playhouse in Victoria the next night. Jack wasn't able to attend,
because he was flying off on a political story, but he gave us a picture
to put on a seat, so as to put me off, he said. Yes, it was good meeting
Jack Webster.

The McPherson Playhouse in Victoria, British Columbia, was built
by an Airdrie man. It was odd to stand outside and read on a plaque
on a wall the name of a place that is really only a few tram stops up

beyond Baillieston where I was born. The manager of the theatre was a Dutchman, which was par for the course in North America. Stage management was minimal, but luckily Alannah was with me and she helped set up as usual.

The Scottish community treated us to supper at Holyrood House, a tartan restaurant not far from the theatre run by a Scottish couple. It was strange to go from its environs to the Empress Hotel which was so very English and might just as well have graced the promenade at Bournemouth as much as it did the front at Victoria.

Next morning we were entertained to lunch by Corinne Sharp of the British Tourist Authority. A lovely lady and just one of the many good officers for Britain who work unsung and unseen in so many places abroad. Bill and Georgie McLeod from Calgary joined us for a drink.

But the biggest surprise for me was in suddenly coming face to face with John Davitt, who had been at school with me in the '40s. He was now translating income tax matters into French for the Canadian Government, and was full of the fact that his daughter had become a famous model. He joined us in the ferry back to Vancouver, where Alannah and I were to take the plane to join the *Canberra* at San Francisco and John was going back to work. We had quite a few drams as we sailed across the Strait of Georgia. But for John and me, snug in the saloon, we might have been sailing up the Clyde. I always remember that at school John had loved Keats:

> Then felt I like some watcher of the skies,
> When a new planet swims into his ken,
> Or like stout Cortez when, with eagle eyes,
> He stared at the Pacific –

The Pacific mentioned by Keats wasn't so different from the Pacific that Alannah and I looked down on from the opulent decks of the *Canberra* as she steamed away from San Francisco en route to Australia.

Burns was once again my business on the trip and he was waiting on the quayside at Sydney in the affable guise of promoter Bob Lapthorne.

Actually Bob came on board to meet us, he was so eager to tell us that the *Burns* had already sold out, and that *Two For A Theatre*, our companion programme, had not. "How many have you sold then?" I asked. "Actually, none," he replied. "But don't worry, there's time yet."

Bob was ever the optimist. That's what made him the successful man he still is. The trouble is we were being sold on two counts. Myself as a solo in the *Burns* and Alannah and I as a duo in *Two For A Theatre*. But people didn't know what *Two For A Theatre* was, and the public doesn't buy what it doesn't know. They knew who Robert Burns was. Unfortunately we had arranged more *Two For A Theatre* performances than *Burns* performances. I suggested we swop them over, but logistically this was impossible as everything had gone to press, so I said why not add on a few more *Burns* performances?

This was done. We played at the Phillip Street Theatre with the *Burns* on Sunday afternoons and I am delighted to say extra chairs had to be brought in and put in down the sides, along the front and along the back. Luckily the fire officer didn't work on a Sunday afternoon.

Despite this wildfire reaction to *The Robert Burns Story* it was a case of Hail and Farewell for the Bard in Australia; yet the fact that I was here at all was all thanks to Mrs Lapthorne.

Ellen Sexton had been in my young brother's class at St Michael's in Parkhead and said he was so dishy even then that he was the one who should have been an actor instead of a football player. According to Ellen I wasn't even good-looking enough to be a football player! However, on a visit home, she had seen one of the television performances and obtained my Burns LP. Returning with it to her home in Sydney, she nagged her husband to bring me out to Australia. Bob's business, Telepix Ltd, was to do with the buying and selling of films for television and had nothing to do with theatre but, as any husband knows, there is no defence against the continual water-drip of a wife's persistence. Ellen got her way and Bob phoned me around the world till he caught up with me on a New Zealand farm. It was arranged we could at least have a brief season in Sydney, if we could fit it in with our cruising commitments with P & O in the Pacific. Dates were agreed and here we were.

This was now my eighth trip around the world. I was starting to get dizzy with it all, but Alannah still had a lot of catching up to do and I was enjoying seeing it all again through her eyes. We also enjoyed meeting the Lapthornes en famille at Whale Beach. Bob unexpectedly turned out to be a marvellous jazz pianist and during parties at his house, some of the best times were when he just sat down and let go. He was a wonderful host, despite the fact that he didn't exactly make a fortune from the Cairneys.

At the end of the season, Bob was mystified. He said, "You know, I can sit in my office, make a couple of calls, and in 12 minutes, I can make what you guys make in three weeks. I think you're in the wrong business."

Dear Bob, he now understands that an actor's life doesn't really make actuarial sense but, in the long run, there are what might be called altruistic benefits; like our friendship. But just to keep him happy, I've promised Bob that one day I'll bring him a modern, full-scale Burns musical to help make up for his skirmish with *Two For A Theatre*. He likes the idea already and we last spoke when he was here on film business at Cannes. "What do I have to do for this Burns musical?" he asked me.

"Just make a couple of calls, Bob," I said.

I had arranged to meet Tommy Docherty in a club somewhere in the factory district of the city. I had last come face to face with him on the playing pitches of Shettleston Hill, 40 years before. Now here he was, the manager of a Sydney football club, having been manager of Scotland and Manchester United, not to mention a player for Celtic and Preston North End. Tommy, as everyone knows, is a wonderful character and natural comedian. Or what Uncle James called a "comeedjin". The East End seems to breed them naturally. Tommy is the archetypal example. I soon ignored the flaccid wine, cold chips and limp veg, as he waxed on story after story from his multi-coloured football past. What a one-man show he would make. I asked him when he was coming to see us.

"Me?" he said. "I never go to plays."

It turned out he'd never been in a theatre in his life.

"Not even with the Boys' Guild?" I asked.

"Especially no' in the Boys' Guild," he replied.

I determined to remedy that. With the help of his new and charming wife, Mary, and she was charming, we coerced him into attending one of the performances. Much to his surprise he enjoyed it.

"But will you come again, Tommy?" I asked him.

"Sure," he said, folding his arms over his bright red shirt. "I'll come the next time you're here."

Given his volatile disposition it was more a matter of whether he would be there. (He left the next season).

Also in Sydney was James Murray, a writer. He was a Glaswegian, but from Govan, not Parkhead. A wild Irish Glaswegian, with a reckless tongue and a sweet pen. He also hated Robert Burns, so this gave us a good starting point. The performances didn't entirely win him over. He thought, as a professional actor, I ought to be able to make the telephone book interesting.

"Ah," I said, "but could I make it rhyme?"

James joined us for some of our gatherings at our Oxford Hotel, though we never succeeded in getting him to the swimming pool on the roof. He was very much a Glaswegian who just happened to live in Sydney, but his conversational agility would have done credit to the palmy days of Dublin pub society. I understand he has written several novels since then, and had a Booker nomination for *The Pale Sergeant*, but I remember him best sitting across the table from me making gorgeous sweeping condemnations, while phrasing his insults neatly.

Quite beside the point, or maybe it is totally apposite, I can mention that he had the happiest of families – six healthy and lovely Australians, and Jenny, a most intelligent and forbearing wife. What lovely memories they helped to give Alannah and me. Nobody knows what memories are, but I know I have the happiest of Sydney. I saw its Opera House, its famous bridge, Bondi Beach, Kings Cross and all the other places the tourist is supposed to see, but my main memories of Sydney are of the Lapthornes and the Murrays.

My divorce came through on 8th May 1980 and became effective 21 days later – 29th May – my silver wedding! The irony was not lost on me.

I don't think it was intended, it was just the way it happened. The anniversary, looming as it was, may indeed have precipitated Sheila into action and was the one thing she had been panicking to avoid. I can understand a reluctance to face the publicity but what of all the presents – all that silver from everyone? But she had gone ahead unilaterally, and that was that. I merely chose to do nothing about it. If that's what she wanted, let her have it. I loved her enough to let her go. And I had loved her.

I toyed with the idea of asking Alannah to marry me on 29th May and so maintain a kind of marital continuity, but naturally she was not all that thrilled. It was then a question of when. We had long ago decided we would marry, and even my mother agreed, but she thought it should be in New Zealand, with Alannah's family. Now it was merely a matter of dates.

Mrs O'Sullivan and Janey (Alannah's aunt) joined us at Oamaru and the diaries came out. Colleen, the number two sister, also had a voice in the discussion. It was a question of whether we should marry at the end of the tour and honeymoon, as it were, in New Zealand, or marry just before we left New Zealand, and make the going-away a genuine departure for the American tour. I favoured the latter, but who was I?

Mrs O'Sullivan said it was a question of enjoying the preparations beforehand or having time to recover afterwards.

"Are you sure your mother can't come over, John? Or your brother Jim?"

No, it was to be another Cairney one-man show. So, let's get on with it. This was a very practical matter. The date everyone seemed to agree on was 20th September, but there was something about that date that immediately gave me a bad feeling, and I said, "I don't like that".

On looking closer we realised it was the Jewish Day of Atonement. Hardly a date for a marriage. Although I don't know . . . but I don't think that it was even that day-long feast which was troubling me. It was a feeling I couldn't explain.

The week later was too near rehearsal time for radio in Auckland and also too near the first performance date in the United States. So, despite my misgivings, we settled on the 20th, and arrangements were put in hand. We were to marry from Alannah's home at Oxford. Neither my mother nor Jim was able to attend for their various reasons, and although my mother was not all that sure even yet about my marrying again from the religious point of view, she loved Alannah, and we knew we had her blessing. Jim just couldn't get away from the paper and the pub in Toronto.

It was only a few days to go when I had a call from Jim – in Glasgow. Mother had suddenly collapsed at home and was in the Royal Infirmary. She had recovered consciousness sufficiently to sit up, so he didn't think he would need to tell me till after the wedding, but then she had a relapse and was now in a coma. Could I come over?

"But, Jim, I'm about to be married . . ."

"I know, John, I'm sorry, but I think you should be here." Then he mumbled, "John, please come. I need you."

There was no question, I had to go. The O'Sullivans completely understood, and dear Janey thrust three thousand New Zealand dollars into my hand, saying, "Go to your mother."

A plane was booked, a ticket was bought, and just before I left the house, Jim rang again from Glasgow in the very early hours of the morning. He was very calm. "She's gone," was all he said.

I went out into the paddocks and howled into the misty morning. I was really alone now. No man is really free until his mother dies. Oh Mother, Mother. And so, on the 20th September, the date I had feared, instead of marrying Alannah, I buried my mother.

Jim had insisted that the undertaker remain open until his brother arrived. "Of course," they said, "of course." Then as their closing-time approached, they kept saying, "Your brother will be here." And Jim kept saying, "Of course he'll be here. Just you keep the doors open."

"But we close at six o'clock," they said.

"I don't care when you close," said Jim, "just stay open till he gets here."

"Has he far to come?" lisped the undertaker.

"Far enough," said Jim. "London, perhaps?"

"No, not London."

"Oh. New York, then? He travels a bit, does he?"

"He's coming from New Zealand."

"Oh my – but we close at six o'clock."

I got in at two minutes to six. It wasn't worth the trouble. It wasn't my mother in that coffin. She was gone, leaving an empty likeness behind. I felt very remote and detached from the whole thing. There was an extraordinary celebratory sense at the Requiem Mass at St Anne's. We knew our mother was all right now and when Father Gillespie raised his hand and said, "The Lord be with you," we replied, "And also with you." "Lift up your hearts," he said, and we answered, "We lift them up to the Lord." Then, "Let us give thanks to the Lord, our God." Our reply was, "It is right to give him thanks and praise."

I felt a spasm of joy as one should feel when a good soul has died, and my mother was certainly that. In the early church they used to rejoice when a person died – and I too was "surprised by joy", as C. S. Lewis put it.

I thought to myself, I should have been married today on the other side of the world, and here I am standing within a foot of my mother's coffin. I reached out and touched it fondly.

At the house afterwards, I let the uncles and aunts and cousins take over. They were good people and they loved my mother, too. There was no need for anyone to say anything. Some just patted my hand or my shoulder, or gave an understanding nod, although when one sanctimonious cousin expressed his condolences, he added, "But I can't wish you luck for your wedding. You being married before, like," I nearly punched him downstairs.

When they had all gone, Jim and I emptied a bottle of whisky each and looked at old photos. We sat up the whole night and when we left I gave the house keys to the neighbours.

He flew back to Canada and I flew back to New Zealand. Alannah was at the airport. She was very pale – and very thin. "Now, what was it I was going to say," I said, "before we were so sadly interrupted?"

"I will," she said.

We were married in the garden by the local Anglican vicar, after a Mass said by the local priest. The table that served as his altar continued as the bar, and the birdbath became our wedding font. The guests attending merely turned their chairs round from the Mass to face the font and found themselves staring at the bank of rhododendron bushes.

Our exotic honeymoon route to the United States was via Singapore, Bangkok, the Philippines and Hawaii. It was hard to return to work on the Lecture Circuit, but I might have been even more reluctant had I known then that the special engagement arranged for the Scottish Festival at Norfolk, Virginia, was to be my last solo performance as Robert Burns.

I had rather foisted myself upon Virginia, but I was determined to be part of this event, even if it was less a festival and more of a scholastic conference. It was sponsored by the Bureau of Conferences and Institutes and the Institute of Scottish Studies, Old Dominion University, and had as its theme, "John Knox and Robert Burns: The Odd Couple".

This was the idea proposed by Dr Charles Hawes, Director of the Institute of Scottish Studies there, who had been a lifelong Scotophile since his student days in Edinburgh and Glasgow. Many prominent Knoxians and Burnsians had been invited, like Drs Kirk and Blake for the former, and Drs Jack and Ross Roy for the latter. Not to mention worthies such as Dr Gordon from Strathclyde and University authorities such as Rosalind Mitchison from Edinburgh. The only artist listed was the inimitable Ms Jean Redpath from Leven and all parts of America. There was no mention of Cairney whatsoever, but I was determined to be involved, so I wrote to them.

Professor Hawes later described my letter as "the most egotistical document" he had ever read. I had often been misconstrued as such, so I didn't really blame him. He perhaps couldn't understand my enthusiasm, or appreciate my eagerness to be of service. I thought I had something to contribute to a discussion of Burns in that setting and there is no greater ruthlessness than righteousness. I also put my wallet where my big mouth was, in that I elected to come out for some lucrative Keedick Lecture dates with Alannah, so that I might be available in Norfolk.

However, thanks to the good offices of Harry Price, a more than adequate fee was agreed with Keedick for my services over the five days involved. In fact, between you and me, it was the highest fee I'd ever been paid for a single performance as Burns. Alannah and I, as was the practice in Virginia, were billeted privately. We were lucky enough to find Mrs Virginia Wilkinson, whose house was at Virginia Beach on the ocean.

She was a most expansive and hospitable lady who had been married to a naval officer ("but don't let's bother talkin' about him," she said). She was something of a character in the community, and no doubt she was selected with us in mind. Or the other way around. On our first morning, she gave us bacon and eggs as any Blackpool landlady would have done. The only difference was she insisted on serving champagne with it. We had to walk it off on the beach afterwards. If this was Southern hospitality, it would be a question of surviving it.

We had lunch with Jean Redpath at the house where she was a guest. She was just the same as ever. That's Jean's charm. Wherever she is she is always Jean. But what a voice! We were to do something together at the Final Banquet, but most of the time we talked about the recording project she had in hand with Serge Hovey. This was to put on disc all the songs of Robert Burns – this could be between three and four hundred titles – on permanent record in the settings for which the original lyrics had been composed. This was a magnificent undertaking, but it was hampered by the fact that Mr Hovey suffered from Motor Neurone Disease and could only work with great difficulty and very, very slowly. Notwithstanding, Jean had already completed two LPs and was preparing another. (At the time of writing she has completed six.)

Jean and I could have talked all day about this, and the courage of Serge Hovey and the importance of Burns as a songwriter for the world, not just Scotland, but I had to remember that I was here as an actor, not as a Burns authority. I had a show to think about.

The Wells Theatre in downtown Norfolk was one of the many Victorian houses built across America to bring the Broadway Greats, like the Drews and the Barrymores, to the ordinary people of America. It later became a vaudeville theatre, presenting people like Will Rogers and even Fred and Adèle Astaire. When vaudeville died, it became a burlesque house and later a cinema. Then with the coming of television the Wells fell on evil days and became a blue movie house with a grotty parlour behind the screen where go-go dancers went. It looked at one time as if the next patron would be the driver of a bulldozer, but just in time it was saved by the town, and once again it was a theatre.

And it was a real theatre. Art nouveau statues, curtained boxes, cherubs and roses and painted ceilings. Any moment one might have expected Al Jolson to strut on, but on Monday 6th April 1981, at 8 p.m., I walked on as Robert Burns.

During the morning rehearsals, a camera crew from BBC Television came into the theatre, led by that stalwart Highlandman from Aberdeen, Donny McLeod. Donny had interviewed me years before at Grampian. Now he wanted to find out how I was surviving in this peripatetic solo career I had chosen for myself, never knowing from one night to another where I would be or who I would be: Burns, Stevenson, McGonagall or even Ivor Novello.

Today I was Robert Burns, both of us were quite sure about that. Donny had a lovely irony and a good way with the spoken word, and I think we got a good interview. The cameraman was Norman Shepherd, who had filmed me for the same BBC in 1965 in the very first filmed interview I ever did for *There Was A Man*. Now here he was more than 3,000 miles from Queen Margaret Drive once again looking down a lens. "Good God, John," he said, "talk about déjà vu. It gives you a turn to feel that."

What Norman was meaning was that in looking down the lens, he saw exactly the same face he saw 17 years before, the only difference being that I now wore a wig where my own black hair had once been. But who wants a grey-headed Burns? I had a sense of the wheel's having come full circle. Was this night to be special?

The boys packed up their equipment. Donny shook my hand. Norman gave me a grin. And Alannah suggested I should perhaps try and have a rest. I went to the dressing-room and lay down. What was it Donny had said? John Barrymore had played here. Fred Astaire. Perhaps I could play Robert Burns in top hat and tails. Tam o' Shanter would look great with a cane. And I fell fast asleep on the dressing-room couch dreaming of footlights and a follow spot with a band in a pit and a full house.

"Beginners, please, Mr Cairney." The voice of the call-boy rang out in the corridors. But in this case there were no beginners, only a beginner. I was the entire cast so they couldn't start without me. I opened as I'd always done as a statue in silhouette against the cyclorama, and as the first shiver of light touched the screen, I slowly began to move and came forward downstage to the table as the lights behind me gradually built up. I then lit the candle at the corner of the table, which prompted further lights. I looked out over the audience as I blew out the match, and unashamedly held the pause as we took each other in. I then started the play.

I must have given nearly 400 performances of the Burns solo in its two versions – *There Was A Man* and *The Robert Burns Story* – starting just like this, all over the world and in every kind of presentation possibility from private room to vast auditorium, for audiences that were hanging from the ceiling and to others that were a mere handful, but I had never given a single Burns performance that didn't have its own particular imperfection.

Something always went wrong somewhere; a lighting cue, a sound effect, I bumbled a line, or took the wrong key in a song. Being live, one is at the mercy of one's own aliveness. The human element is very fallible indeed and never more so than in the acutely stressful situation such as a theatre performance is, especially in the one-man convention. But I want to put on record now that that performance that April night in that lovely old theatre in Virginia was as near perfect as I and the audience and stage management and God could make it. I swear to that.

I don't think I fluffed a line. Certainly not a cue was missed and all the laughs were there. The understanding silences. And the purple emotional end was very much there. It so affected me that at the end, sitting down at the dressing-table mirror, I said to Alannah, "That's it."

"That's what?"

"That's the end of Robert Burns."

"Are you sure?"

"I've never been more certain of anything."

It was a glowing feeling. I don't think I'm a fool about my profession, but after almost 30 years I could tell a good show from a bad one. I've had my share of each, although to be immodest, a lot more good than bad over the years, but the last Burns was as good as anything I had ever done, so I resolved to leave it at that.

And I've kept my word. Even today I still get requests to play *The Robert Burns Story* in the scripted, costumed form. But I still say no. I want to keep untarnished that golden Virginia night – even if it were only theatrical gilt. But perhaps the truth was, I had been looking for a good excuse to stop.

EPILOGUE

The scene is St Giles Cathedral during the Edinburgh Festival of 1986. I was playing Thomas Becket, otherwise Archbishop of Canterbury, in T. S. Eliot's *Murder in the Cathedral*. On this night, I was progressing solemnly from the crypt to the nave at the beginning of Part Two, about to give the famous Interlude sermon. I was draped in priestly vestments, head bowed, concentrating hard on the Eliot text I was about to utter, but no doubt giving the appropriate appearance of sanctity and solemnity. I was preceded as usual by my three "angelic" twelve-year-old Edinburgh choirboy attendants, their hands clasped in prayer, all looking suitably meek. We had halted at the first pillar waiting for the music cue to take us on to the altar, when the smallest boy suddenly whispered to me in his hoarse, Gorgie Road accent, "Do you get peyed for this?" "Mind your own business," retorted "Becket" in a hoarse whisper. There was a slight pause. The music sounded and we resumed our dignified procession, but that didn't stop the wee choirboy. "No' that you need the money," he muttered. "My mammy said you made a fortune oot o' that show you did on Robin Hood." By this time we had reached the sanctuary and were genuflecting more or less in unison. The boys moved to their places, but the audience must have wondered why "St Thomas" suddenly had a fit of the giggles as he ascended the pulpit.

217

*The Memory Lingers On – A Cairney/Burns impression
by Ronnie Brown of the Corries.*

L'ENVOI

An honest man has nothing to fear if he has been in life no more than the sport of his own instincts. He returns to a God who gave him these instincts and well knows their force.

No doubt, though, I will have much to answer for. Yet my philosophy was simple enough: whatever mitigates the woes or increases the happiness of others, that is my criterion of goodness, whatever injures society as a whole or any one person in it, that is my measure of iniquity.

And if I could, I would wipe all tears from all eyes.

ROBERT BURNS
(1759-1796)

Writing for STV's Burns plays

FILMING began last week in his brother, Gilbert, are each ...
Ayrshire for an STV series of ... portrayed by Gordon Low ...
on one-hour plays on the life of ... Cousins Schoolboy Burns is bey ...
Robert Burns. There are to be ... younger John Burns by Law ...
shown by STV early next year. ... Cousins Burns, after young, and ...
John Cairney will star as Burns ... John ... Burns are employ ...
and Colette O'Neill as over a ... and mature Burns. This venture ...
hundred ... There is a cast of over a ... sisters of young Robert Burns are ...
whole life ... to the poet from his ... played by a further television ...

stage. dec. 67

BURNS'S DOUBLE IN IRVINE

Scottish Television producer Liam Hood kneels to study Irvine
Burns Club's mural watched by actor John Cairney and Burns
Club President Andrew Hood during recent filming in Irvine
for a new television series. (See Local Echoes.)

Glasgow Herald 8 dec 1967

In 1968 we'll see a STV serious dramas on STV ...
the life of Robert Burns.
Cairney is starring as Burns.
lette O'Neill as Jean Armour,
a cast of well over a hund ...
including many of Scotland's ...
known actors, spanning the life ...
poet from his birth at Alloway ...
59 to his death 37 years later ...
umfries.

John Cairney, the actor, crawling from the sea over
Ayrshire, after shooting a bathing scene for a television
on the life of Robert Burns.

A MAN CALLED BURNS
by HUGH GRAY

's 'double' bows

By CLARE BROTHERWOOD

THE ROYAL
MFRIES

nt with the Guild of
Players)

te the anniversary of the
t Burns on 21st July, 1796

Robert Burns

OHN CAIRNEY
AS ROBERT BURNS

e famous one-man play by Tom Wright

"HERE WAS A MAN"

TAINED FOR ANOTHER WEEK
AY, 29th July, to SATURDAY, 3rd Aug.

Commencing 7.30 p.m.

ALL SEATS 10/-

At home, John is a great family man. Here he is pictured with his
wife, Sheila, and his four lovely daughters.

JOHN CAIR

daily at Theatre Royal, Shakespeare
day (Saturday), 10 a.m. to
2 p.m. to

An Exclusive Interview With DICK TATHAM